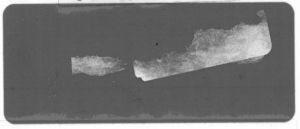
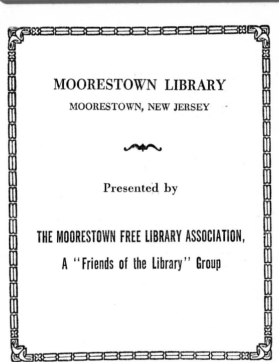

MY
DEAREST
FRIEND

Also by Nancy Thayer
in Thorndike Large Print

Spirit Lost
Three Women at the Water's Edge

MY DEAREST FRIEND

Nancy Thayer

Thorndike Press • Thorndike, Maine

LP
Fiction
Tha

Library of Congress Cataloging in Publication Data:

Thayer, Nancy, 1943-
  My dearest friend / Nancy Thayer.
  p. cm.
  ISBN 0-89621-994-1 (alk. paper : lg. print)
  1. Large type books. I. Title.
[PS3570.H3475M9 1990]   90-10847
813'.54--dc20   CIP

Thorndike Press Large Print edition published in 1990 by
arrangement with Charles Scribner's Sons.

Cover design by Catherine Minor.

**The trees indicium is a trade mark of Thorndike
Press.**

This book is printed on acid-free, high opacity paper.

For Jessica,
Joshua, and
Charley

and you want her
and she wants you
we want everyone
no one no one no one
ever is to blame

—HOWARD JONES

FALL

1

Hudson's brown Volvo took the last curve in the rutted Vermont dirt road, and within a few yards the public road narrowed to a private lane overgrown with sumac, grasses, laurel bushes, and maple saplings. The little trees, their trunks as slender and silver as flutes, shivered as the car passed among them. The dirt lane ended abruptly in front of a clapboard cottage that had once been painted white but that had become with age so streaked with dirt and weathered and peeled that it was now at an interesting tortoiseshell stage.

Hudson stopped the car, turned off the engine. For a moment the silence was complete. The cottage stood before them, its every flaw blazing at them through the clarity of the fine early-September day. It was shabby, asymmetrical, crooked, humble. Never grand, it had been worn down by age.

"This is it?" Hudson asked.

"This is it!" Daphne answered enthusiastically, and got out of the car. "A small thing, but mine own."

Hudson still sat in the car.

"Hudson, you are such a stick!" Daphne said to him calmly. She walked around to the other side of the car and stuck her head in the window. "It's better inside. It's really cute."

"Cute," Hudson said.

"Yes, cute!" Daphne grinned. "Now, come on!"

She yanked the door open and Hudson reluctantly unfolded himself from the car. Daphne watched, and a helpless smile of pleasure spread across her face. Really, Hudson was such a thoroughbred, with his very long lean limbs, and he looked so fine in his clothes, that pink oxford-cloth button-down shirt with the sleeves rolled up, khakis, leather loafers on his long skinny feet. Daphne was wearing rubber thongs and a wraparound strapless sundress she had made from some flowered material she had found on sale for eighty-nine cents at Zayres. She didn't dare think about the responsibility she'd given to the three little black snaps that were holding the dress on her body.

"Come on inside," Daphne said, taking Hudson's arm. Now, this was a different thing: Hudson *looked* great, so skinny, elegant in his clothes, but she hated the *feeling* of his thinness, it worried her. His arm felt skeletal to her hand, too frail to bear all its burdens. Instinctively she pulled him against her affectionately.

"Do you know, this is the first house I have ever owned? Forty-six years old, and a home-owner for the very first time." She caught Hudson's glance. "Well, of course you could say I owned a house when I was married to Joe. My name was on the deed, but I never really *owned* it. *Joe* owned it." She felt the bitterness, like a sleeping snake inside her — always such a quick thing, always on the alert! — ready to uncoil and strike, releasing its poison throughout her body. She shook her head, she kept walking, she pulled Hudson to the first concrete step that led to the front door. "But this is mine," she said triumphantly, and the snake lay back down. "It might have taken me a long time, it might not be a mansion, but it's mine."

After all the years of their friendship, Daphne could read Hudson's mind. Just at this instant, as his courteous hand reached out to open the door for her, his fastidious mind was thinking with dismay: The screen door is made from aluminum instead of wood.

"The floors are all hardwood!" she cried, offsetting his silent criticism. "Look, aren't they beautiful? Now, Hudson, you have at

13

least to agree that the floors are beautiful."

Hudson walked through the house. It didn't take long. The front door opened into the living room, without even a pretense of an entrance hall. The living room was generously proportioned, with a large flagstone fireplace in the middle of one wall, and two windows on either side of the fireplace, giving views of the seedy grass and deep forest that ranged at the side of the house. Immediately to the right was a door leading into a bedroom, and Hudson circled the house through the bedroom, into the bathroom, which (he shuddered) had been tiled in pink plastic and papered with swans playing with bubbles, out the other side to the kitchen, which was spacious and bright (but had metal cabinets). From the kitchen he peeked in at what seemed to be an afterthought built on as a back bedroom, and at a small concrete-floored shed with a disconcerting step down to it, and at a stairway hidden behind another door.

"That leads to the attic," Daphne told him. "It's the best room in the house. Really. Go on up and see."

The stairway was narrow, the only railing a thick twisted rope attached to the wall. But the attic room was charming, because of its slanted ceiling and the windows, one at either end of the room, which were oval and paned

14

with diamond-shaped glass set in lead.

"Nice," Hudson admitted.

"It will be hell getting furniture and boxes up there," Daphne said. "I might use the little back bedroom as a storage room and make this attic the guest bedroom. I'd like to sleep up here some nights — to see how the moonlight falls through those panes."

"Where will Cynthia sleep?" Hudson asked.

"I don't know, really," Daphne said. "Up here when she comes to visit, I suppose. I'm not counting on having her here permanently again." The snake struck. Bitter pain shot through her stomach on its way to her heart. She counterattacked by digging her nails into the flesh of her hand. She hurried down the stairs, thinking: Action. Movement. That's how you deal with the pain. You just keep moving right on over it. That way you still have the pain, but sometimes you get somewhere.

They were back in the living room. Now Hudson could take a long look at the oak floors, which had been sanded and polished until they gleamed like bronzed satin.

"Good floors," he said. "Where will you put the piano?"

"I've sold the grand," she said, moving away from him, keeping her back to him.

15

"But that's fine! I've found a darling old baby grand. Not a Steinway, but . . . "

Hudson was looking at her. She could feel his eyes on her back. "I've always told you, if you needed money — "

"I know. And I'm grateful. But this isn't an emergency, Hudson. This is just life. Come on, come out back. There's a place for a garden there, and a sweet little stream running just inside the woods."

They went out through the door leading off the kitchen. The backyard was largely taken up by a garden fenced off by chicken wire. Orange marigolds and multicolored zinnias bobbed along the edges; discouraged potato plants and obstinate zucchini grew among the weedy rows.

"The chicken wire's ugly, I know," Daphne said. "But the former owners, the Wests, say it's absolutely necessary out here. Otherwise raccoons, skunks, even deer get in and eat the entire garden. Well, they couldn't do much this year. They're old and ill. But next year I plan to plant the entire area. And look over there — raspberries! The Wests said they're called 'ever-bearing' and they bloom from June into September. Here, Hudson, taste!"

Daphne came to the bushes before Hudson and, squatting down, reached in through the thick green leaves and pulled off several fat

16

ripe beaded red raspberries. She stood up, picked the best berry, and put it in Hudson's mouth. Her fingers touched his soft lips, his white teeth. He bit down and she felt the gentle tug of his mouth as she pulled the green hull back. She stood, the sun hot on her back, the unruly grass tickling her bare legs, Hudson looking at her through his wire-rimmed glasses, his brown eyes huge through the distorting lens. She crushed the green hull between her two fingers and turned away. It was possible Hudson loved her. It was certain that he wanted her. But he was married, to a woman who had a chronically bad back, and he was of New England Puritan stock; he could not leave that wife, and he could not betray her by sleeping with Daphne. Though they had wanted to for many years now. Well, perhaps it was for the best: they certainly had stayed good friends. And Daphne had had David. In a way. For a while.

"Delicious," he said, at the same time she said, turning away from him and the sensations he caused inside her, "Let's go unload the car!"

They brought in laundry baskets filled with clean sheets, clean clothes, blankets, pillows and a sleeping bag for tonight, boxes of kitchen staples, paper cups and plates.

"This is a nice kitchen, isn't it?" Daphne said.

The floor was brick-red tile-patterned linoleum, the walls colonial blue, the metal cabinets and appliances all old-fashioned white.

"It's patriotic, at least," Hudson said. He walked off into the living room, came back to stand just inside the kitchen door. "Daphne, I can't see you living here. It's so isolated. It's so much of a change."

"Well, my dearest friend," Daphne said, "there's not much I can do about change, is there? I mean, *change* seems to be the order of the day for me recently. We've been over this all, Hudson. I had no choice, what choice was there, some dreadful rented box of an apartment? Besides, with Cynthia leaving, I had to do something special. Something different. You know that."

"I would have given you the down payment for a house in town. I still would. I could easily, just a gift. You would never have to pay it back."

Daphne looked at Hudson and knew that as much as he loved her, and for as long as he had known her — seventeen years now — he would never understand that she could not take a gift of money from him. Life must be lived by certain rules.

18

"Hudson," she said. "Don't. Just don't. We've been over this all before, too many times." She looked at her watch. "Anyway, you have to go."

It was five-thirty. Claire worried if Hudson didn't get home in time for drinks at six. Claire relied on order in her life, and she relied on Hudson.

"You are sure you want to stay out here all alone tonight?" Hudson asked as he headed for the door.

"I'm sure," Daphne said.

"No car, no phone. Dickens isn't here. Won't you be frightened?" Hudson turned to look back at her.

"Oh, Hudson, what should I be frightened of?" Daphne said, thinking: What else can be taken from me?, sighing. Then, seeing his face, she made herself brighten. "Don't be silly!" she said. "This is just what I want! I've told you that. I've been looking forward to it all week. The movers come tomorrow with all my stuff, and then this house will be transformed, taken over by me and mine. But tonight it's bare, just itself, and I want to get the feel of it. Well, think, Hudson, it's like me being alone. Without Joe or Cyn or my friends or you. Or it's like what you might be, if you suddenly were alone somewhere and you weren't a college professor or a hus-

19

band. Elemental."

"I swear I don't know what you're talking about," Hudson said.

Daphne crossed the living room and leaned up to kiss his cheek. It was the most they permitted themselves. "Thanks for bringing me out."

"Shall I fetch you in the morning and take you to your Jeep?"

"Yes. Please." Daphne smiled. Their eyes met, held.

"All right, then," Hudson said, turning to go.

Daphne watched as the brown Volvo turned around and moved down the lane. Her own car, a "new" car for her, for this place, was a 1979 red Jeep, scarred and bouncy, but with four-wheel drive for the winter. She had traded her Citation in on it, and the automobile salesmen were just finishing up what they called the "prep" job. The Jeep would be hers tomorrow; until then Hudson had offered to chauffeur her around. He always did what he could to help.

Her old home, the house she had rented for fourteen years, was down in Westhampton, just over the Massachusetts border, on a pleasant residential street lined with trees, near the college where she worked, within calling distance of other houses, other people, within walking distance of friends. The same week that her daughter had decided to go live with her father, the father Cynthia had not seen, had not received a birthday card from for fourteen years, Daphne had been told by the owners of the house that they were going to raise the rent by four hundred dollars a month, the exact amount of child support Daphne had been receiving all those years from Cynthia's father. The exact amount that, now that Cynthia was going to live with him, he would not be sending any longer. Daphne could not afford to stay in the rented house that had become home to her and her daughter. And she didn't know if Cynthia would ever live with her again.

Life often did things like that, hit you twice in the very same place — Daphne didn't know why people believed that lightning wouldn't strike twice in the same place. Of course it would.

Frantic, in shock, Daphne had wanted to run, to move, to change her luck, her life, and the most she could do was this wild thing: she had rushed out and discovered and made a down payment on this inexpensive and ugly little cottage set off a dead-end road partway up a rolling mountain in Plover, Vermont.

She was seriously thinking of naming the house Dead End. Her life had, after all, come to a dead end, had it not?

No. She would not dwell with bitterness.

Daphne went back through her house, which at least now without furniture seemed quite spacious, and into the kitchen. She opened a bottle of inexpensive champagne, which made a lovely celebratory pop, and poured it into a paper cup, then took it outside. She sat on the top step and surveyed her property. The sky was still a bright blue bowl overhead, but evening was on its way, in the blue air, and in the long sea-green shadows that floated on the heavy grass.

I have a house, Daphne thought. This house is mine. She liked those words, that thought. She rose, and slowly sipping her champagne, she circled her house.

God, what a place. It was crooked, angled, lopsided, it needed sanding and calking and filling, and especially it needed painting. She would not be able to get that job done this year, not with fall and winter approaching.

Well, this would not be the biggest house she had ever lived in, nor the most expensive or elaborately decorated. But it would be the best. She would see to that.

She raised her glass and toasted her house. Her ramshackle house. As if in response, a cardinal called out and flew past, its passage reflected in the kitchen windows. Daphne turned in time to see the bird swerve off into the trees behind the garden.

She loved cardinals. They were perhaps her favorite bird. She thought of them as omens of good luck. Or once had. That was when she was a believer: in the luck of houses, in wishes coming true, in fortune-cookie fortunes, the I Ching, shooting stars, and God. And love. It was a relief to give up all that, and yet it left her strangely limitless; it was odd to have nothing left to pray to in a crisis, nothing superstitious to do when in agony.

But here would be comfort. In this house would be comfort. She was going to wrench this much from life.

How Cynthia would have scorned this place, Daphne thought. The chicken-wire fence was truly ugly. The encircling forest made the house seem more isolated from the world than it was — and Cynthia would have hated that, because she craved the world. Now sixteen, Cyn could never get enough of friends and boyfriends, of admiring teachers and children to baby-sit, tests and challenges, parties, dances, tennis games, recitals, plays . . .

Of course, Daphne would not be here if Cyn had not first decided to leave. So the question would never have arisen.

The snake struck: bitterness and anger raced through her veins. Think of something else, Daphne ordered herself; something else, quick. She turned from the house and looked at the sweep of ground around her. She now owned an entire acre of land — so much grass to mow!

Setting the cup down on the back stoop, she crossed the yard to the wooden shed that stood near the garden, leaning toward the house as if it missed it. As she pulled the doors open, she noted from the squeaks and drag that they needed new hinges. The whole shed needed painting as much as the house. Inside, the concrete floor seemed in good condition, not cracked, but covered with general crud bequeathed to her by the former owners: leaves, dust, seeds, manure, bits of paper, small objects rusted past recognition, bits of rubber, dented empty oil cans, and what had once, not so long ago, been a mouse.

An old hand lawn mower was also inside, and, delighted to discover it, Daphne eagerly pulled it out from where it was entangled with rakes, spades, and shovels in various states of dilapidation. Taking hold of the splintering handle, she pushed it; it shrieked and caught and would not move. She turned it around and pushed it the other way. It shrieked again, caught, then something gave, and as she pushed it, it whirred noisily around as if it had remembered what it was meant for.

Daphne made three swaths across the yard, the mower clattering along merrily, before she looked down to see that it was doing absolutely no good at all. The heavy grass was only bent. The blades were too dull, she supposed.

She sagged a moment, balancing her weight against the little old mower, waiting for the despair to pass. It was at times like this, when some slight thing thwarted her, that she most strongly felt the need to give up. It was at times like this that she could feel how her entire life, all her talent and potential and hard work, her devotion and perseverance and courage, had brought her only to this: loneliness so deep, tribulations so dense, like the sea of grass around her, that she could never fight her way out. And the things she counted on, hoped for as objects of assistance, like this mower, failed her every time. She sighed, rolled it across the yard, and put it back in the shed. She grabbed up her cup of champagne and headed for the front of the house.

The view was less demanding here. No unworked garden to chide her vision, no sagging shed. She sank down on the top step and tried to clear her mind, to observe. Light was fading from the sky, colors deepening. Birds were calling out and flicking through the trees. Daphne relaxed, leaned back against the screen door, stretched out her legs. Really, it was very nice here, like living in the middle of a Pissarro. Life imitated art, and the leaves on all the slender or thick-trunked trees were like so many millions of dots, silver-green, blue-green, jade and chartreuse.

Shadows shifted across the grass like ghosts, then vanished, absorbed into the gray late-evening light. Behind her, her house was dark, and this seemed somehow to make it loom bigger, to take on size and density. In a minute she would go in, turn on the radio, turn on the lights, live in the present. In a minute.

For now she sat staring. As darkness became complete, the individual trees of the forest were blotted out, one by one, until she saw the edge of her property as all of a piece, one dim and motionless mass. Now if she walked toward the woods, the trees as she came closer would take on life, silhouettes, individuality. Just as in her mind, when she walked deep into memory, the people she had loved and lost and let fade came clear, presented themselves to her in the flesh with their old alluring charm and smiles and voices, and the clarity of their margins, the expressions on their faces, and what they had meant to her, and meant to her still, could pierce her like a hook. For they were inside her, after all, a black mass of significance that she carried everywhere, unlike the forest around her, outside her, which she could always escape, if only by closing her eyes.

Cynthia. Joe. David. Laura. And Hudson too, though she saw him still, saw him every day. All gone from her now, yet never far away from her thoughts. What was her life about? Shadows?

Boy, it was amazing how fast a life could get fouled up, Jack Hamilton was thinking. It was amazing. He pulled his old silver Honda into the drive next to his wife's white Mustang convertible (a present from her father), gathered up the sacks of easy deli foods — salty meats, oily salads, oniony buns — beer, and milk for Alexandra's bottle, and made his way up the gravel drive into the A-frame house, the first house he had ever owned.

Here he was, coming home. Dr. Jack Hamilton (although they didn't use that title here in the East), a college professor, the newest member of the Westhampton College English department, dapper and trim in his gray flannels and blue blazer. Arms laden, still he managed to open the front door. It swung inward, and his two-year-old daughter, dressed in pink, came flying across the room to him.

"Daddy! Daddy!" Alexandra tackled him at knee level, almost knocking him off his feet.

Jack set the groceries on the table and bent down to pick her up. He tossed her above his head, brought her down to nuzzle her stomach, his mustache tickling her soft skin so that she giggled and writhed with helpless glee. Her soft fat tummy smelled of baby powder and she wriggled like a puppy.

Across the long sweep of room, an actress in a dress coated with sequins glittered on the television screen, drinking champagne and looking scornfully at an actor in swimming trunks and a gold necklace. Carey Ann pulled her attention away from the drama and came to greet Jack. Barefoot, she made her way carefully across a floor littered with what seemed to be three million wooden and rubber toys: rock-a-stack rings, puzzle pieces, building blocks, bright pink naked baby dolls.

"Hi, darlin'," she said.

Whatever else Jack would ever think of his wife, he would always think she was the most beautiful woman in the world. She had long blond shimmery hair, huge blue eyes, a perfect figure. Now she was wearing jean shorts and a white T-shirt, and Jack loved the way her nipples showed like buttons through the

28

soft cotton. And Carey Ann loved him too; that showed in her eyes.

"Glad you're home," she said, and leaned forward to kiss Jack, who tried to tuck Alexandra into one arm, but didn't succeed; their daughter put out her fat hands to push her mother away, crying, "No! Mine!"

Sighing, unkissed, Carey Ann stepped away, discouraged. "I just don't know when she's going to stop that," she said. She followed Jack into the kitchen to help him unpack the groceries. "I'm sorry the place is still such a mess. I did get all the towels and linens unpacked today. While Lexi napped. And believe it or not, I had all her toys in the playroom, but she insisted on bringing them in here. I don't know. How was your day?"

"Cracker!" Alexandra yelled, seeing Jack bring out a box.

"Fine," Jack said, handing his daughter a fist of crackers. "Look what I brought for dinner."

"Oh, Jack," Carey Ann said happily, seeing the beers he pulled from the sack. "You sweetie. I've been wanting one so much."

"Me drink too!" Lexi cried.

"Here's your drink," Carey Ann said lovingly, getting the bottle from the refrigerator and handing it to Alexandra.

"*No!* That!" Lexi pointed to the beer bottles in her mother's and father's hands.

"Babies don't drink beer," Carey Ann said sweetly. She tried to distract her daughter. "Here, want a bite of salami? Lexi *like* salami."

"*That!*" Lexi cried. Her peaches-and-cream face scrunched up and turned rosy with anger.

"I don't suppose it could hurt her to give her a little sip, do you?" Carey Ann asked, looking at Jack.

He could see blue circles under his wife's eyes. "Probably not," he said. Then he grinned conspiratorially. "Actually, it might make her a little sleepy."

"Oh, Jack," Carey Ann said, but grinned back. She squatted down and held the bottle to her daughter's lips. Alexandra took a big suck, her eyes widened, and she spat.

"Yucky!"

"Thank God," Carey Ann said under her breath, wiping the spit off the mouth of her bottle. "Now I can have it for myself. Here, Alexandra, here's *your* bottle."

They spread their feast out on the paper wrappers on the dining-room table. Thirty feet away, at the other end of the room, the great wall of window glowed with early-autumn light, green leaves just turning gold, blue sky. It was after six, but still bright.

"So?" Carey Ann said eagerly. "How did it go?"

"Great," Jack said, smiling. It both amused and pleased him that Carey Ann was so awed by his work, as if teaching freshman English and neoclassic literature required the bravery and courage of an astronaut. She couldn't imagine how she'd keep a class of twenty-five young people quiet and interested for an hour. As he spoke of students and schedules, she listened intently, shaking her head in admiration. Jack was thirty-one, Carey Ann twenty-four, but she seemed so much younger. Sometimes she seemed so terribly young. (And sometimes that was good, and sometimes not.) "The composition classes will be fun, and easy — I can do that with my eyes closed, it's what I did at UMKC. But the neoclassic class — God, it's such dull stuff I'm still worried about how to get the students interested. But hey, I forgot to tell you — we're invited to a party next Friday night."

"Oh," Carey Ann said, looking down. She began to busy herself with Alexandra, who for once was silent, lying in her mother's lap, content with her bottle. "Well, I don't know. I mean, we'd need a baby-sitter for Lexi, and I don't know anyone yet . . . " Were those tears in her eyelashes? She kept looking down.

Jack stared at his wife. She didn't raise her head. *Here we go again,* he thought, then with a burst of self-controlled energy jumped up from his chair. "I'm going to run up to the bedroom and change out of these clothes." He took the stairs two at a time, needing to burn up the anger that had burst inside him. *What* would make that woman happy? She'd been afraid to leave Kansas because she didn't know anyone back east and didn't have any friends in the Westhampton area, and she was a woman who loved being with friends, but here was a chance for her to meet people and she acted as if he'd just suggested a visit to the dentist.

In a frenzy he stripped off his clothes and hung them up neatly, trekking into the bathroom to put his socks in the hamper; Carey Ann sure wouldn't be able to say he had left the room a mess, had left his socks for her to pick up. Turning, he caught sight of his face in the bathroom mirror. Boy, did he look grim. He sighed and put the toilet lid down and sat there a moment in his Jockey shorts, trying to calm down.

He didn't want an instant replay of last night. Last night had been terrible. He had driven home from the college through a sun-dappled September day, as brilliant as any day he had ever known, and, arms laden with briefcase and groceries, had burst into his beautiful and overwarm house to find his wife and child seated in front of the TV.

"TV?" he had yelled. "Hey, you guys, what are you doing in front of the TV on a beautiful day like this?"

It had been a spontaneous outburst, purely curious. He had meant no criticism and had thought there was nothing but enthusiasm in his voice.

But, "What's wrong with watching TV?" Carey Ann had said, bursting into tears immediately. "Where am I supposed to go? I don't know anyone to go visit. There isn't a neighborhood around here. We're stuck out in the old country! What am I supposed to do with a toddler? Do you have any idea how hard it is to follow a little kid around all day? It's backbreaking. Besides, I like watching TV! It makes me feel better to see all those people whose lives are worse than mine!"

"Worse than yours? But, Carey Ann! What is so bad about your life?" Jack had asked, amazed. Again, he had meant only a question, not criticism.

But Carey Ann had shaken her head and turned away. "Oh, *you* can't understand!"

She had sunk onto the sofa, head in hands, and cried. Alexandra had watched a few moments, enthralled, then, looking up at her

33

father, had burst into confused tears herself, and there Jack had stood, in his splendid new home, with two of the most beautiful blondes the world had ever seen, bawling their eyes out.

He had calmed them down, and eventually, after dinner, they had all gone for a walk down their bumpy dirt road. Jack had tried to cheer Carey Ann up with descriptions of his day, his office, the other faculty members and the students, and thought he had been successful. But later, when they were climbing into bed, with Alexandra for once miraculously asleep in her crib, he had reached out for his wife, wanting to make love to her. But Carey Ann had pulled away and begun crying again.

"Oh, I'm too ugly for anyone to make love to."

"Carey Ann!"

"Well, look. I guess I'm going to have this blubber on my stomach for the rest of my life."

"Carey Ann, you're beautiful. You don't have any blubber. You're perfect!"

"Oh, don't you lie to me," she had said, offended, pulling away from him to sit on the side of the bed. "I know. I know how you get to look at all those pretty young carefree flat-stomached coeds all day long, those girls who

34

have nothing to think about but getting dressed!"

"I think Westhampton College students have slightly higher intellectual concerns than that," Jack had said, and all right, that had been stuffy, but it had just come out.

"Oh, right, and I don't!" Carey Ann had snapped irrationally.

He had tried to charm her out of her sulks, but nothing he could do worked. "Just leave me alone, please," Carey Ann had said. "I don't want to make love. I'm tired." She had curled up on her side of the bed and fallen asleep instantly, while Jack lay awake for long minutes, staring into the night.

How had he and his wife become so antagonistic? Were all marriages this way? He wished he had someone to talk to. He was getting the strangest feelings about his life, that it was *fouled up*, going the wrong way, that he was out of control, that he couldn't do it right.

Wouldn't Carey Ann's old father back in Kansas be thrilled to hear of this? When Jack had formally asked for her hand in marriage, Mr. Skrags had said, "Jack, I have to tell you that I think I have a pretty good idea of what Carey Ann needs in life to make her happy, and when I look at you, I don't see it." Pompous old fart. He and his wife had spoiled Carey Ann terribly; they proudly admitted it.

And even if she had married someone who made more money than he did — which would be just about anyone — she'd still have to learn how to boil water and keep house and take care of a baby: *she* was the one who wanted the baby. She was the one who wanted *lots* of babies. Not that he didn't love Alexandra. He loved her more than his own life. But since her birth, just ten months after their marriage, everything had gotten so difficult. Carey Ann, who in her parents' home had never made her own bed or done her own laundry, hadn't been prepared to cope with a baby's never-ending needs, the crying, the wetting, the fevers, the dirty clothes, the endless tending. Not that Carey Ann ever was anything but infinitely patient with their daughter. Still, Jack was beginning to think that she — they — were doing something wrong. These days Carey Ann found it impossible to do any kind of shopping for groceries with Alexandra along because the baby started screaming if she didn't get what she wanted — cookies, candy, and so on — and yet Jack had seen mothers with babies Alexandra's age riding along in the baskets of grocery carts, so *other* mothers must be able to do it. Why couldn't Carey Ann? But if he tried to talk to her about it or offered to help, she grew furious or teary-eyed and ending up crying because her mother had always had help around the house. So maybe Mr. Skrags had been right after all: maybe it was all Jack's fault that his wife wasn't happy.

He wanted to make her happy. He wanted that more than anything else in the world. Although he could see how she would think that wasn't true. After all, he wouldn't work for her father, and he had made her move here so that he could teach where he wanted. Raised and educated in the East, Jack had finished his Ph.D. at Yale and started his grown-up life with two dreams: to teach English at Westhampton College, where he'd been an undergraduate, and to write novels. He knew he had to save up some money before he could seriously try to write, but in his fantasy/plan for his life he didn't think that would take him too long. Then, after he'd written a few novels and become famous, he'd be asked to teach creative writing and modern fiction at Westhampton. When he had been asked, right after finishing graduate school, to teach freshman composition at the University of Missouri at Kansas City, he knew his plan was starting to take shape. He'd never lived in the Midwest before, and he thought of it in terms of "vitality" and "brashness." He thought he would find material there for his future books.

What he found there was Carey Ann. He hadn't been prepared for this. Probably there wasn't any way to be prepared for such a thing — for falling in love so fast. He had met Carey Ann at a party, and that was it. He fell in love with her at once, and fell more in love with her every moment he was with her. She was so beautiful, and so much fun. She was such a happy person, so spontaneous and loving and quick and eager. He had fallen in love with her fast and deep. He'd never stop loving her.

Carey Ann had fallen in love with him too; loved him still. He believed that, had to believe it to go on. She admitted early on that she, too, had been attracted to Jack for superficial reasons: he was handsome, and had such an elegant New England accent and all those prep-school manners. Then, too, his last name, Hamilton, had appealed to her. It seemed aristocratic and British, unlike the embarrassment of a last name she was stuck with. Even though her father owned a chain of posh department stores all over the Midwest, so that now that name had, if nothing else, a kind of power attached to it, still . . . Skrags — why, it sounded like a kind of disease a person got from sleeping around too much, Carey Ann had laughingly said.

And Jack taught English literature. He was always quoting British writers. This just made

38

Carey Ann swoon, for they had met the year that Prince Charles married Lady Di and a wave of Anglophilia swept the world. In her deepest heart, Carey Ann thought of herself and Jack as *sort of* like Prince Charles and Princess Diana. After all, Jack was dark and handsome and she was fair and beautiful. Not that Carey Ann was a fool. She was just romantic. She was smart in many ways, and intuitive. She *listened* to Jack when he talked about his work, and she could be clever: once, when she was reading a little hands-on book to Alexandra, which involved rubbing a section of the book, then inhaling and getting a good strong whiff of peanut butter or bubble gum or peppermint, Carey Ann had grinned up at Jack and said, "Just think what kind of a scratch-and-sniff book Chaucer would have made!" When she was happy, she could make love like the Fourth of July. But what she was . . . well, what she really was was spoiled. She was her parents' only child, and so pretty to look at that anyone would spoil her, but it helped that her father was so wealthy. She had gone to college in Kansas City but hadn't been able to figure out what she wanted to do with her life except that she wanted to get married and have *lots* of children (another thing, Carey Ann said, that she shared with Princess Diana). After college she had moved back home into her parents' vast house in Shawnee Mission, Kansas, and she had worked at one of her father's department stores on the Plaza, selling stuffed animals. It wasn't what she wanted to do forever, but she enjoyed it, she was good at it, and no one could tell her she didn't work, couldn't hold a job.

Jack had "courted" her — that was how Carey Ann liked to think of it — for the first year he taught in Kansas City. When his contract was renewed, he had asked Carey Ann to marry him, and had been warned by her father that he could never make her happy. Not a college professor. Not someone who made so little money and lived such a prissy (Carey Ann's father's estimation) life.

But he had made her happy, that first year, when he taught at UMKC and she was pregnant. It was after Alexandra's birth that things got difficult. Not that Lexi was a difficult baby, but any baby took a lot of care and work. And then Jack heard there was a position opening at Westhampton College and he'd applied for it and gotten it. Carey Ann didn't want to leave Kansas City and her family and friends; the Skragses didn't want her to leave, even though, in their own old-fashioned way, as they told Carey Ann, they believed a woman was obligated by marriage to follow her husband wherever his work took him. In the meantime, Jack had developed a depression of his own, over the realization that now that he had a child and wife to support he'd *never* be able to take a year off to write, at least not until he was in his eighties. His plan for his life was all turned around. But when he tried to tell Carey Ann that, she had burst into tears and said, "Well, all right, if that's how you feel, let's just get a divorce." Which wasn't what he wanted at all. "No, no," he'd said. "I've always wanted to teach at Westhampton." And that was true. He just hadn't expected it so soon. And not with a wife and child, on a tiny salary.

But together they had decided to make the move, and once the decision was made, they went toward their future optimistically. They almost had been happy again. But when they had come east that summer to look for a house, leaving Lexi with her grandparents, more problems had arisen. Westhampton had become such a resort area, with people flocking there in the summer for the cool mountain air and in the winter for skiing and winter sports, that the cost of real estate had skyrocketed. There was no way that young faculty, paid pittances to teach at Westhampton (but teaching there anyway, because of the prestige), could afford to buy a house. Carey

Ann's vision of herself as an American Princess Diana rapidly slipped away as she was confronted with the realistic view of a two-bedroom rental apartment with walls so thin they could hear the couple arguing next door, or a large rental house with windows that wouldn't open, doors that wouldn't close, mouse droppings in every room, and a kitchen with appliances that were rusty or moldy or broken or all three.

The realtor had suggested they try Vermont, just a few minutes away. The school system wasn't as good as the Westhampton one, the realtor told them, but Carey Ann proclaimed they'd be long gone from this area before her daughter was old enough for school. And the A-frame was a spectacular buy. Nestled in the side of the hill, it overlooked a green and winding valley. The living and dining rooms had a splendid two-story-high cathedral ceiling. Two doors led off the area, one to the small kitchen, one to the room that would become Alexandra's playroom. A staircase led up along one wall to a sort of gallery where the two bedrooms and bathroom were. The banister and railing were all knotty pine, sturdy, unshakable, and the space between the balusters was too small for Alexandra to stick her head through. Whoever had built the house had taken care that a child not be able to fall from the high second floor. The bedrooms had wall-to-wall carpeting, as did the playroom; the living-room and kitchen floors were beautiful flagstones; and the entire house was full of light. There was even a fireplace built into the living-room wall, and Jack had been afraid that it would be a long time before he could buy a house with the luxury of a fireplace.

Best of all, they could afford it. Barely. With Carey Ann's father's help. Jack agreed to borrow the down payment from his father-in-law; what else could he do? And to give the old goat his due, Mr. Skrags went out of his way not to make Jack feel second-rate or obligated or indebted.

So now here they were, in their beautiful house in the mountains. Jack had his job and Carey Ann had her baby, and she was down there crying and he was up here sitting on the toilet in his underwear. He rose, made a face at himself in the mirror, and went into the bedroom to put on his sweats. Then he took a deep breath and went downstairs.

Carey Ann and Lexi were sitting on the floor with a wooden puzzle. Carey Ann rose and went up to Jack, nuzzling against him. "I'm sorry, honey," she said. "I mean about getting all maudlin about the party. I'm just having a real insecurity attack, I guess. I don't know anyone here, and the faculty wives I met when you interviewed here . . . well, people are just so different. They're so cool and boxed up. They make me feel like I'm funny-looking or something."

"You could never be anything but gorgeous," Jack said, hugging her to him. (It flashed in his mind at just that moment, however, that he had noticed — and he wasn't usually aware of women's clothes — how different Carey Ann had looked next to the faculty wives when they were all out to dinner when he was being interviewed in the spring. All the other women wore little gold shells in their ears if they wore any jewelry at all, and there Carey Ann had been with her earrings swinging back and forth like pieces of a chandelier amidst her shimmery hair. But he couldn't tell her that, could he?) He tried to be helpful. "Listen, when I interviewed, we met only the old faculty. There are lots of young faculty wives around. I know you'll make friends."

"I want to show you something!" Carey Ann said, pulling away from him, a smile on her face.

Honestly, Jack thought, when his wife smiled she could light up the night. She led him to the little room under the stairs, which was to be Alexandra's playroom.

"Ta-*da!*" Carey Ann said, opening the door.

The shelves along one wall, which had been meant to hold Lexi's toys, were stacked now with Jack's collection of books, mostly textbooks and novels. Their old card table was set up against the window looking out over the valley, and on top of that was his old faithful portable manual typewriter, and next to that an unopened box of bond paper. There was a coffee mug on the card table, holding pens, pencils, scissors, his letter opener. Behind the card table, within easy reach, were his dictionary and thesaurus.

"I wanted to put your leather desk set out," Carey Ann said shyly, "but there was really no place for it, since you don't have a desk at home. Besides, I know you like to write on the typewriter instead of longhand."

"Come here," Jack said, and hugged his wife against him, hard. He was overwhelmed with emotion.

"It's nice, isn't it? Now you've got your own study. Now you can write your novel."

"I thought . . . Lexi's playroom . . . "

"Well, I could see I wasn't going to have any luck getting Lexi to keep her toys in just one room. She likes to be wherever I am, so she'd always be dragging her stuff out into the kitchen to watch me cook, or to the living room. Besides, she's got enough room in her bedroom for all her stuff. And she doesn't like being stuck away from everyone. But you do. You need a room all to yourself to get your writing done. Do you like it?"

"I love it, Carey Ann. This is really sweet of you. This is really thoughtful." He kissed her.

"Go on," she said. "Sit down. Look at the view."

Jack sat on the old wooden chair in front of the card table and looked out at the sweep of valley. She just doesn't have a clue, he thought. How could she imagine he'd ever have the time to write a novel when he was teaching such a heavy load at Westhampton? He didn't want to hurt Carey Ann's feelings, but God, didn't she understand the first thing about his life? Now that he was married and had a child, now that his life was all turned around, he had to get tenure. He dreamed of tenure like Percival dreaming of the Holy Grail. Tenure meant security, a wonderful financial and emotional security that would set him free later to write his novel. If he could get tenure, he could get a sabbatical, and in seven years he'd have his year off to write. But getting tenure these days, especially at Westhampton College, was about as easy as getting hold of the Holy Grail. It required hard work and dedication and publications, not fiction, but critical essays in the

46

best and most erudite journals. Publish or perish. If he did any writing, it had to be critical. And he wouldn't have a chance to get to that sort of thing until Christmas vacation.

No, he wouldn't find time to write fiction for years.

But now was not the moment to break this news to Carey Ann.

Jack pushed back his chair, rose, took her in his arms again. "Thanks," he said. "Thanks a lot."

They kissed, and moved closer to each other, and Jack would gladly have shut the door and made love to Carey Ann on the floor right then and there, but Alexandra came toddling into the room, waving a plastic elephant. Wanting to please his darling daughter, wanting to please his wife, he swooped Alexandra up in his arms and carried her upside down out into the living room. He roughhoused with her for an hour, giving her pony rides on his knees, tickling her till she howled, playing with her until he was exhausted. Then he gave her a long bath and put her to bed with her bottle.

Later, though, when Jack and Carey Ann went up to bed, Alexandra awoke, as if from an instinctive alarm, called out, climbed out of her crib, came into their bedroom, and merrily climbed into bed with them. She sat between her parents, grinning happily.

"I don't know what to do," Carey Ann sighed. "I can't get her to realize she's got to sleep in her own crib."

"Let's just put her in there and shut the door," Jack suggested.

Carey Ann looked at him as if he'd just become one of the criminally insane. "We can't do that! She'd cry. You know how she's cried whenever we've tried it before." She cuddled the baby against her. "Oh, Lord," she said. "She's wet again."

It was after eleven when they fell asleep, all three of them, in their chaste bed.

The next morning was Friday, and Jack awoke at six-thirty. He had such a routine, had awakened so regularly for so many years now, that he almost couldn't *not* wake up at six-thirty, except for a week or two in the fall and spring when daylight-saving time threw him off.

He looked over at Carey Ann, who looked dead. When she slept, her skin did the same weird thing Alexandra's did: it paled out so completely that it seemed her heart had stopped pumping and had withdrawn all the blood in her body into a tight hot chamber in the center of her heart. If he touched Carey Ann now (which he wouldn't — she'd cry

48

with exhaustion if awakened so early), he knew she'd be hot at her stomach, burning at her crotch, but her face was so drained of color that it looked frosty. Her long blond hair was every which way all over the pillow, and her long eyelashes curled down onto her cheeks. She looked innocent, a child herself, too young and helpless to be taking care of another child.

Alexandra lay in the middle of the bed, as zonked-out as Carey Ann, sleeping on her stomach with her bum sticking up in the air and her thumb at her mouth. The back of her neck was damp with moisture, her blond, almost silver hair curled from the moist heat of her little body. She had her thumb poised right at the edge of her mouth, as if even in sleep she kept it near for emergencies, and her bottle, a plastic thing that used to look like a bear but had lost some of the markings, lay next to her, drained.

His little girl. His baby. When Alexandra saw Jack, her face lit up with ecstasy, every single time. No one else adored Jack as Lexi did. It really was something to have the power to make another human being so happy. It was also a responsibility.

Carey Ann used to say, before they married and in that first year, that she could never *ever* be happy without him, but now he wondered if she could be happy *with* him. He would do anything in the world to make his two females happy. If only he knew what to do!

He slipped from the bed, grabbed up his jogging things where he'd tossed them on a chair, and went into the bathroom. Then he crept out of the room, down the stairs, and out of the house. The sun hit him like a spotlight. God, it was a warm and brilliant day. He stood in his driveway, doing warm-up stretches. He'd been jogging five times a week for six years now. He'd started jogging at Yale when he was working on his Ph.D., feeling the need to stretch out the body that spent so many hours bent over a book, crooked and cramped at a desk or typewriter. He used to go every weekday morning to the gym, where gradually he worked up to jogging four miles around the track. He kept it up for a while when teaching in Kansas City, because he found the morning run exhilarating and refreshing. He taught better, his mind worked more quickly, his responses were sharper. After his marriage, and especially after Alexandra's birth, he just couldn't find the time — or the energy — to keep up those four miles. So he had settled for two, which took him only about fifteen minutes, even when he was taking it easy.

He'd gotten in the car and measured a route

up here the first day they moved into the house. It was almost exactly one mile from his doorstep to the end of a funny little lane giving onto an old cottage, and back again; then a mile in the other direction, down to the remains of an old barn, and back. It was a pretty run along a country dirt road, perfect for jogging, not as hard as street pavements, but well-packed, with no other houses in sight, mostly forest bordering the road, and dusty wildflowers and grasses, and an occasional view through the trees, as the road turned, of the valley so far down below.

The realtor had shown him and Carey Ann the cottage. "Only forty thousand dollars," she had said. "You just can't find anything at that price anymore. But it's been sold. Just like that, this spring. After being on the market for over a year."

"Ugh," Carey Ann had said. "It looks like something imported from the Ozarks."

In a way, Jack liked the property the cottage sat on better than his own — they had no land, just a small yard — and although the view out the front was spectacular, Jack was already worrying about the heating bills and the winter wind. Their A-frame felt exposed. The little cottage, on the other hand, was sort of nestled down in among an orb of trees. It seemed so cozy, protected, a fairy-tale place

51

cut off from the world.

Now he headed down the dirt road, taking it easy, concentrating on his breathing. The road narrowed to a lane, the grass and saplings flickered closer to him, and the taller trees arched over, cutting off the sun. He ran through the shadowy tunnel, and, coming out into the light again, saw, with a shock, a woman seated on the steps of the cottage.

In the instant before she opened her eyes in surprise, he saw that she had been leaning against the cottage door, wearing a short white terry-cloth robe, her long bare legs stretched out in front of her. She had been soaking in the sun, and, perhaps, the silence, before he broke it. His breathing sounded like roaring in his ears. He supposed he was trespassing. In any case, he couldn't just turn around and jog away; it would be rude. It would look strange.

"Oh, hi, sorry!" he said, coming just a little closer to her, jogging in place. "I didn't know anyone was here yet. I'm sorry if I startled you."

"That's all right," she said, smiling. "You gave me just the shot of adrenaline I need to start the day. I didn't know anyone lived around here." She had short dark hair, large blue eyes, and freckles. Freckles all over, from what he could see.

"I'm Jack Hamilton," he said, and stopped jogging. Breathing deeply, he walked toward her, holding out his hand. "My wife and daughter and I just moved into the A-frame down the road. You have to pass it to get here."

"Oh, wonderful!" she said, shaking his hand. As she reached forward, her loosely tied robe fell open slightly so that he couldn't help but see a great deal of her heavy, swinging, plump, and freckled breasts. "I'm Daphne Miller. I'm moving in today. My furniture's coming up this morning. I was just having coffee, enjoying a few more moments of peace before the madness hits. Would you like some coffee?"

She gestured toward the Styrofoam cup next to her on the step, and he realized the wonderful rich dark smell he had been unconsciously enjoying was coffee. Brewed coffee. Carey Ann didn't like coffee; didn't drink it. She would get up in the morning and pour herself a tall glass of warm diet cola, without ice, or, if it was winter, she'd put a spoonful of instant-iced-tea mix in a mug and stir hot tap water into it, making a lukewarm murky brew. He used to think the sight of her doing that, drinking that stuff, was surely one of the things people got divorced over. But now he knew that was nothing; there were much more serious matters.

He shouldn't drink coffee now, in the middle of a run. On the other hand, he'd interrupted his run already and it wouldn't be polite for him to take off again right now. He'd walk back to his house.

"That would be really nice," he said.

Daphne Miller smiled and stood up. "I'll be right back," she said. "Cream, sugar?"

"Black," he replied. Her robe came only to the top of her thighs. She was as tall as he was. Her limbs were not fat, but they were full, and so white, with a sprinkling of freckles. Cream. Sugar. His mother used to cook a heavy white candy that she called divinity; he could sink his teeth into a piece and it was as substantial against his teeth, for a moment, as dough; then it would dissolve, filling his mouth with an explosion of sugary sweetness. My God, why was he thinking of that?

The woman went in the house, came back out with a cup of steaming coffee. She handed it to him and they sat down together on the step.

"It's beautiful here," he said, looking around.

"Yes," she replied. "So peaceful. It will be a great change from the college."

"You're at the college?" he asked.

"I'm a secretary," she said. "For the history department."

"Well, maybe I'll run into you there," Jack said. "I'm going to teach there. In the English department. This is my first year."

Daphne smiled. "We're bound to run into each other. The English and history offices are in the same building, on the same floor. We even share" — she lowered her voice dramatically — "the same Xerox machine. Quite intimate, you see. And your wife? Does she teach too?"

"Oh, no. Alexandra — our daughter — is only two years old. Carey Ann wants to stay home and take care of her. Carey Ann's from Kansas. We just moved here. I . . . hope she won't be lonely. She doesn't know anyone here," he heard himself confessing.

"Oh, there are *lots* of young faculty with children," Daphne said. "She'll have friends in no time. Read the faculty newsletter. There should be some parties for new faculty anytime now, and also there will be parties at the faculty club, which many of the townspeople belong to. She'll meet all kinds of people."

"I don't know about the parties," Jack said. "With the baby, it's kind of hard to get away."

"Oh, you just bring her to the parties," Daphne said. "To most of them, anyway. I mean, these are family parties, cookouts and so on. And the town's crawling with nice teenage girls who want baby-sitting jobs."

She went on talking, and Jack drank the coffee, which was strong and aromatic and filled him with an instant complacency. Or was it this woman? She was making everything sound so easy. Now he knew why he had thought of the divinity: this woman had made him think of his mother. Not that she was that old — although she was older than he. There were the crow's-feet around her eyes, and the skin on her neck and chin was not smooth and taut. But she was a comfort to be around. Here she sat, friendly, talking, smiling, flicking a flying insect off her bare knee, as if she had complete confidence in the workings of the world.

Suddenly his whole future looked as promising and bright as the day that was now opening up around him. Birds were singing, dipping, flitting across the grassy yard, calling . . . the sun was high enough now so that the grass seemed to glow and the trees to flicker and blaze like candles . . . he was warm from the sun and the coffee . . . Why, he was *young!* He was only thirty-one! And he had a beautiful wife and a healthy, happy baby daughter, and he had been hired to teach at a prestigious college, and he'd do a brilliant job — there had been wise people who had called

him brilliant — and he'd write a novel someday, and the entire world, the rest of time, lay
before him, as the valley lay spread out below,
just on the other side of those trees.

"I'd better go," he said. "I've got work to
do. Thanks for the coffee. And stop down and
meet Carey Ann sometime. I know she'd be
glad to meet you." In her white robe, with her
heavy white limbs as subtly rounded as if
carved in marble, Daphne seemed Greek,
prophetic, wise.

They said good-bye. Jack intended to walk
back to his house, because he'd drunk the coffee and didn't want it sloshing in his stomach.
But before he knew it, he was running again,
and whistling as he went.

2

Daphne was beginning to regret her impulsiveness. It was Friday morning, and pouring rain, and she'd spent the week unpacking boxes and rearranging furniture and was tired of it. The following Monday she'd start back to work at the college, and then she'd be in the thick of people again, and she didn't want that much now; she just wanted a little break, a little conversation. Her friend Pauline was working today, getting ready for classes. Daphne stared out the window, remembering rainy days when Cynthia was a baby. Then, how luxurious and necessary had been the times she had spent with her best friend, Laura. Remembering Laura, Daphne had picked up the phone and called Carey Ann, introduced herself, and asked if she and her daughter would like to come up for some tea. The other woman's voice had been soft, drawling, and hesitant. But she had agreed, and soon a white convertible crept through the lane and stopped in front of the cottage.

Watching out the window, Daphne reflected that in Carey Ann's place, she would have put raincoats on herself and her daughter and splashed down the road through the rain, giving the little child some exercise before entering a stranger's house. Then, too, it was always fun to walk in the rain, stomping in puddles so the brown water flew up in the air like crickets. All the times she and Cyn had walked on rainy days, holding hands, sticking out their tongues to catch the raindrops, sometimes barefoot on the warm days, such a yummy feeling, squishy mud and tickly wet grass against their feet!

Carey Ann raced from her car to the door with Alexandra in her arms, both enclosed in squeaky yellow slickers. Carey Ann's hips were so tiny Daphne couldn't imagine how she had managed to carry a baby. Carey Ann seemed shy at first, but Alexandra didn't; as soon as her mother released her from her arms, she began running through the house, grabbing hold of everything, and Carey Ann hurried along behind her, rescuing vases, straightening bedspreads, trying in vain to interest her daughter in a book she'd brought along. When Alexandra saw Dickens, who was asleep under the table in the kitchen, she shrieked with such delight that the dog sprang to his feet in terror.

"Doddie!" the little girl yelled, and, racing over to him, she began to pummel his back with her little fists. Both she and the dog were about the same height. Dickens could easily have taken a bite of her, but he only looked up at Daphne with a disoriented and puzzled look.

"Alexandra just loves dogs," Carey Ann said, watching her daughter grab Dickens's short black fur and pull. She sank into a kitchen chair, obviously grateful to have her baby's attention captured for a moment so she could rest.

Daphne watched her dog warily, not sure just how much he would put up with. He was a young dog, only five, and he had been around children before, but never around this kind of child, who was now trying to crawl on his back.

"Good Dickens," she said to him. He was standing very still as Alexandra mauled him.

"Eye," Alexandra said, poking her finger against Dickens's eyelid. The dog blinked and turned his head away.

"That's right, Lexi!" Carey Ann said. "What a smart girl you are."

What an idiot *you* are!, Daphne thought, then chided herself. No, she had to give the woman more of a chance than this.

She had brewed a pot of apple-cinnamon

tea, knowing that often children wanted to drink what the adults drank, and since Carey Ann was already collapsed on a kitchen chair, Daphne picked up the tray and put it in the middle of the table. On a flowered plate were some cookies for the little girl, and crumbly pieces of applesauce cake for everyone. Daphne chatted easily about moving in, getting settled, and poured tea for herself and Carey Ann. In the meantime Alexandra had lost interest in the dog and clambered up on one of the wooden kitchen chairs to see what was going on at the table. Dickens, released, hurried off into Daphne's bedroom. She could hear the clicking of his nails and the funny scooting noise he made as he crawled beneath her bed to hide.

"Would you like tea?" Daphne asked Alexandra, smiling.

"*Me!*" the little girl yelled. She was standing on the chair, leaning over the table.

"Is it all right if she has tea?" Daphne asked Carey Ann. "It's apple cinnamon, but I've got plenty of milk if she wants it."

"Well . . . " Carey Ann said, drawing the word out as she tried to make up her mind.

Daphne waited. Alexandra screamed, "*Me!*" A vision flew through Daphne's mind as quickly as a bird; she saw herself stuffing a huge piece of applesauce cake into the little girl's mouth.

"I suppose it's all right," Carey Ann said.

"*Me!*" said Alexandra.

"Yes, you may have some tea too," Daphne told her, leaning over and picking up the bright pink flowered mug she had set out especially for Alexandra.

"No — *me!*" Alexandra yelled, her face growing red.

"I think she wants to pour her own tea," Carey Ann said, smiling. "Alexandra's such a big girl," she said to her daughter in an adoring voice.

Daphne put the teapot on the table within Alexandra's reach. It wasn't an expensive teapot or one rich with memories, but it was china, made in England, and it would break easily. It was so heavy Daphne didn't know how the child was going to manage to pick it up. But she sat down at her place at the table and watched as Alexandra picked up the teapot with both hands, and suddenly quiet with effort and concentration, began to pour herself a cup of tea. She got the spout near enough to the mug that some of the tea actually went in, but more of it flowed down the side of the mug, across the table, and in a thin brown stream from the table onto the floor.

Alexandra kept on pouring. Daphne looked at Carey Ann.

"Lexi spill," Carey Ann said, smiling. "Let Mommy help." She reached for the teapot.

"No! Me!" Alexandra screamed, jerking the teapot away, glaring at her mother with rage.

Carey Ann withdrew her hand. She sat watching until Alexandra had emptied the pot. All the tea things and the plates and napkins were swimming in a sea of liquid that now dripped down on the side and also in the middle where the two oak leaves met.

Carey Ann looked up at Daphne. "The books say children learn faster if you don't interfere," she said, almost meekly. "And Alexandra is, you know, so bright. We think she might be a *gifted child.*"

The gifted child had dripping elbows and a wet shirt from leaning on the table in the tea. She set the pot down, and kneeling on the chair, picked up her cup and drank. She smiled, a radiant smile. "Good," she pronounced.

"Aren't you a good girl!" Carey Ann said. Then she sighed and took a sip of her own tea.

Now, am I getting old or what?, Daphne thought, for it bothered her to sit there as tea still spilled over the edge of the table and made puddles on the floor. Well, God, it would all wipe up with paper towels. But the floor in this old kitchen slanted slightly downward in one direction; if she didn't stop it now, all the tea would end up in a puddle underneath the refrigerator.

"Excuse me," Daphne said. She rose and sopped up the mess with paper towels.

Alexandra began to bang her spoon on her mug. Daphne looked up from the floor to see the little girl beam a seraphic smile at her mother. *"Bang!"* she said merrily, delighted.

"Yes, bang," Carey Ann said, not so merrily. "Lexi want cake?"

But Lexi didn't want cake. She wanted to bang her spoon on her mug, and she continued to as Daphne duck-walked on her haunches around her kitchen floor, wiping up the tea. Alexandra found a rhythm and got into it: BANG BANG BANG! BANG BANG BANG! BANG BANG BANG! The mug would surely break. Daphne rose, put the towels in the trash, and sat down at the kitchen table. She was surprised not to see chips of china flying around the table. I didn't realize how old I've gotten, she thought. This is driving me crazy.

"Jack told me you work at the college," Carey Ann said, smiling, her voice raised to carry across her daughter's noise.

"Yes," Daphne said. "In the history department. I'm a secretary. I've been there for fourteen years now."

"You must like it," Carey Ann said.

64

"Well, yes," Daphne answered. "I suppose. You see, I was divorced when my daughter was two, and I had to have some kind of job to support us both, and the people in the history department were friends — some of them — and it worked out all right. And then Cynthia grew older and all her friends were here, and the school system is so excellent, it seemed best for her if I stayed in the town. Although it's not what I ever envisioned myself doing when I was younger. Being a secretary. And now that I'm older . . ."

Daphne let her voice trail away. It was just too difficult to make herself heard over Alexandra's banging, especially since the little girl had miraculously managed to increase the volume. And now she was shouting, *"Bang, bang, bang!"* as she pounded, obviously unhappy that her mother's attention was focused elsewhere for a few minutes. Exasperated, Daphne pointedly looked at the little girl, then looked at Carey Ann.

Carey Ann responded by looking miserable. But she leaned over to her daughter. "Alexandra," she said softly. "You're hurting Mommy's ears."

For a moment mother and daughter looked at each other, frozen in a standoff. Then, with a smile that flashed radiance across her face,

Alexandra said, "Sowwy, Mommy!" and put down the spoon. She crawled off her chair and up into her mother's lap. She kissed her mother's ears. "Lexi make boo-boo okay!" she said. Then she snuggled into her mother's lap, put her thumb in her mouth, and let her eyes glaze over.

"She's a pretty little girl," Daphne said gratefully.

"Thank you," Carey Ann said. "We think so. She's awfully energetic. Sometimes . . ." She dropped her eyes and looked down at her daughter. Then she looked up at Daphne. "Sometimes I just don't know if I can keep up with her," she confessed.

"I remember feeling that way myself." Daphne laughed. "It never did seem fair to me that the babies got all the energy that the parents needed." Although I had my child under more control than you do by a long way, she thought.

"Where's your daughter now?" Carey Ann asked.

"She went to live with her father. In California." Daphne felt pain shoot through her, and poison, as the bitterness within her flicked its tongue. She took a deep breath. "Well, she's sixteen years old. And it was something she needed to do," she said. "She hadn't had a chance to get to know her father before."

"You must miss her," Carey Ann said.

"I do," Daphne replied. "Very much."

"I know I miss my parents," Carey Ann went on. "Especially my father. He always took care of me. Sometimes — "

"*Bottle!*" Alexandra yelled, popping her thumb from her mouth. She turned around and grabbed her mother's face with her two small chubby hands. She wrenched Carey Ann's face around to hers. "*Bottle!*" she said again, directly into her mother's face.

"Oh, dear, I didn't bring her bottle," Carey Ann said. She rose, letting her daughter slip to the floor. "Let's go home, Alexandra," she said. "Your bottle's at home. Thank you for the tea," she said, turning back to Daphne.

"Perhaps she'd like a glass of milk?" Daphne offered.

The little girl left her mother's side and ran off into the living room, her hands flying out sideways to hit whatever she passed. "*Bottle!*" she yelled as she went.

Carey Ann shook her head. "No," she said. "It's not really the milk she wants, you know, it's the bottle. Maybe she'll take a nap now. Then I'll be able to get something done around the house. It's so much work unpacking, isn't it?"

The two women moved, as they talked, into the living room. Alexandra had discovered the piano and was suddenly up on the piano bench, pounding out chords that would have made John Cage weep.

"What I don't understand is how you decide where everything goes," Carey Ann said wearily. "I mean, the kitchen things go in the kitchen, of course, but where? I mean, should the dishes go in the cupboards next to the sink, or the food? I mean, they both have to be near the sink, right? Oh . . . " she said, a smile breaking out over her face. "That sounds like 'Frère Jacques,' doesn't it? I wonder if we should get Alexandra a piano. She's so smart that way."

Daphne thought that what the child was hammering away at sounded nothing at all like any organized musical notes she'd ever heard before, and she was amused and somehow strangely saddened that Carey Ann thought they should get a piano for the little girl now. "She's only two," Daphne said. "I think that's really too young for a piano. Even if she is smart. Their hands have to be a certain size in order to reach the keys, or it's frustrating for them, you know."

Carey Ann said, "But didn't Mozart perform when he was three?"

"It's difficult to hear you!" Daphne said. "Perhaps we should — "

But suddenly she sounded insane, as her

voice, which had been raised to carry over the sounds of Alexandra's banging, roared out in the quiet living room. Alexandra had abruptly stopped playing. She was staring, her adorably rosy face rapt with delight, at something on top of the piano.

Many valuable things were on top of the piano. This house was so small that Daphne had of necessity used the top of the baby grand as a surface for the certain objects of her life she wanted to have near her, available to sight and touch every day. Mostly there were pictures: of herself as a young graduate student, a picture that had been taken for the school newspaper and that showed her as she had really been at that time in her life — devoted, studious, profoundly serious, and radiantly beautiful. It was almost her favorite picture of herself, and it was in a silver frame. There were pictures of her with Cynthia at different stages of their lives together, when Cyn was a baby, when they were at the Cape or riding horses, and then a huge azurite-framed picture of Cynthia in costume as Maria in *West Side Story*, which the local high school had put on last year and in which she had been cast in the lead role even though she was only a sophomore. Cynthia had dyed her long blond hair black for the part, and in this photo she looked devastatingly beautiful and utterly *dramatic*. Daphne still was amazed to think, every time she looked at the picture, that this creature was her daughter.

There were other objects on the piano top too — it held so much. An alabaster box trimmed in brass, fading from emerald green to pearl. A large Chinese vase, a reproduction, but costly — for Daphne — nonetheless, which Daphne had filled with multicolored zinnias from the back garden.

It was the flowers that Alexandra was focused on.

"Pretty fwower, Mommy!" the little girl said.

And in a flash she was clambering up from the piano bench, and then onto the piano keyboard. For a moment she stood with both feet in their tiny pink rubber sneakers, balanced on the piano keys. The piano plinked and plonked as she shifted forward, reaching for the flowers.

Daphne looked at Carey Ann, who was calmly watching her daughter with adoration on her face. "I don't think it's wise for her to stand on the piano keyboard," Daphne said. But the words were scarcely out of her mouth when Alexandra, unable to reach the flowers, stepped on the music rack and crawled up onto the piano lid. Then, scooting along on her knees, she made her way toward the vase of flowers, knocking picture frames to the left and right as she went. The picture of Daphne's parents, poised rigidly inside an old gilded wooden frame, thwacked to the floor. The alabaster box, struck by the child's knee, flew to the edge of the piano and hovered there. Alexandra reached out for the flowers, and Daphne took three giant strides and grabbed the vase just before it toppled, as Carey Ann raced across the room and scooped up her daughter.

"Oh, sweetie, *be careful!*" she said. "You could fall and hurt yourself!"

Daphne stood, the vase of flowers in her arms, staring at Carey Ann. Carey Ann turned, holding Alexandra in her arms, and, at Daphne's expression, her own turned immediately into one of childish alarm.

"Is something wrong?" she asked. Her daughter was trying to squirm away from her to get back to the piano; her arms were waving frantically and she was kicking her feet. *"Fwower!"* she screamed.

Daphne took a deep breath. "Carey Ann, I think you need to learn to control your daughter more, at least when she's in someone else's home. She almost broke several valuable things of mine, irreplaceable objects."

Carey Ann gasped at Daphne's words, and Alexandra must have felt the shock waves in her mother's body, for the little girl went quiet suddenly and stared up at her mother's face.

"Oh!" Carey Ann said. Suddenly she was trembling all over, and her face had gone white, drained of all color. "Oh! No wonder your daughter won't live with you!" she cried. Her lower lip quivered and her mouth opened as if she were about to say something else, when instead she swept across the room, clutching her baby to her tightly, pulled open the door, and hurried out into the rain. Alexandra, face round with surprise, gazed over Carey Ann's shoulder at Daphne and then at the house.

Daphne stood, the vase of flowers in her hand, and felt such a wave of despair sweep over her that she, too, began to shake. Tears sprang to her eyes. She felt both violated and guilty. Something about Carey Ann reminded her of Cynthia — perhaps it was just her youth — although she knew she had taught Cynthia better manners. Cyn would never act this way in someone else's home, though she might act this way around Daphne, in her own home.

Daphne strode to the front door and stood watching as Carey Ann bent into the passenger side of the car, strapping her daughter into her car seat. Then she went to the driver's side, got in, and drove off. Soon, where the white convertible had been, only a wall of pouring rain remained.

Daphne shut the door and leaned against it. She grinned, for the yellow rain slickers of both Hamilton females were still hanging on the antique oak coatrack in the front corner of the living room. Those rain slickers made Daphne feel triumphant, made her feel that she had *won*.

But won what? My God, Daphne thought, what had happened? She put the vase of flowers back on the piano lid and set up the picture frames again. Nothing was broken. Suddenly the room seemed very empty, *emptied*, and she was overcome with an extreme and immediate exhaustion.

The soggy tea things were strewn all over the kitchen table, but she left them and walked into her bedroom and lay down on her bed. Here it was dim and cool. She kicked off her shoes and pulled a quilt up over her. Rain streamed down the windows, the outside walls, enclosing the house in a steady, heavy thrumming noise; and it was like being on a ferry or in an airplane with the engine drumming away incessantly. She had that sensation of being trapped for a while in something bigger than she was, something moving, carrying her someplace, and she could only calmly let

73

herself be carried, while the droning around her assured her that something else around her was persevering, and she could rest.

Memory was bizarre: it was so *defensive.* How many times had she tried to remember a time, an event, with David, or even being in Joe's arms — and her memory threw up walls of brick, clouds of fog. She couldn't get through to her own past life! Or she would try and try to focus, only to find herself becoming irritated, agitated, restless, and without the memory she was craving.

But Carey Ann's dramatic exit, and the sight of Alexandra at the piano, a small blond girl child at the piano, had released a memory in Daphne that was as ripe and full as the present. Or, rather, it had released Daphne into the memory, and as she lay on her bed surrounded by the sound of rain, it was as if she had just sunk down into a pool of remembrance.

Three years ago (three million years ago, so much had changed since then), Daphne and David had been seated in the Grange Hall with half the other people in the town, waiting for the local spring student music recital to begin. David had gone to Westhampton College, and like many other alums, had loved it so much he had come back to Westhampton to live. He was a lawyer, a handsome and eloquent man, but he was an alcoholic. Two wives had left him because of his drinking. Now, in his forties, he and Daphne were lovers. He wanted Daphne to marry him, and Daphne had promised him she would — as soon as he managed to get himself sober and to stay that way. His states of ugly drunkenness did not come often, but when they did, they were terrifying, and she would not inflict them on Cynthia, who adored David.

Tonight David had promised that he had had only the two gin-and-tonics that Daphne had given him, and she thought she believed him. He was being very quiet and contained as he sat upright on his uncomfortable metal folding chair next to her. It was early May, and although the spring had so far been unseasonably cool, today the temperature had shot up to nearly eighty and the humidity and pollen made the air dense with invisible, irritating motes and flecks. Daphne had leaned over to put her hand on David's arm to let him know she loved him now and was grateful that he had come with her.

It had always seemed to Daphne to go against ordinary logic and even Christian compassion that student music recitals were held in such mundane and insufficiently ventilated rooms, where the audience shifted their

75

numbed bums on tiny ancient folding metal chairs that threatened at every moment to collapse beneath them. These recitals were always, at the best, horrible torturous events, while earnest or uninterested little children pecked and blatted their way through asinine little tunes that no one over the age of ten ever wanted to hear again in her life. Daphne's vision of eternity was listening to Heather Goldman, who was six years old, turgidly plonking her way through "Twinkle, Twinkle, Little Star" while her parents, who also had the poor child taking ballet, ice skating, tap dancing, and art studio, slunk to the front (bent over so as not to deprive the rest of the audience of the sight of their daughter at the piano) to snap pictures of her hitting every single note.

Oh, David did love her, Daphne thought, to sit through all of this, and if he could put up with this for her, why couldn't she put up with his bad patches? As the other cute or nasty little children appeared to maim and camouflage "Lightly Row," "Old MacDonald" (Oh, Christ, oh, Christ, why hadn't all the music teachers in the world long ago conspired to eradicate "Old MacDonald" from the music books?), "Little Indian Dance," "Frère Jacques," and "Pop Goes the Weasel," Daphne occupied herself by going over in her mind for the millionth time just why it was she was not marrying David when she loved him so and he loved her. The answer was always the same, and irrefutable: she did not want Cynthia exposed to David drunk.

After a brief intermission during which all the parents sprang from their chairs as if released from the rack and stretched their arms and rubbed their backsides and yawned and made a lot of noise, it was time for the older students to play. This was almost pleasurable, even worth waiting for, but now of course all the younger pupils who had already performed were seated in the audience, giggling and picking their noses and falling off their chairs and making paper airplanes out of their programs. Dorothy Kasper, the head teacher, came out onstage to say a few words about the proper behavior at a concert, then disappeared behind the curtain, leaving the older students to perform to a room that sounded vaguely like a mutinous insane asylum.

Daphne managed to filter out the other noise and focus on the pianists. She thought it was just possible that Cynthia might make a career out of music, for she wanted to do something in the performing arts, and she had lost interest in ballet. Cynthia was thirteen, and taller than a lot of her classmates, and filling out with what Daphne considered astonishing rapidity. Seniors in high school were already calling to ask her out (Daphne wouldn't let her go). So far she had not hit that humiliating "awkward" stage so many teenagers hit. She was tall, and slender, and tonight wore her long blond hair in an elaborate French braid that hung down her back and was entwined with tiny lilac flowers. Her best friend had done it — if Daphne had done it, it would have been pronounced, for some reason, *wrong*. Daphne had offered to buy Cynthia a Laura Ashley dress even though they were so damned expensive, but Cynthia had rolled her eyes in disbelief and said, "Oh, Mom, you're so *archaic*," and left the room exhausted with the burden of her mother's hopeless gaucherie. Now, as she came across the stage to sit at the piano, she was wearing layers of clothing that actually looked like layers of old sheets and tablecloths and that made it impossible for anyone to believe there was an actual human body hidden inside, which was probably, after all, Cynthia's intent.

Cynthia played "Für Elise" and part of the Moonlight Sonata. The old favorites, the old standbys. Unless absolutely butchered, these pieces were crowd-pleasers. As Cynthia began to play, Daphne stopped breathing. If Cynthia faltered or hit a dissonant chord, Daphne

78

knew she would die on the spot with embarrassment for her child. Her hands were sweating so terribly she had to keep wiping them on her skirt. David, sensing Daphne's nervousness (how could he not? — she was practically bleeping with anxiety), put his arm around her shoulders and gave her a small reassuring hug.

And after a while, it was obvious that Cynthia was not going to make any mistakes. She had these pieces down pat. Daphne knew this — she had heard Cynthia practice probably *billions* of times by now — but still . . . Still, it was such a relief to hear the music rippling, waterlike, fluid, sparkling, from her child's hands.

It was worth it. All those years of lessons. All the things Daphne had forfeited in order to pay for the lessons, all the grueling moments she had reminded — forced — Cynthia to practice. Now Cynthia was playing the Moonlight Sonata, and the music swelled and opened like the color lavender deepening on a dusky summer night. Now, no matter what else happened, in times of sadness or pain, Cynthia would be able to sit at the piano and play these eternal Beethoven pieces, which with their amaranthine melodies would lift her from the present into a pure and peaceful space.

Daphne's cheeks were wet when her daughter finished. The applause was spontaneous, enthusiastic, deafening. My God, sometimes life really was worth living, sometimes it really gave you something back!

Other teenagers played, none as well as Cynthia, and Daphne listened halfheartedly, actually resting from the euphoria to which she had been lifted. Then Tammy Benton sat down to play the final selection, the first movement of Beethoven's *Pathetique* Sonata, the longest and most complicated piece to be performed that evening.

Daphne was impressed simply that the girl, at Cynthia's age, was attempting it. Secretly she hoped the girl would do terribly, that she would foul up and hit clunkers and even end up sobbing with humiliation onstage in front of everyone. (Cynthia and Tammy were rivals. Tammy really was a horrible little bitch — she had been trained well by her mother, who was poisonous and nasty and snobbish and who had reduced Daphne to secret fits of rage and weeping many times.)

But in spite of all the ill will Daphne could summon up and send out into the air, Tammy played beautifully. Masterfully. She was splendid.

"Wow," David said to Daphne when the girl had finished (he didn't know how Daphne

80

and Cynthia felt about Tammy and her mother). And the applause was stunning; some people even rose to give the girl a standing ovation.

Then the applause fell down to a pattering, and the concert was over. Mothers and fathers and teachers carried long tables out into the hall and set out punch, paper cups, brownies, and cookies. Little girls who had played piano with huge pink bows in their hair raced around the room pursuing little boys, while the older children sauntered around the room looking desperately bored.

"I need a drink," David whispered.

"You deserve one after this," Daphne replied. But they waited until Cynthia had received all the praise it seemed she could get that evening and the hall was emptying of people. Then Daphne and David crossed the room to collect her. But just before they reached her, horrid simpering Tammy slid up in front of Daphne.

"Hello, Mrs. Miller," she said with cloying sweetness.

"Hello, Tammy," Daphne said. "You played beautifully tonight."

"Oh, thank you, Mrs. Miller," Tammy said.

The girl would have stood there smirking and twittering, but Daphne said, "We're late for something else, must go, goodbye," and swept around Tammy, devoted darling David following in her wake. "Ready?" she asked Cynthia, who was now staring at her with a face like the plague.

David drove (he had the loveliest Mercedes, gray-blue and as deep and smooth as a good dream), Cynthia slid silently into the back seat, and Daphne turned from the front passenger seat to talk to her daughter.

"Oh, Cyn, my angel, I am so proud of you, do you know that?" she said. "You played so beautifully tonight!"

"Yeah, that's what you told Tammy too," Cynthia said.

At once Daphne knew that her daughter was about to treat her to something from *The Exorcist*. Of her many roles, this was the worst. Actually, in a way it was her best, for she played it with a power that would have put Linda Blair to shame, but it was the hardest for Daphne to deal with.

"Oh, honey . . ." Daphne began.

"You didn't have to tell her that," Cynthia said. "You know how I feel about her!"

"And I agree!" Daphne said. "I think Tammy Benton is a piece of *slime*. But, darling, this is the world we're living in, and she did come up to me. What could I do, spit in her face?"

"You didn't have to tell her she played *beautifully*. You could have said she played *nicely*. You didn't have to say *beautifully*. God."

"Oh, Cyn, I'm sorry, I didn't mean it, it just popped out," Daphne began.

"Yeah, the way it popped out when you told me *I* played beautifully." Cynthia's voice was full of scorn.

"Cynthia," Daphne said, injecting firmness and common sense into her voice, "there is no reason for you to ruin this wonderful night by fussing about that awful Tammy Benton. You were so wonderful, you should be so proud of yourself, I'm so proud of you, it would just be a waste of our lives to spend another second even thinking about that stupid little twit, let alone arguing about her."

"Oh, now you're trying to get out of it."

"Out of what?" Daphne asked, baffled.

"Out of telling me the *truth*. Like you always do, evading the issue, trying to sneak away from telling me the truth."

"Cynthia," Daphne said, "the labyrinth of your mind is a thing of wonder to me."

No response. Cynthia sat staring at her mother with righteous anger vibrating from her entire body.

"All right." Daphne surrendered. "What is the truth that you think I'm trying to evade?"

"That you think Tammy played better than I did."

Now Daphne was stumped. How was she going to get out of this one? For Tammy *had* played better than Cynthia. In her deepest, *deepest* heart of hearts, Daphne thought not only that Tammy's piece was more difficult but also that she had played it with real feeling, with subtleties and nuances, whereas her own daughter had merely played with expertise.

"Cynthia," she said, sighing, "I do think that Tammy's piece was more *complicated* than yours. Of course I would be lying if I said otherwise. And it does seem that she is just a little more advanced than you are. Perhaps she's been taking lessons longer. Perhaps she practices more. Perhaps she's driven, perhaps she wants to be a concert pianist, I don't know, how can I know, and I don't even care. I don't care about Tammy! I don't think she played *better* than you. I don't even want to consider this evening in those terms. I don't want to think about that horrible girl. Oh, darling love, why can't we forget her and just be so happy that you did so well? You know, I felt like my entire life was justified when I heard you play. I felt like you had just recompensed me for all those hours in labor."

By this time they had reached home and

David was sitting silently, keeping the engine running, unsure whether Daphne would invite him in or ask him to leave so the two of them could carry on with their fight in privacy. He had been around them long enough by now to know that while usually Cynthia and Daphne were compatible, companionable, like the best of friends, there were times when Cynthia went berserk like this; he and Daphne had decided it had to be teenage hormones running amok and taking Cynthia with them. Daphne looked back at her daughter. She was still angry, so angry her head would start spinning around in circles any minute while bile exploded all over the car. This is what it's like having a teenager around, friends told her, and we just have to put up with it, because our own parents went through the very same thing and let us live.

"Come on in the house, Cynthia," Daphne said. "David, why don't I call you tomorrow? Thanks for coming, thanks for driving."

As they entered the house, Dickens came groveling and wagging up to meet them, drooling with joy to see them again. Fred Smith, their ancient stupid black male cat, was sitting in the corner of the living room, staring at the wall. He did not acknowledge their presence. Usually Cynthia bent to stroke and fondle Dickens, to smother him with baby talk, or at the least she would go over and stroke Fred Smith's head and say, "Now, calm down, Fred, I'll get you some Valium." Usually after outings like this (which were getting fewer and fewer), when mother and daughter had been in a room with other people, they would collapse in chairs and gossip like friends, criticizing everything everyone wore, the way Mrs. Kasper's teeth hung out — why didn't she get braces!

But tonight Cynthia went stiff-backed, without a word, up the stairs and into her bedroom.

Daphne thought: I'm not sure I have the energy for this.

But she went up the stairs and stood in her daughter's doorway — Cynthia hadn't shut her door; that was something.

"Cyn," she said, "Cyn, come on. Give me a break. I love you. I am so proud of you I could pop. I think you performed better than Tammy, and besides, you *looked* a million times more beautiful. You make her look like a *lump*."

Cynthia's back was to Daphne; she was fussing with books and papers on her desk. Suddenly she turned to face Daphne, and her face was shining with tears.

"Oh, you don't have to say all those things. You don't have to lie like that. *I* know what the truth is."

Daphne was dumbstruck. Her daughter was *riven* with misery, and where had it all come from? Why? What had she done?

Was it only a year ago, two years ago, that Cynthia, at eleven and twelve, had rushed in the door after school to hug her and tell her every detail of her day? They used to sit together on the living-room sofa watching TV, and all at once Cynthia would cuddle up to her, giving her a rib-breaking hug. "My Moochie," she would say. "My Coochie," Daphne would answer, and they would go on that way, cuddling, Daphne stroking her daughter's shining hair, the two of them saying infantile, nonsensical favorite phrases that they would never have spoken in front of others.

"Cynthia," Daphne said at last, going carefully. "You keep mentioning that you know the 'truth.' What is the 'truth'? Would you please tell me?"

Cynthia raised her head and looked at her mother, pride and anger and scorn radiating from her face. "The truth is," she said, "that I'm not good enough for you. I'll *never* be good enough for you. That's why you don't *really* love me."

"Cynthia," Daphne said softly. "Honey. My Coochie. How can you say those things?

You know I love you. You *know* I love you. Darling child. What's wrong? Why are you so upset?"

"You talked to Tammy before you talked to me, you told her she played beautifully before you said anything to me."

"Oh, I see. Well, I'm sorry I didn't speak to you first. I'm sorry I told Tammy she played beautifully. If it's any comfort, I *did* walk away from her, I walked around and past her, I practically walked *over* her." She looked at Cynthia's face to see if it had lightened any. It hadn't. "Oh, honey, you've got to know how proud I am of you. I love you. I adore you. You are the light of my life. Don't you know all that?"

"No," Cynthia said, and tears came flowing again. "I don't know that. I know you used to love me. But now all you do is criticize me. And *I can't stand it!* Don't you think I know I'm not good enough for you, I'll never be good enough, I'll never be what you want me to be?"

"Cynthia, what are you talking about? What do you mean? What do I want you to be?"

Cynthia sprang up from the bed in one quick movement, all her layers of clothing frothing and flapping around her, as if she'd taken the bedsheets with her. She crossed the room to her desk to grab a handful of tissues.

Her shoulders were shaking. "The best. That's what you want me to be. The *best*. You're always saying, 'I want you to be the best you can be.' Well, what if I can't be the best? What if I'm not an A-plus person like you are, what if I'm just a B-minus person? Or even a C-minus person?"

"Cynthia, Cynthia, calm down. What are you saying? I don't *grade* people." (That wasn't true, and Cynthia knew it; they often compared and "graded" people.) "I certainly don't grade you. Or if I do, I always give you an A-plus."

"No, you don't! Or you shouldn't! Because I'm *not* an A-plus. I don't think I'm anything at all! Oh, Mommy, I know I can't be a concert pianist. I'm not completely stupid. I have ears too. I hadn't heard Tammy play before. She's *really* good, she's a trillion times better than me. No matter how hard I work, I'll never be that good, and that's the truth. And I can't be a concert pianist, and I don't think I'll ever be anything! I *thought* maybe I could be a concert pianist, but now I know I can't, and I don't know what else to try to be."

"Well, that doesn't matter!" Daphne exclaimed, relieved to have her child talking, sorrowed by her words. How had Cynthia come to be so harsh on herself? "Oh, sweetie, that doesn't matter. You can quit lessons if you want. I just wanted you to learn to play for pleasure. I never meant for you to be a concert pianist."

"No, but you want me to be something. Something *special*."

"No, no, no, I don't care what you become. I think you already *are* something special."

"That's not true! That's not true, and you know it." Cynthia was shouting now, crying again, and her nose was running and she was wringing one of her long cotton shirts in her hands. "How many times in my life have I heard about how different your life would have been if you had finished graduate school and gotten your doctorate and taught instead of marrying Dad? How many times have you said to me, 'Cynthia, you've got to *be* something . . . Cynthia, you're special, you're the sort of person who could star in this world . . . Cynthia, I want to help you so you don't end up like me'?"

"Oh, honey," Daphne began. For she had said all that, but she had meant it differently than Cynthia was taking it, she had meant it as praise, as help.

"And I'm not even as smart as you were! I couldn't even *get into* grad school! My science grades suck this term. My spelling is dragging down my English grades. And I can't be a concert pianist. I can't be anything!"

90

"Cynthia, you're thirteen years old," Daphne said. "Give yourself time. No one expects you to be anything yet. And the time will come when you will find your special talent, your special quality. But I'll love you no matter what — even if you become a . . . a gas-station attendant." Desperate, Daphne flashed on an article she had read recently about unusual jobs. "Even if you become a worm farmer."

"A worm farmer?" Cynthia asked, her curiosity caught. So then it was all right. They were on the other side of the argument. Cynthia calmed down, Daphne soothed her, and they became friends again.

But not constantly. After that night, which seemed to have been some kind of watershed in their lives, so that everything could be measured as "before" and "after," Daphne knew that Cynthia had moved beyond the bounds of her control. And what had happened was what always had to happen in life: Cynthia moved into the wider world where her mother could not arrange complete happiness. So of course she took her unhappinesses out on Daphne — whom else *could* she take them out on? Daphne watched as her child became more and more successful in her life: she was very popular, invited to all the right parties, she had several close girlfriends, and eventually a few handsome and awkwardly polite and endearing boyfriends. She was always lovely to look at, she was on the honor roll (but not high honors, because of her spelling). She was forever being asked to baby-sit, because children and parents alike adored her — and then, at fourteen, she started acting, in school productions and in the local theater productions, and it was obvious that so early in her life she had found her talent. To the outside world she looked like a golden girl, enviable, with everything, and she walked through that outside world radiating confidence. But when she was inside, in her own home, she was overcome with doubts and self-hatred and self-criticism, and because she was so young still, she couldn't seem to understand how hard she was being on herself.

Perhaps the problem had been that Cynthia had never had her father around to dote on her. Perhaps it had been a deep and tangled Freudian thing. Now Daphne shifted on her bed in her dim bedroom, where the sound of rain was lessening, coming in gentle patters as if little frogs were hopping against the house and windows. Cynthia had left in late June, as soon as school was out. Daphne still expected her to appear any moment, asking something like, "What's that word that means it doesn't last, passing away quickly, oh, *you* know. I need it for my homework." "Transience?" Daphne would offer. "Oh, yeah, right," Cynthia would respond, wandering back to her room.

But Cynthia had no room in this house. Cynthia was in California with her father, and Daphne didn't know when she would ever see her daughter again.

Jack had had a rotten day. Hudson Jennings, the head of the English department, Jack's former professor, now his boss, had dropped by Jack's office to see how he was settling in.

"What is *that?*" Hudson had said.

Jack knew what Hudson was asking about — an almost life-size cardboard stand-up of Prince and his purple motorcycle. Jack had a friend who ran a record store and got stuff like this as publicity gimmicks; the friend knew how Jack felt about Prince and had given him the stand-up. It wasn't obscene or even provocative (well, maybe provocative); Prince had all his clothes on for once, in fact he had on elaborate clothes, a purple satin suit, thigh-high black boots, an Edwardian white shirt, and white lace gloves. Very fine. He looked dangerous and ready to break all the rules, and his motorcycle was three times as big as

93

he was, and that was the wonderful thing about Prince, who was, after all, a little man, even a tiny man. He swaggered and flaunted and wouldn't let *anything* make him look small.

"It's a stand-up of Prince. The musician," Jack said.

"Oh, yes. I know who he is," Hudson said. "But what is it doing in your office?"

"My wife won't let me keep it at home." Jack caught his boss's expression. "Just kidding."

"I must say it occurs to me to wonder whether the office of a professor of English literature is the place for it."

Jack swallowed. He couldn't believe this. Was this Russia? "Well, I thought it might make me more . . . accessible to the students."

"I believe the point of college is to raise the students to our level, not to sink to theirs," Hudson said.

Jack looked at Hudson. Hudson looked levelly back at Jack. When Jack had been an undergraduate at Westhampton in the seventies, he had admired the hell out of Hudson. No, he had worshiped Hudson. He had wanted to *be* Hudson. One of the main reasons he had wanted to teach at Westhampton College was Hudson Jennings.

"Would you like me to remove it?" Jack asked, letting his bafflement show on his face, trying to say in that way: I didn't realize you'd gotten so inflexible.

"I think so, yes," Hudson said, smiling now. (Was he amused by Jack?) "By the way, I dropped by to tell you that we hope we'll see you and your charming wife at the faculty picnic next Friday evening. At the faculty club. It will be a cookout unless it rains."

"Great!" Jack said. "We'll be there. I know Carey Ann's eager to meet some of the other wives."

Hudson went on down the hall then, and now here Jack was, driving home with Prince and his motorcycle jammed in the back seat of his car. He felt that Hudson had been uptight and dictatorial and that he himself had been a wimp. Prince wouldn't have given in to Hudson so fast. But what could he have done? Jumped up and poured out his soul? "Well, you see, sir, I think this big stand-up of Prince that few other people have kind of helps out my *image;* it's sort of like my mascot, especially now that I have to teach this neoclassic crap, which is so cut-and-dried. Jesus Christ, Alexander Pope! Prince has more *poetry* in his left sideburn than all of the neoclassicists put together. But you've hired me to teach the stuff, and I will, and I'll do a

95

good job of it. I'll lie about it and pretend I like it, but God, at least let me let my students know that I'm not like that, that I'm modern, alive, I don't like a cold, closed, rigid literature."

Well, of course he couldn't have said all that. But perhaps he should have tried harder. Not given in so easily. Saying what? "If you'll look closely, sir, you'll see that Prince's clothing is not unlike the clothing of the lords and bards of the neoclassic age. My instincts are that when my students see this cut-out, they will *subconsciously* become more receptive to the work of the eighteenth century because it will be linked in their minds with this 'poet' of the twentieth century." That would have been good, that sounded pretty reasonable, he should have tried that. After all, what if Hudson had only been testing him to see how much of a yes-man he was, or if he had the guts to stand up for what was right?

He was getting paranoid. Hudson wasn't doing that. Hudson hated that stand-up of Prince; it was as simple as that. Now Jack didn't know where he'd put it. He wanted it somewhere visible to him daily, as an antidote to his life, which was so bound up by rules.

Oh, God, how awful, to be thirty-one and already as stuck in life as if both feet were sunk in cement! He couldn't change now, he

96

couldn't take risks now; he had a family to support. Although that was not fair, not fair to Carey Ann and Alexandra; he hadn't been an adventurer before marriage; he'd never been an adventurer at all. He had always been so *careful* that, looking back, he saw that he had been just short of cowardly. It was his parents' fault, probably (he loved both his parents and knew if he accused them of this, they'd agree): they had been happy, in a mundane way (although, a voice in the back of his mind argued, don't you know enough by now to know that happiness is never mundane?). They were both college professors in Boston — his father taught English literature, his mother taught in the history department. They had married just out of college and had two children, a boy and a girl, and their lives had been neatly packaged and scheduled by the college's calendar, and really it had been a very fine way to live. And so *safe*. The parents taught during the day and the children went to school (until they went off to prep school, which was also scheduled and safe). The parents read or worked on their courses in the evenings and the children did their homework. The entire family went together to the college's celebrations of Christmas and graduation and then for two weeks in the summer to the same rented wooden seaside house on

Cape Cod; oh, they had lived a repetitive life of harmony and balance and serenity — my God, Alexander Pope would have loved it. Jack had lived a neoclassic life!

He hadn't even fought very much with his sister. Diana was two years younger than he was and they had always been chums. Still were. He had always liked having Diana around with her stuffed animals and baby dolls and later with her nail polish and hair rollers, in the same way he had liked having Carey Ann around during the first year of their marriage: women seemed to be so much more optimistic about their control over the world than men. They seemed always so certain that they could arrange things to their satisfaction. If nature — fate — gave them straight hair, they could make it curly. If nature gave them curly hair, they could make it straight. They could paint their fingernails or not, and have babies or not, they could go into a room and put the furniture where they liked it and then they'd call friends on the phone to tell them what they'd just done or were planning to do and the entire world settled down and fit its bulging boisterous bulk into the delineated limits the women painted with their polish and their plans. Men were supposed to go out and fight the world, explore it, poke at it, but women got to soothe and tame and restrain it, and then sit down and relax in it. There was no use talking about "women's lib," "men's lib"; that's the way it really was. When it came right down to it, the truth of the matter was that Carey Ann was not responsible for getting the money that paid for the food and the mortgage and the heat. Jack was. The truth of the matter was that Carey Ann didn't have to arrange her home to please anyone else, but Jack had to arrange his office to suit his boss, and he had to do it in the right way, so that he wouldn't anger the man who had the power eventually to give him tenure or not. He could not have said some brilliant rebellious obscenity and stalked, Prince-like, out of the office and onto his motorcycle and off into the sunset, because he was responsible for his family. Although this was the life that, after all, he had chosen. Not only chosen, it was the life he had craved all through his childhood. He couldn't help it, he was by nature, if not by fantasy, a family man.

When he pulled into the driveway of the A-frame, he noticed that Carey Ann's white convertible was gone, and immediately a wave of pleasure swept over him — followed quickly by a seizure of guilt. But he so seldom had any time alone in his house, it was never quiet in his house, and he was really tired and still a little upset from the episode with Hudson.

He wrestled Prince into the house and into the anonymity of his study under the stairs, then headed for the kitchen. He really needed a beer. Or a vodka and tonic. With some pretzels.

But when he opened the refrigerator, he found that there was no beer. Or tonic. He searched through the cupboards and then through the cardboard boxes (Carey Ann still hadn't unpacked much). The refrigerator held some canned pears and half a gallon of whole milk and some Popsicles and some eggs, and that was all.

Perhaps Carey Ann had gone to the grocery store. He hoped so. He walked around the house, stepping over Alexandra's toys. What a messy child she was. He stood a moment looking out the great glass window down at the valley. Now he wished Carey Ann were home. He was lonely. He really would have liked to sit down with his wife, to share a drink, to tell her in detail about his day, and about his episode with Hudson. He felt the need for some comfort, just the simple comfort of a friendly conversation with a person who was on his side. And a drink, a vodka tonic or a beer. He really could use one.

The more he thought about it, though, the more he guessed that when Carey Ann did get home, she might not be in the mood to sit down and listen to his woes. Then he remembered the woman down the road, the secretary from the history department. Daphne. He remembered the taste of the strong, rich, brewed coffee she had given him a few mornings ago. He remembered sitting on her concrete stoop, enclosed by a circle of woods that made her place seem cut off from the world and its problems. Well. Maybe she wouldn't mind if he dropped by for a drink. At least he could ask her if he could borrow some tonic.

The road to her place was pure mud. He should have changed into his sneakers, but he was in such an obstinate mood that once he set out, and saw immediately that his loafers were getting rimmed with muck, he just kept on going. It was slippery; he tried to walk along the high ridges of the ruts, but kept almost sliding down into the channels between the ruts, which were full of brown water. Finally he climbed over to the shoulder of the road and picked his way through the high grasses, brambles, and goldenrod. It was hot now, and humid. Green steamed at him from the forest and ground; it was no longer raining, but occasionally a fat clear pendant of water would fall from a tree.

Jack was almost soaked by the time he reached Daphne's house. What hadn't hit him from above had gotten him from below as the tall wet grasses squeaked and slapped at his legs. The front door was open. He stepped up and knocked on the aluminum screen door. "Hello?" he called. There was no answer. Damn, he thought, but she had to be home. There was an old dented, rather valiant-looking red Jeep parked at the side of the house. "Hello?" he called again.

"Come around back!" he heard Daphne call. He noticed then that a narrow jagged rough path had been cut through the high grass; more of the grass had been pushed over than actually cut. Following it around the side of the house, he saw Daphne at the edge of the forest, on her knees, reaching into the raspberry bushes. A large blue-and-white-striped bowl was on the ground beside her, almost full of berries. Daphne was wearing blue shorts, an old, too-large (perhaps originally a man's?) T-shirt, no shoes. When she turned and stood up, strips of grass and flecks of dirt clung to her damp white legs and feet.

"I'm so glad you came!" she said. "I've got more berries here than I can ever use. I'll freeze some, of course, for the winter. I love making a raspberry pie in the middle of winter. For a few moments I can taste summer again. But even with freezing them I've got more than I can use. Come in the house and let me give you a bowl to take home." She led the way to her back door. "How are you?" she asked over her shoulder.

"Oh, fine," Jack said politely. "How are you?"

Daphne laughed. "Well, as my grandmother used to say, 'Fair to middlin'.' I think the rain got me down today. It seemed to go on *forever*."

"Why, look at your place!" Jack said. He gazed around the kitchen, then stepped through into the living room. A really amazing transformation had taken place. This was a *home* now, this was a *refuge*. Here was a case of the whole being more than the sum of its parts, because it was not just that there were now rugs here, and curtains, and furniture, and pictures and books and magazines and vases and andirons and fireplace tools. It was the way they were all there together, in a wonderful bright harmony that was at once soothing and invigorating.

"My God," Jack said, "how did you do all this? You didn't even have your furniture in here at the beginning of the week."

"Oh, well," Daphne said, "it was just about all I did all week." She looked carefully at Jack. "And I didn't have anyone else to take care of or cook for or anything — and I didn't have Cynthia's opinions to bother me. I just put things where I wanted them."

"That must be a good feeling," he said. It was almost as if she knew about the Prince stand-up. He let his shoulders sag a little, his mouth tense.

"Would you like a drink?" Daphne asked. "You look like you could use a drink."

"Yes, I would. I would very much like a drink," Jack said, following her back into the kitchen. (What a wonderful place, with plump blue-and-white-checked cushions on the captain's chairs and Dutch-looking canisters lined up all in order on the clean counters, and a vase of wildflowers in the middle of the table.) "In fact, I'll be honest, I came down here just hoping you would offer me a drink. Carey Ann's off somewhere, shopping with Alexandra, I imagine, and there's not a drop of anything alcoholic in the house. And I've just had a run-in with the head of my department."

"Oh," Daphne said. "What did Hudson do?"

Jack told her about his episode with Hudson while Daphne fixed his drink (she even cut and squeezed a wedge of fresh lime into it — why didn't they ever have fresh limes at home?) and set it before him, and then, easily, with her effortless sort of gliding movements, she put some cheese and whole-wheat crackers on a wooden tray and set those on the table too. He loved this, loved having someone take care of him a little bit (and at the same time he felt a little guilty for being so glad to be with a woman other than Carey Ann).

When he had finished talking about his Prince stand-up, Daphne sat there a moment thinking. Jack waited, knowing she would say something supportive.

"Well," Daphne said at last, a slight wrinkle between her brows, "you know, Hudson is a reasonable man. I think that if you had insisted, he would have let you keep the thing, and he would not have harbored a grudge. Hudson's good about that. He may be a bit of a stick, but he doesn't hold grudges. Well, I guess you can't if you're part of a department. A successful department." She was gazing in the general direction of the refrigerator when she said all that, but now she turned toward Jack and looked at him as she spoke, smiling, and relaxing her limbs, crossing her arms on the table, leaning forward in a conspiratorial pose. "You know, Jack, now that I think about it, I do think Hudson's instincts were correct. I'll tell you why. I think something like that is more a display of ego than of . . . whatever, anything else. I remember so well, when I was a junior in college. We had a biology professor who looked *just* like Paul Newman. God, he was handsome. He was really something to look at. The same blue eyes. Perhaps he was a little taller than Paul Newman, I don't know, I've heard that Newman's short, but you can't tell from the movies. Anyway, all the girls had terrible crushes on him, and we talked about him all the time. We wondered if he knew he looked like Paul Newman. Then a horrible thing happened. Oh, it makes me squirm to think about it. We had to go into his office to pick up our midterm tests and discuss our biology projects with him. Everyone had to do a special project. So I walked into his room, just swooning and shaking with excitement to think I'd be alone with him for even five minutes, and . . . oh, God, it just makes me cringe to think about it: he had a small office, and his desk was right in the middle of the office, facing the door, and right behind his desk, taped to the wall, facing us, was a *huge* poster of Paul Newman. It must have been ten feet by five feet, and Paul Newman was staring right out at you, so that when Mr. Ryder looked up from his desk, both he and Paul Newman were staring at you. Oh, God, I was so embarrassed for him! I just wanted to scream, I wanted to say, 'Oh, please take that thing down, we know you're handsome, we've got eyes, we can see you look like Paul Newman, don't be so vain or insecure or whatever it is, you really do not have to pound it into our heads like that.' Of course, I didn't say those things, but afterward, when I talked to everyone else in the class, males and females, *everyone* was just laughing at him. Everyone just thought he was the biggest joke. No one respected him anymore. He must have wondered. He must have sensed the change in the attitude in the classroom. God. The poor man. You know, it's often the incredibly handsome men who are the most insecure. It's a riddle, isn't it?"

Daphne sat sipping her drink for a few moments. Jack sat digesting all she had said. He wasn't quite sure what to make of it, but he didn't feel soothed. He didn't feel supported. He almost wondered if he'd been insulted.

"Not that you look like Prince!" Daphne laughed. "And not that you wanted it in there for reasons of vanity. I think you wanted it there to give your students an idea of what you are like, to let them know that you're young, and thus on their side, and you can have a real meeting of the minds, and all of that. But, Jack, you know, the students who come to this college are really *bright*. Most of them. They appreciate subtlety. They can even use a bit of mystery. You don't have to advertise anything about you — and I guess that's what that Prince thing would seem like to me, a sort of advertisement — and believe me, you don't need that. Well, I've only just met you, but you've got the right feeling about you. You look preppy and Ivy Leaguey and all that, but you don't look stuffy, you don't *feel* cold, and that's what they'll respond to about you. Your warmth."

Jack was chagrined to feel a flush crawl up his neck and across his cheeks. No one had ever spoken about his "warmth" before, and he was flattered. And he *was* warm, too, sitting here in this kitchen on a humid hot day, the alcohol, in spite of the ice, heating him a little. He thought about what Daphne had just said, and he thought she was right. She was so perceptive. And, put in her words, he could understand more clearly Hudson's reaction to the Prince stand-up, and now all his anger at Hudson dissolved. He felt young but not hopeless; new, but not stupid.

"It really helps to talk to you," he said. (Was he drunk? Should he be talking this way to this woman? Would it make Carey Ann jealous? Was he doing something *wrong*? But it was so nice to have someone on his side.) "I can see it all in a different perspective now." He rose. "Thank you very much. You have been so kind. This was just what I needed — a drink and a good talk. Someday you'll have to come . . . oh, borrow a cup of sugar or something. And I really want you to meet Carey Ann and Alexandra."

"Actually," Daphne said, rising also, "I met them. I called and asked them to come over this morning. I've been trying to think how to tell you this, Jack, and I hope it won't cause any bad feelings."

Oh God!, Jack thought. What happened?

Daphne was still talking, and moving back into the living room. "Your little daughter climbed up on the piano and crawled across it and knocked everything over, and I'm afraid that I told Carey Ann that she shouldn't let her child do things like that. I'm very afraid I upset her, your wife, I mean, and I'm so sorry, because I liked your wife, and your daughter, and I didn't mean to make her angry."

Visions of the temper tantrums Carey Ann was capable of throwing flashed before Jack's eyes and he was mortified. After a few seconds he found his voice. "Carey Ann got angry?"

"Well, justifiably so," Daphne said. "Jack, all mothers are like tigers when it comes to their children — they can't bear criticism. I don't blame her a bit."

Shit, Jack thought, what a day. "What did she do?"

Daphne smiled. "She just . . . said she could

understand why my daughter doesn't want to live with me."

Jack flushed again, and went mute with misery.

Daphne reached her hand out and gently touched his arm. "Oh, please, don't worry," she said. "I shouldn't have even told you, but on the other hand, I didn't want it to become some awful secret. It was really nothing at all. I shall feel very sorry if I've upset your wife, and I really do like Carey Ann and Alexandra, really I do, Jack. I was rude to say anything to her. I was wrong. I wish I had remembered how difficult it was for me, as a young faculty wife, with a baby."

"I think Carey Ann's having a hard time," Jack said, feeling he owed Daphne an explanation for his wife's behavior — he didn't want her to think Carey Ann was a nut or had no manners; at the same time, he felt bad, as if he were betraying Carey Ann. "Away from her parents and all her friends."

"Oh, I'm sure of it," Daphne said. "After all, you've got the people at the college to talk to, who know you and what you're about. But she's new here, and it takes quite a while to make good friends, real friends. And it's such hard work taking care of a little child. Jack, would you do me a favor, please?" Daphne headed for the front door, and Jack followed.

She took two yellow rain slickers from the coatrack. "I meant to call her, but perhaps it's better coming from you. Give these back to her and tell her I'm very sorry about this morning. Tell her I'd really like for her and Alexandra to come visit again . . . we'll start all over fresh. Tell her I was probably just tired after working so hard all week to get my house in order."

Jack slogged back home over the muddy ruts, the rain slickers squeaking over one shoulder, a bowl of ruby-red beaded raspberries in his hands, the berries glistening from the recent rain. As soon as he was hidden from Daphne's sight, in the overarching avenue of trees, he popped a few berries into his mouth: they were sweet and tart at once. Now he was really tired. Thoughts and images were colliding in his head. He ate a few more berries, thinking as he did so how his daughter would like them: they were pretty and little and could be eaten with fingers, and they were bright: they looked bright, and they even *tasted* bright. Each berry was a cheerful surprise — like the male cardinal that now flashed across the road right before his eyes.

3

It was a perfect evening for the picnic, Daphne thought, for the college had been in session for two weeks now and the satisfying routine of a term under way was established. The weather, which had been mostly cool and rainy and cloudy, fall-like, keeping them in the mood to beaver away indoors, had changed just today. The sun had come out and the humidity had disappeared and the evening was blue and gold and warm.

Marcia Johannsen, who was in charge of the faculty-club affairs, had set the bar up on the wide side porch of the club. She'd put tables and chairs there too, so that the older and more ramrod faculty could keep their dignity and reserve. This unfortunately had the effect of dividing the faculty and the members of the faculty-club into the old guard and the new peons. Those who had chairs and sat above, looking down, and those who had to squat, humbly, on blankets on the grass, being looked down upon. Well, there really wasn't any way around it, Daphne and Marcia agreed, standing off to the side, talking in low voices. The old guard was, after all, *old*, many of them, dignified and revered scholars and professors, with arthritis or some ailment that made it difficult to lower themselves all the way to the ground. Hudson, who was not so old, sat among them, partly because of his status, partly because his wife, Claire, with her bad back, chose to sit there.

Then, too, the new faculty were the ones with the little children, who did somersaults down the hill and chased each other around the faculty club. The youngest children lay on blankets, sucking bottles or their thumbs, or happily mashing up potato chips. Here these younger professors were parents first, of necessity, and they had worn slacks and skirts and dresses that could easily be washed, unlike the older faculty, who shone in their white linen trousers and blue blazers and silk flowered sundresses.

Daphne was wearing a blue cotton dress, one of her favorite warm-weather dresses. She had on low heels, respectable enough for the porch, sensible enough for the grass. She was — and always would be — an "in-between" person; because she was only a secretary, she'd never be able to sit on the porch even when she was old. Well, maybe they'd let her sit there when she was *really* old and infirm and had become an "institution." There were enough people here (all on the porch) who remembered her as the wife of a professor and therefore deserving of a certain amount of respect, although that group was gradually shrinking and that memory fading. But she was popular, in general, with everyone; she was a good secretary, she didn't play games, she didn't gossip, she didn't try to sleep with any of her bosses, and she was nice. The only people who snubbed Daphne were two or three very old faculty wives who had been here from the time when the college was for men only and who needed to snub *somebody* to keep their feeling of superiority in a world where they'd lost their looks, and their husbands were losing their power; and some of the youngest faculty and their spouses who wanted it made clear to everyone that as professors (even untenured), they ranked higher on the ladder of respect than a mere secretary. The older group snubbed Daphne by nodding and looking away without smiling; the younger group simply looked away, fast, almost terrified to make contact, afraid someone would think they were *friends* with a secretary.

She knew the new young untenured history teacher, of course, because that was her department, but there were several other new families out on the lawn who were unfamiliar to her. Marcia pointed them out: chemistry, poly sci, art. The new English professor, Jack Hamilton, and his family, hadn't arrived yet. But it wasn't too late, the faculty-club chef was only now putting the hamburgers and hot dogs on the charcoal grill while the rest of his staff, pudgy women in white uniforms, carried out plastic-covered bowls and set them on the long paper-tablecloth-covered tables.

Daphne walked across the grass, a glass of white wine in her hand, and sank down on the blanket with Pauline and Douglas White. She would always be welcome with them; Pauline was her age and her good friend. Pauline had taught in the English department since before Daphne began as a secretary, and Douglas had been David's best friend. And, long ago, they had both known Daphne and Joe in a social way.

"How do you like Jack Hamilton?" Daphne asked.

"Oh, he's just fine," Pauline said. Pauline had gone a bit square (she was shorter than Daphne) and let the gray thread through her dark hair. Tonight she was wearing a plaid shirtwaist that made her look even squatter and thicker than usual, but Daphne had given up trying to get Pauline to dress better.

Pauline was through with vanity. "He's so energetic, you know, as we all are when we're new. I've seen him in his office, in the halls. He lets the students talk to him endlessly — they're just eating up his time."

"Oh, he wants to be popular with them!" Daphne said.

"We had dinner with Claire and Hudson last night. Daphne, it was awful. Claire is becoming wicked, I really believe it. All that elegant restraint we used to admire her for has become twisted, hardened, and I think she's proud of it. She's getting so . . . isolated. She relies on Hudson for everything, but treats him as if he were some kind of servant. She watches him like a hawk. I could be spilling government secrets to her and she'd turn away in the middle of our conversation if she saw that Hudson was involved in a conversation with someone else. You know, really involved, talking about something that interested him or made him smile. 'Oh, Hudson,' she says, 'would you get my pills?' Then she says, 'I know it's awful that Hudson has to help me so much, but if I were at home in England I'd have relatives around. Instead . . .' Then she sighs and tries to look like a martyred saint. It makes me shudder. Why does he stay with her? And when do you suppose was the last time poor Hudson got laid?"

Daphne laughed, feeling terribly sad at the same time. "From what I've gathered, I think he's just decided to forget about all that," she began, but then her attention was diverted by a rustle that passed through the picnickers.

"Oh, God," Pauline said.

Daphne turned her gaze in the direction it seemed that now almost everyone else at the picnic was looking. Jack Hamilton, his cute little daughter on his shoulders, was striding down the lawn from the parking lot. Carey Ann was walking along beside him. Jack had on khakis, a red-and-blue-striped cotton sweater, and leather loafers without socks; he looked casual yet decorous.

Carey Ann was wearing thin sandals that crisscrossed and tied around her slender ankles with pink ribbons, and her legs flashed bare and sleek all the way up to her very short pink shorts. Tied at her shoulders with pink bows was a tiny white top so short that as Carey Ann walked, it rose and dipped, rose and dipped, teasingly exposing a flash of her flat silky waist. She was not wearing a bra. Her shimmery blond hair flew out around her and she looked totally beautiful, intensely sexy, and completely inappropriate. She looked ready to attend the Indianapolis 500, not an Ivy League college affair.

The Hamiltons had come halfway down the

hill before Carey Ann realized her mistake. By that time Daphne was muttering a silent rapid prayer: Oh, dear God, don't let her notice. But Carey Ann noticed. As her big blue eyes swept over the lawn and porch and she saw the women in dresses, skirts and blouses, or at least long, loose silk or cotton slacks, her face took on a look of panic, a rosy glow spreading from her forehead down to the little top.

People were still laughing and talking, but most were frozen, watching, knowing they were witnessing a faux pas that would be remembered and discussed for years. And who was going to jump up and welcome the Hamiltons, talk to them? Not many wives there would forgive Carey Ann for being so stunningly, movie-star beautiful. They would have no mercy — and would not let their husbands show any. And the younger faculty did not want to appear guilty by association.

"God damn him, God damn him!" Daphne said. "Why didn't he tell her? What is the matter with him?"

"He didn't know, Daphne," Pauline whispered. "He still doesn't know. He doesn't know about women's clothes. Look at his face, he's completely unaware."

"He's *stupid*," Daphne said. "Pauline, go get them. Bring them here. I would, but you'd be better, you're faculty."

But while Pauline was still struggling to rise from the blanket, another senior faculty member came down from the porch, hands held out, to greet the Hamiltons. He could not have been more welcoming or jovial. It was Hudson, and he brought the Hamiltons up onto the porch to greet the old guard seated there.

"Oh!" Pauline said, breathing a sigh of relief. "Oh, bless his heart. Oh, God bless him. Daphne, you ought to sleep with him for that."

"You know, you're obsessed with Hudson's sex life!" Daphne said, laughing. "I think *you* want to sleep with him!"

"Oh, I don't, not really, but I do care for Hudson, and I'd like to see him happy. He's such a good man. And I know how his face gets when he looks at you, Daphne. He's loved you for years."

"And you and I have discussed this for years. He's married, Pauline. He's an honorable man. For that matter, I'm an honorable woman. Oh, let's eat," Daphne said, jumping up from the blanket in her sudden impatience.

After the meal everyone relaxed as the sky paled and then darkened with the deepening night, and the babies fell asleep on their blankets. The oldest of the old guard tottered home, and the adults left moved among each other, talking, having another drink, one last drink. The end of summer was in the air. Tomorrow there were duties, tomorrow they must face classrooms full of rampant youth who had the world before them, while they, the professors, had already used up a good part of their lives and were entrenched in marriages or relationships that they cherished, or didn't cherish, but had chosen and must get on with. But tonight they were outdoors, and the stars came out, more and more of them; tonight was expansive — and kind, and warm. They lingered.

Daphne, another glass of white wine in her hand, approached the Hamiltons, who were sitting on a blanket with Robert Butler. Butler was in the chemistry department, a nice man, but almost astonishingly boring, and once he found someone who would listen to him for a minute, he clung for hours. Jack was nodding and responding politely, but Carey Ann's eyes were glazing over, and Alexandra had fallen asleep in her lap.

"Hello, everyone," Daphne said. "No, don't get up, please. Carey Ann, I thought you might want to come with me and let me introduce you to some of the women who have children Alexandra's age. They could tell you about play groups and preschools and pediatricians and all that sort of thing."

In response, Carey Ann looked miserable. "Well," she said hesitantly, "Alexandra's sleeping . . ."

"I'll hold her," Jack said, and before his wife could reply, he reached over and took his daughter from her. Alexandra sighed, a singing little sound, nestled against her father's shirtfront, and stuck her thumb in her mouth.

Warily Carey Ann rose to her feet. She and Daphne had not seen each other since the day Alexandra crawled across the piano.

"Do you want another glass of wine?" Daphne asked, thinking: Why don't you have three or four, maybe you'd relax.

"Well . . ." Carey Ann said, uncertain.

Daphne took her gently by the arm then — it was the only way, she decided, like leading a timid beast, perhaps one of those quivering, gorgeous, skinny Afghan hounds with lots of messy blond hair (one had to take gentle but firm control) — and half-pulled her to the bar. Daphne chatted the entire way about the mothers Carey Ann would meet, and their children, and finally got Carey Ann to the blanket where the young mothers were gathered, some with babes in arms. Daphne knew some of these women, not all, and she remembered how it had been to *be* one of these women, with life passionately, messily, almost insanely centered on one tiny human being. She introduced Carey Ann and then excused herself to get more wine — she felt that Carey Ann would be more relaxed without her around, and indeed, that probably all those women would. She could remember how she had felt when she was in her twenties and early thirties — women over forty seemed antediluvian.

When she reached the wine table, she realized she really didn't want any more wine. She was tired. Now she felt her singleness and it weighed her down. When she and Joe had divorced, her friends had at first rallied round her and made her join them on their forays to the faculty-club affairs. At first she had been a "cause" for her friends, and after all that died down, she felt comfortable enough to brave the affairs on her own. She had known so many people. Then she started working for the history department and had her own membership. For a long time she had come with David. And now, again, she came alone. When she had been younger, divorced, it took courage, real determination, to walk by herself into a room crowded with couples, but now that was the easy part, for there were so many people who were glad to see her. It was the leaving that was difficult — not awkward, for no one noticed, but simply painful, because she was alone and had no one to gossip with about the evening, no one to ride with through the dark night: no one to cuddle up with in bed.

Daphne found her straw summer purse where she'd left it on a blanket. Everyone else, in couples or groups, was engaged in intense conversation, it seemed. Pauline and Douglas had already left. There was no one for her to call or wave good-bye to. She left the party in silence, trailing up the lawn past all the people like someone unseen, like a ghost.

Ghosts. They were everywhere. They materialized all over: from a piece of jewelry or a piece of furniture or a wisp of song curling from a radio or a nightmare. They sprang up like geysers, right out of the top of Daphne's head, and spilled down all around her, enclosing her in their falling fluid silvery sheen so that she became a ghost herself, trapped in the past, in her past.

Daphne, in her teens and early twenties, had lived in a dream world. She had been absolutely retarded. Retarded, indeed, by her times, by her parents, by her religion, and by the nature of her own personality; retarded in the true sense of the word: slowed down.

Retarded and, later, demented.

If she were to tell Cynthia, her sixteen-year-old daughter, who had friends taking the pill (who might even now herself be taking the pill out there in fast-paced, action-packed California, for all Daphne knew), that she had been a virgin at *twenty-three*, Cynthia would fall off the sofa with laughter. Or, more likely, these days, when Cynthia was so bound and determined that she and Daphne would *not* get along, Cynthia would seriously, with the deadly earnest patience of a true martyr, point out that this was just one more sign of the difference between mother and daughter, the proof that there was no way Daphne could ever understand Cynthia, ever *come close* to understanding Cynthia.

But the twenty-three-year-old Daphne, still a virgin, had been a happy one — actually, an oblivious one — drifting along in a world all her very own. Since then she had seldom been as happy, certainly not as peaceful.

She had been an English major. She had finished her bachelor's degree and was working on her master's, with every intention of going on for her doctorate in medieval literature. Her body made the necessary motions of going through ordinary life in the town of Amherst, where she was a student at the University of Massachusetts, but her soul and mind and imagination belonged to the literature of the Middle Ages. It was 1962, and her world was peopled with knights and faeries and dragons and sorcerers and love stories of mythic dimensions. The legends of Sir Arthur and the Round Table. *Sir Gawain and the Green Knight. Aucassin and Nicolette. Tristan and Isolt!* What in modern life could compare with the romances of ancient times, especially those romances with pure and noble and faithful and chaste and yearning lovers?

While her friends were lying in their apartments listening to Johnny Mathis, Daphne lay on her bed truly lost in another world, swooning as she read for the fiftieth time the poem *The Nut-Brown Maid*. While her friends were twisting to Chubby Checker, Daphne's mind was full of medieval ballads sung in a high clear voice, accompanied by lute.

She was, really, just a little bit nuts. Something in her then longed for the romantic, the epic, the impossible, wanted love in the twentieth century to be like love in the Middle Ages. She wanted a knight, she wanted true, pure, superior love.

Her wish had come true, as wishes sometimes have a way of doing. Oddly enough — humorously enough — it had been a cock that had brought her love, true love. It had been her naive and romantic handling, so to speak, of a cock, that had brought her romance and love and marriage.

While working on her master's degree, Daphne held a teaching assistantship. She was paid an insignificant sum of money to teach beginning literature to freshman students. Every Monday, Wednesday, and Friday morning at eight o'clock and again at nine o'clock (while the professors with tenure slept late) she taught poetry, essays, and short stories to freshman students who were not especially interested, but who were required to take basic English in order to get a degree in anything at all. She went into her teaching determined to make her students love the language, determined to open to her students the ethereal, majestic, magical world of fiction.

The poetry in the fat text chosen by powers above her was arranged chronologically. The first poem she chose from the text was one written in the fifteenth century. It was brief, and very easy to read. And, as Daphne told her class, it was wonderfully subtle and clever! She read it aloud:

I have a noble cock,
Who croweth in the day.
He maketh me rise early,
My matins for to say.

I have a noble cock,
Whose breed is nothing low.
His comb is of red coral,
His tail of indigo.

His eyes are shining crystal,
Rimmed all around with amber;
And every night he perches
Within my lady's chamber.

"You see how devious the poet is," Daphne (enraptured by her own sensitivity and by anything written in the fifteenth century) said to her students. "Now, what does he say in the first stanza that the cock does? Why, he wakes his master up. Of course that is what a rooster does, but we can imagine this as a pet rooster, a beautiful bird with a comb of coral and an indigo tail, who crows in the morning and wakes up his master. Why does he love his rooster so much? Why is this rooster so special, so *noble?* What is the poet trying to tell us by innuendo? What does the poet tell us in the last stanza? Where does the rooster go to sleep at night? 'In my lady's chamber'! So you see, the poet is subtly, inventively, telling us that he is sleeping in the bedroom of his ladylove — the rooster who wakes him in the morning goes to sleep at night in 'his lady's chamber.' It is the indirectness of

127

poetry, the clever sidestepping of it, the sneakiness of it, if you will, that often gives poetry its power. The poet is writing a love poem to his lady, but instead of praising *her*, he is praising an object that is related to her and to the fact that he is sleeping in her room."

On and on she went, while her students stared down at their books, strangely quiet that day. She began to wonder if she had embarrassed them, because they said nothing. She went on from that poem to other love poems by Donne and Shakespeare, and was just beginning Andrew Marvell's *To His Coy Mistress* when the hour was up. She taught the next period — the same subject, the same poetry (with the same strangely numbed reaction on her students' part) — and then, when her class was over, she walked down the long hallway to the private lounge where the faculty and staff, including the lowly T.A.'s, gathered for coffee and quiet conversation.

She was just outside the door to the lounge when she heard such an explosion of laughter that she paused. If the room was full of men, and only men, she wouldn't go in. There were only three other female T.A.'s, and she often felt timid around the male T.A.'s when they were in their group, laughing with their low voices, gesturing extravagantly, bellowing out their opinions, fighting over their explication of *The Waste Land* like bulls butting for territory. She listened for the sound of any moderating female voice. What she heard was:

" . . . Gawd, I stood outside the door for fifteen minutes without taking a breath. I couldn't believe my ears! 'I have a noble cock'! I have a noble *cock,* and she thinks he's talking about a *rooster!* Those kids must have peed down their legs with laughter when they got out of there." The speaker (Daphne thought it was George Dobbs, a freckled red-haired arrogant Mark Twain specialist) paused to cackle. "She tells these freshmen, who are, you know, the horniest people on God's green earth, that 'in my lady's chamber' means the bedroom. She thinks that a cock in a lady's chamber is a rooster in a bedroom! Haw haw haw haw . . . " The laughter rose, billowed, burst. "Dear *Christ,* how can one woman be so dumb! How can they let her teach freshman literature? She should be teaching first grade, maybe kindergarten!"

Daphne felt her entire being shrinking, collapsing into herself, like a star falling inward and becoming a cold void. Not until this very moment had it occurred to her that there might be more earthy interpretations to that poem. And now she saw how wrong she had been — how unbelievably ignorant and naive.

Her students must be laughing at her. And now that Dobbs was telling everyone else, how would she ever face her colleagues? They would all think she was a fool. And she was, she really was. Oh, dear God, her life was ruined. She wasn't a teacher, she was a little idiot.

Suddenly another voice imposed itself upon her panicked mind, and to her amazement, she heard a man saying, "Oh, George, you are such a mental slob. Just because you read vulgarity into everything you see doesn't mean that everyone else does. Now, how do you *know* that the poet was talking about his cock and not a pet bird? Huh? How do you know? And even so, do you expect a beautiful classy female like Daphne Lowell to stand in front of a class of horny freshmen and talk about penises? I'm sure she can be sexy when she wants, but a woman teaching freshmen can hardly choose to be lewd. And we're supposed to be teaching *poetry*, don't forget, you know, we're supposed to be *trying* to introduce the sublime, the majestic, the angelic — 'the music of the soul, and above all of great and feeling souls' — to these poor earthbound clods. What a crud you are to make fun of that elegant woman just because your own vision is so crass."

Now Daphne really couldn't breathe. She

130

clutched her books to her breast, truly nearly fainting: my God, she had suddenly become a damsel in distress overhearing her knight in shining armor rallying to her defense. She was weak with astonishment.

"Jesus, Joe, you should be studying debate, not English literature!" George Dobbs said, laughing. "Give me a break — you sleeping with her, or what?"

"I haven't even spoken to her, you asshole!" Daphne's hero said, and then Dr. Frazier, the Shakespeare professor, came down the hall and caught Daphne standing outside the door, rigid with shock.

"Are you going in, Miss Lowell?" Dr. Frazier asked, and before she could move, he had pulled the door back, intending to allow her to pass through before him, unintentionally exposing Daphne to the lounge full of English T.A.'s.

Daphne stared — and saw one person, Joe Miller. And he was seeing only her. She turned — she fled. She ran from the building and across campus and down nameless streets until she came to her apartment. Not until she was safely inside, in her bedroom with the door locked, on her bed, did she feel safe.

Daphne lay there and caught her breath, and replayed the entire morning in her head — and began to smile, and could not stop.

She had longed to have a knight, a hero, and she had one. She had been defended. She had been praised. It was obvious, it was undeniable — she was loved from afar! She felt radiant, ethereal, she felt like Guinevere reincarnated. And in her mind from that moment on, she thought of herself and Joe in impossibly romantic ways, like Tristan and Isolt, like Aucassin and Nicolette.

Finally she came around to thinking about Joe himself, Joe Miller, her knight. She hadn't really thought about him before, ever, had seldom seen him — there were, after all, twenty-three T.A.'s in the department, and scores of other Ph.D. and master's candidates.

She summoned up a vision of Joe in her mind: he was blond, with thick hair that he wore longer than most men these days, and he had blue eyes and a straight nose and a great smile — why, he was handsome! Why hadn't she noticed that before? He wasn't very tall, unfortunately, and perhaps that was why she hadn't paid much attention to him; Daphne was tall for a woman, five-eight, and slender, but big-boned, and she was attracted to very tall big men. Joe was probably the same height she was. Probably the same weight, too, though she'd never tell him so — but could he pick her up? Could he carry her in his arms? He was the serious type, she remembered, very serious, even fierce, and competitive, and, now she remembered, he was rumored to be quite brilliant. Well, wow! How wonderful. How *romantic*. A brilliant man had come to her defense. Had proved that the age of chivalry was not dead.

When the phone rang, she knew it would be Joe, and it was.

"Hi," he said. "I think that after this morning it might be nice if we could get together."

And so they did.

It really had been a wonderful thing that Joe had done for Daphne. She had told Cynthia about the way they met, because the psychology books said to tell the child of a divorce about the time when her parents loved one another. She told Cynthia how after just three months of going together they were married, and how they laughed together and understood each other and shared everything, told each other everything. They were the dearest friends, but they were husband and wife too. She did not tell Cynthia in exact words, but let her understand that sexually the marriage had been fine and rich: it was a treasure. (She did not tell Cynthia about the time that she finally said, laughing, wet all over her body from different bodily moistures

— sweat and kisses and sex and tears: "Oh, Joe, you have a noble cock!" How they had laughed, so pleased with themselves.)

And who could take that away from Daphne now? What could make it change, what could make it false? Because Joe had betrayed her and left her for another woman, did that mean he did not truly love her then, in those young years? This was the mystery of life, not how death transforms us, but how life transforms us, even our memories, even our most radiant memories — if what Joe gave Daphne in their youth was golden, did his later betrayals tarnish it, demean it, debase it? So that the gold fell away, a lie, leaving only base metal, leaving a cheap pretense, tin?

Daphne sat alone in her cottage, wrapped in a light summer quilt, rocking in the curved wicker rocking chair in which she had rocked Cynthia when Cynthia was newly born. Daphne had put the chair here, by the long window looking out at the field and forest, just so she could sit this way, and look, and think, and remember, and be calmed by the way the lawn slanted and the woods stood firm, guardians of her realm. So long ago, she had been romantic. She could still be romantic. In fact, she was. Some of her friends, especially her new friends, saw her life as a sort of cliché, a cautionary tale to younger women: Look at what poor (foolish) Daphne Miller did with her life! Such potential, such a brilliant student — and she threw it all away, by trusting a man, by falling in love. They would say she had been duped and even robbed, and in a way that was true, for when she married Joe, she had stopped taking courses, had stopped working toward her doctorate. Joe was poor, and two years older, and was closer to finishing his doctorate than she. So she had worked for four years as a secretary in the chemistry department so that they could pay the rent on a little apartment and eat and wear clothes. Then he had gotten a teaching position at this prestigious college — wonderful for him, but what was Daphne to do? For their plan was that when he had gotten his doctorate and had a teaching position and was earning money, then she would go back to school. But this small college gave only undergraduate degrees; she could not get her doctorate here. The only thing for her to have done was make a long commute, an hour-and-a-half drive over treacherous mountain roads, back to U. Mass. at Amherst. She would have done that — but she got pregnant with Cynthia. So her life had become a perfect feminist tract: the woman who gave up her career to support a husband who then left her with a small child and little money. She had to work as a secretary to support herself and Cynthia (Joe paid child support, but college professors didn't earn much); there was no way she could work and take care of a small child and study for a Ph.D. Now here she was, forty-six years old, a woman who had been a brilliant student with a promising career — and she was a secretary, just a secretary! If the feminists knew about her, they would take her like a dog-and-pony show around the country to show her off to young women as an example of promise denied.

But it was not the teaching that she missed now. It was not a career that she yearned for. If she could have what she wanted right now, on this starry end-of-summer night, she would simply wish to be loved. To be held right now by a man she loved who loved her in return. Oh, well, she was still a romantic, still hopelessly mushy. She supposed she always would be. She wished David were still alive. She had cared for him so deeply, even when she was furious at his drinking. And he had loved her. His arms . . . his embrace. David had been a huge man and his body had been a kind of shelter for Daphne, but more, and terribly, it had been a shelter for his disease. He had died, as everyone feared he would, of cirrhosis of the liver, when he was only forty-seven, just two years ago.

She had not been held by a man for two years. There was Hudson to talk to, and she knew he cared for her. They had a kind of silent communing, a caring and affection that were expressed tenderly and obliquely, as if they were together in a pool of life, and although they did not actually touch one another, their feelings caused life to lap at them like gentle waves, giving them soft sensual satisfaction. But it was not the same as making love, as being held in a man's arms. Daphne missed that. She often thought of trying to seduce Hudson, because she knew they could give each other pleasure and comfort and even joy, but no, there was Claire.

And really, most of all, Daphne missed her daughter. She missed Cynthia terribly. She had lived her life around her daughter as if around a glowing fire, and she had spent all her time bringing fuel to that fire, feeding that fire, tending it, watching it flourish and flame, and standing back in amazement sometimes at how brightly it burned, how high it flared! And now Cynthia was gone. Daphne was left with a void, a hole where the fire had been.

She ached, missing her daughter. Not being loved by a man did not defeat her, but this did. Not having Cynthia in the house defeated her. She could understand why Joe had left her, and she could bear that. She could understand why her daughter had left her, but she could not bear that. It hurt to think of it. It was as if her heart had been torn from her body, and nothing in the world would stanch that wound.

Daphne huddled in her chair and cried. The old release. She was a lonely woman, a woman who had been left and left again, a woman who was growing old. She was a lonely woman wrapped in a cotton quilt sitting in a rocking chair crying in the moonlight, and no one heard her cry. And never, not even in all the romances she had ever read, did someone come to the rescue of such as she.

Down the road in their A-frame, Jack and Carey Ann were fighting. Again. Still. It had started in the car, when Jack had asked pleasantly (hopefully), "Well, did you have a good time?"

"Oh, *sure*," Carey Ann had replied, her voice low with sarcasm.

Jack sighed. He hated it when Carey Ann's voice got like that. "What does that mean?"

"What do you think it means?" Carey Ann replied, and before he could answer, she had said, "Let's just be quiet till we get home, okay? Alexandra's just about asleep and I don't want to wake her up."

So they had ridden home in silence, silently fighting every mile of the way. Carey Ann had hunched over against the door, as if afraid his arm might touch hers, inflicting injury or disease. Her face was stony. When they came to the house, she didn't wait for Jack to come open the door and help her and Alexandra out, which he usually did, which he enjoyed doing. She awkwardly nudged the door open with her elbow, then kicked it open the rest of the way, crawled out, and walked past him into the house.

Jack poured himself a beer and one for Carey Ann too while she put the baby into her crib. He was sitting on the sofa in the living room when she came out. "Here," he said, indicating with his hand the beer, the cushion next to him. "Sit down. Let's talk."

Carey Ann picked up the beer but didn't sit down next to him. She chose the chair across the room next to the stone fireplace. She sat down and crossed her legs and swigged her beer and swung her leg back and forth in a maddening little rhythm and stared into space as if she were all by herself riding on a subway.

"All right," Jack said finally, "now tell me, what's wrong? What didn't you like? Who didn't you like?"

"What didn't I like?" Carey Ann asked, turning to look at him — to glare at him. "Who didn't I like? Everything, everyone, that's what, that's who!"

"Well, I thought there were a lot of nice people there — " Jack began.

"Fuddy-duddies!" Carey Ann said. "Jack, they were *all* fuddy-duddies!"

"Well, I know some of the older ones — "

"Oh, I'm not talking about the older ones," Carey Ann said. "I don't care about them. I'm talking about the ones our age. That Madeline Spencer. For example."

"She seemed very nice. And her little boy is just Alexandra's age," Jack said, wondering what on earth Carey Ann could have against Madeline Spencer, who seemed to him to be an awfully nice woman.

"Well, did you notice her hair? Did you even notice it? How it just hangs there on each side of her head? It's just so *limp*, and she wasn't wearing any makeup and she had on horrid shoes like retarded people wear, and her little boy wouldn't let Alexandra play with the teddy bear — "

"Madeline did say it was his special bear," Jack said. "You know, like a blanket, a security thing." When Carey Ann went silent, he said, "I thought the two of you were getting along fine."

"Oh, she wasn't so bad, but the others with her. You didn't hear them, you were talking to the men. 'And what do you do, Carey Ann?' " she mimicked. "And when I said I took care of Alexandra, they said, 'I mean what do you *really* do?' Like being married and having a family isn't *really* anything. They're all so *serious*, Jack, talking about how hard it is to be a faculty wife here and not be able to 'pursue their interests,' and making cookies for the students during exam week, and hospital committees and stuff. They're so *earnest.*"

Jack looked at his wife, feeling hopeless. What could he say? How could he defend his colleagues and their spouses? In fact, they *were* a pretty earnest bunch. They had had to be to get their Ph.D.'s and be asked to teach by this college. He could see, too, how they might look pretty drab to his wife, all his colleagues with their thinning hair and horn-rimmed glasses and pimples and pipes. They were all like he was, riddled with worry and concern: how to support a family on a minuscule amount of money, teach a bunch of aggressively bright students who were paying a fortune to be taught by them, and write profoundly original essays that would bring critical praise — and tenure.

" . . . doesn't anyone here know how to have fun?"

"Well, Carey Ann, maybe when we get to know some of these people a little better — you know, this was a faculty affair at the college, so everyone had to be on good behavior."

"Oh!" Carey Ann wailed. "I don't want to get to know any of them! And they don't want to get to know me!" She took a deep breath, and then, to Jack's dismay, she burst into tears and crumpled in the chair. "Oh, Jack, I'm not blind. I may be pretty but that doesn't mean I'm a complete fool. I saw the way some of those women looked at me, and I know I was underdressed, but at least I looked pretty, and women out here don't care anything about looking pretty. I can't imagine ever talking to them about . . . oh, my hair, or what kind of dress to buy, or anything at all! Do you know what one woman said? I went up to her because she had a little baby and I thought we could talk about babies, but she started telling me all about how her husband was studying 'quarks.' What the fuck is a quark? I thought she was joking so I laughed and she got such a stuck-up look on her face like she was so much better than I am. Oh, Jack, are there such things as quarks?"

Jack rose then and went over and put his

arms around her. He brought her with him back to the sofa and sat and held her while she cried. "It will get better. You'll make friends. I know you will. You'll be a great faculty wife, you'll see."

"A great *faculty* wife?" Carey Ann raised her head and stared at Jack in dismay. "You want me to be a great faculty wife? Oh, Jack, sometimes I don't think you know me at all."

"What do you mean?" He was trying to be careful.

"I mean, I don't want to be a faculty wife! I know you, and no matter what you think you feel, if I get all old and limp-haired and saggy and intelligent, you'll stop being in love with me."

Jack thought a moment, racking his brain for the perfect answer. "No. I would be in love with you even if you were old and limp-haired and saggy and intelligent," he said.

Carey Ann was quiet for a moment and Jack thought she was trying to decide whether she had just been insulted or complimented. "Oh, honey," she said at last, and hugged him. "Sometimes . . . sometimes I just feel so . . . young or something. Like I don't know what to do around those people. Jack, I try, I want you to know that, I really am trying. Like I was really polite to that Daphne Miller tonight even though she insulted me and Alexandra."

"I told you, Carey Ann, she — "

"Oh, let's not go into that again, I don't want to talk about that again, I'm trying to say something here," Carey Ann said. She reached up and put her hand, gently, softly, over his mouth. At the same time she kept her arm around his waist and leaned her hips in against his. "All my life I never had to change," she said. "Then I met you and all I seem to have to do is change. Get married, get pregnant and all fat and swollen, have a baby, move halfway around the world from all my friends . . . oh, Jack, and now you say you want me to be a faculty wife."

"Well, I am a member of the faculty. And you are my wife."

"You know Daddy always said he'd support us so you could write."

"And you know I've got more pride and sense than to accept that offer."

"Yes, I know." Carey Ann sighed. "Men."

Jack moved his hands down her back to rest on her buttocks. "Women," he replied.

They were kissing when Alexandra began to cry. Honestly, Jack thought, does that child have some kind of built-in sensory device?

"Let her cry," he said. "She'll cry herself back to sleep."

"Jack! I couldn't let the poor little thing do that!" Carey Ann said. "Let me go just a minute. I'll just rock her back to sleep." She pulled away from him.

Jack watched some late news, waiting for his wife, but when she didn't come down, he took off his shoes and tiptoed up the stairs to their room. The hall light shone on their queen-size bed, where Carey Ann lay in one of her lacy nightgowns, and Lexi lay in the curve of her arm, crooning softly to herself, trying to ward off sleep, fighting to stay awake. When Lexi saw her father enter the room, she grinned mischievously. Looking at Carey Ann, reclining, made Jack desire her terribly, and feel base for this desire, and feel wretched because he could tell that tonight his desire would not be fulfilled — and because she did not equally desire him. He could almost feel his penis shrinking into his body, unloved, rejected, disappointed. As he went into the bathroom to wash up for bed, he felt his sex against him, a small bobbing sack laden with displeasure and resentment and frustrated desires, like some heavy symbolic object in an ominous ancient tale.

4

Daphne thought that friendship carried with it an enormous responsibility. She had not always thought that, she had learned that. As a girl she had wanted a lot of "friends," but as she grew older she became more careful — not unfriendly, and many people in Westhampton would call her a friend — but that true friendship involved a form of intimacy, in some cases an intimacy different from but more naked than that of marriage, for there were things you would tell a friend that you would never tell your husband. Things about former lovers, or jealousies or fears or fantasies or even just foolish feminine thoughts about your thighs. Or the time when you, married, were at the grocery store during another routine day and a young man in line looked at you and then smiled at you and then offered to carry your groceries for you and tried to talk to you, so that for one moment in the middle of a day during which you only thought: Dry cleaning, get the tires checked, go to the bank, groceries, you suddenly thought: Oh, I am still an attractive woman! how nice, how nice, if I were free and single I would be able to get to know that handsome man who is now getting into his Porsche; if that happened, and of course it did happen, you could not tell your husband. It would seem as though you had somehow been unfaithful, flirtatious — cheap; he would be angry, or, worse, he would look scornful (Christ, my wife's thrilled because some creep in a *grocery* store talked to her; where's her sense of dignity?). When all the time you had been looking at your grocery list and at the items piled in your cart and wondering whether or not to buy a candy bar and had looked up to see that man studying you, with interest in his eyes. When this happened, you could not tell your husband, but you could tell a friend, and you needed a friend who would understand this appropriately, who could understand because it had happened to her too, so she would not think that you derived pleasure from it because you didn't love your husband. It was so nice to have a friend who was your equal in experience and who shared your values; and it was so rare.

And it was such a responsibility. When you met a person, and the chance to become a real friend arose, there were decisions to make immediately: Do I want to know this person's secrets? All of them? Do I want to tell her mine? Do I want her to help me — and then will I be obligated? Do I want to help her?

But of course finding a true friend was in many ways like finding a lover, or rather, not just a lover, but a true love. Chemistry was involved: it often happened at once, out of your conscious control, your body went ahead and did it for you, you liked the person at once, that was it. You met your friend and could tell her everything, hear everything, help and be helped.

That was the way, strangely enough, that Daphne felt now about Jack Hamilton. She had never felt that way about a man before. Her friends had always been women. And she could not pretend to herself that she wasn't also sexually attracted to him — very much so. But there would never be any question of an affair; he was so much in love with his wife, and Carey Ann was so flawlessly beautiful, a walking centerfold of a girl, and Daphne was so much older, she was fifteen years older than Jack, and twenty-two years older than Carey Ann — she was old enough to be Carey Ann's mother! Oh, how embarrassing even to have sexual thoughts about Jack Hamilton. But there was no doubt that the instinct was there, the surge, the joyous, even gleeful

148

sense of discovery every time she saw Jack Hamilton, and it was true that when she came home from work every day she felt buoyed up and cheerful rather than tired, anticipating the moment when Jack would come jogging through the tunnel of trees up to her front door for a quick drink and a friendly chat.

Her friendship with Pauline White had not come hot and quick, in an explosion; it had been more of an accretion, like a tree growing its rings of years. The last time she had felt this sort of triumphant fireworks sort of friendship had been when she had met Laura.

That had been in 1966. Almost twenty years ago! Daphne was twenty-seven and Joe was twenty-nine, and had finished his doctorate in English literature and had been hired to teach at Westhampton, in the very department where Jack Hamilton now taught, where Hudson Jennings still taught and was now chairman. Daphne and Joe had just moved to Westhampton from Amherst and had bought their first house and were stunned with what seemed to be the beginning of their real grown-up life. They weren't wealthy, but they could eat something more now than tuna-fish casseroles and they could unpack their wedding presents. They hadn't even seen a lot of the loot for four years; it had been packed away in storage while they lived in tiny rented apartments. They hadn't realized they had so much.

They were barely able to buy a little old "colonial" in a good neighborhood; they were able to afford it because it had been owned by an impossibly old brother and sister and the sister finally died, leaving the brother to sell the house and move to a rest home. The outside of the house, which was red brick with blue shutters, was fine, but the inside hadn't been painted or redecorated for thousands of years.

That first semester in Westhampton had been a frazzling time for Joe, who was trying so hard to do everything perfectly so he could get tenure; Daphne wanted to be there when he got home from work or for lunch or dinner to listen to all he had to tell her. Daphne didn't know what she wanted to do — she didn't think she wanted to start commuting for her Ph.D. work now, not when Joe needed support and peace and quiet at home so he could concentrate on his work. She didn't want to go to work either, in some secretarial job; she had just done that for four years. She enjoyed being able to stay in her robe, finishing her coffee in the mornings; she enjoyed watching the old house spring to new life under her hands. Now when Daphne tried to remember that first semester . . . when she had no women friends . . . what came into her mind first and most vividly was the pattern of wallpaper she had finally chosen for the kitchen, a luscious melon-colored print of basketed fruit — apricots, plums, pears, apples, grapes, all shades of orange and lavender and ruby. She had papered the walls with that, then trimmed the woodwork in melon-colored paint, and washed and painted the inside of the cupboards, even the insides of the top cupboards that no one could see. She ordered quilted fabric that matched the wallpaper and made cushions for the captain's chairs as well as place mats and napkins. She made crisp heavy white cotton curtains for the windows. She played classical music on her stereo while she worked, and let her head fill with daydreams. She began to think that being a "homemaker" might be very pleasant.

Yet she knew she was lonely for women friends. She had had good friends at U. Mass. and still phoned them occasionally, but her life was now centered in this town, in this house. Joe wanted the inviolable security of the tenured faculty members, the complacency with which they moved through the world, the respect. Joe and Daphne yearned to be like those tenured faculty, all of whom, it seemed, had an old Jag or Rolls or MG or at least a Cadillac that had belonged to their parents, all of whom had summer places on the Vineyard or the Maine coast. The couple the Millers admired and envied the most, like everyone else at the college and, for that matter, in the town, was Hudson and Claire Jennings.

The Jenningses were just a few years older than the Millers, but they had tenure, the house on the Vineyard, the antique auto in the garage. Hudson was handsome, in a giraffish way, with long legs and limbs and long-eyelashed huge gentle brown eyes. He had thick dark hair that fell over his forehead, and he was kind. He was also brilliant and well-liked, and it puzzled Daphne that Hudson was married to Claire, who was rather large and awkward and mannish in an English, Virginia Woolf–intellectual sort of way. Claire was very pale. She had blond hair that she wore in a twist at the back of her head, and a long face from which her lower front teeth protruded somewhat. Her eyes were a piercing blue, with heavy lids, and she radiated intelligence and "breeding."

The younger faculty, all Anglophiles, said only Claire, of all the people they'd ever met, was "the real thing." She knew all about birds and flowers and dogs. Claire and Hudson had no children, but somehow that seemed right to those who knew them. Claire and Hudson seemed to have sprung full-blown from the womb, married, aristocratic, educated, elite, and terribly self-possessed. Claire had a long thin mouth that seldom moved, and a remarkable smile, during which her lips did not move sideways as others' did, but simply turned up slightly at the corners while her eyelids drooped down correspondingly over her great long oblong blue eyes. So one never knew if one was amusing Claire or boring her into a state of agony. But this all gave her tremendous power and everyone wanted to please her, and Hudson was erudite and full of clever tales, so the Jenningses were invited everywhere.

When Joe and Daphne received the invitation to the Jenningses' for New Year's Eve, they were wild with delight. They felt like the Chosen, and wouldn't have traded places with anyone in the world. The Jenningses lived on one of the most prestigious streets in this prestigious town. They had a great tidy French Provincial set in three acres of lawn and garden. Joe and Daphne nearly swooned with pleasure when they were shown into the library — the *library!* And it was paneled in mahogany, with shelves and shelves of books and hunting or seascape oils hung around the fireplace and an old but not shabby Persian rug on the slate floor. This was how all college professors should live, the Millers thought: this is how they would live one day.

At one end of the room, on an elaborately carved table, stood oversize art books and small brass or porcelain sculptures set out very formally on its surface. At the other end, by the window, was a walnut drinks cart with a silver ice bucket and some ornate crystal glasses and a bottle of Dry Sack. Daphne and Joe were just settling into a deep sofa before the fire when Hudson came into the room, bringing another couple from the college with him, the Krafts.

Otto taught German; he and Laura, whose real name was Hannelore, were both from Germany. Otto was stocky and bald even though he was only in his early thirties, with ice-cold blue eyes and amazing white teeth. He would have been thrillingly handsome except that he looked and sounded and carried himself like a Nazi. He was stiff and his speech was ponderous. In contrast, Laura seemed warm and bright and vivid, with her long dark hair held back with a paisley silk scarf and perfume wafting from her. When she crossed her legs her black evening skirt made slithery sounds as it exposed her legs almost to the hip. She was wearing patterned black hose and her thighs were long and slender; all during their friendship Daphne would envy Laura her thighs. During that long evening when Daphne and Laura first met, Daphne didn't know whom she wanted to look at the most: dark-haired, vibrant Laura, or cool, blue-blooded Claire, or gorgeous, gentle Hudson. She tried not to stare. She tried not to feel tongue-tied. Everyone else seemed so cosmopolitan and self-assured.

They discussed college matters and college gossip. They talked about the major events of that year, and their hopes for what was to come. Claire held forth at length on the tradition of celebrating the new year, which was a celebration of the victory of order over chaos. Cultures had always celebrated the new year, she told them, as a time of purging and mortification in order to have renewal and revitalization. William the Conqueror had decreed in the eleventh century that January first was the start of the new year, but in medieval times the new year had started, more appropriately, in the spring, when the earth was coming back to life. The noisemaking, Claire thought, was probably originally from the Chinese, who exploded firecrackers and lit torches to frighten off the evil spirits.

She is so learned, Daphne thought, looking at her hostess, who sat at ease in her wing chair, her dogs at her feet. But could she be friends with Claire? She didn't think so.

Claire seemed so ... humorless. Perhaps, though, Daphne was being unfair, perhaps Claire was in pain. It was Hudson who served them their drinks and brought in the tray of cheese and crackers, and Claire had said, with a wave of her hand, "Hudson has to do these things, you see; I have a bad back." Perhaps that accounted for Claire's stiffness. *I wonder if she can enjoy sex*, Daphne thought, and looked over at Hudson, who to her horror was just at that moment looking at her as if he were reading her mind. She felt her face blush and immediately looked back at Claire, freshening her face with an expression of interest.

" ... the Scots have their own tradition of serving haggis on New Year's Eve," Claire was saying. "Have you ever eaten haggis?" Without pausing for a response, she went on. "It's made from a pudding of sheep's innards and oatmeal and other such things, stuffed into a sheep's stomach, and slit open at the table."

Daphne looked away again, this time at Laura, and to her surprise, Laura smiled and made a funny face, rolling her eyes. Daphne grinned and looked away. She didn't want to be disrespectful, not here. But she was glad to see that smile of Laura's; it reminded her that this *was* New Year's Eve, and the tradition in the twentieth-century United States, she

156

wanted to say to Claire, was to drink too much and dance and party and eat, not to attend lectures. Daphne shifted in her chair. How old was Claire anyway? She and Hudson both seemed to be in their early thirties, but Claire acted as if she was and always had been some petrified grande dame. How could she make Hudson happy? For he was not as deadly as she. Daphne looked at Hudson as he sat in his wing chair across from Claire. Did Claire ever walk in front of this elaborate fireplace and kneel on this gorgeous Persian rug and unzip her handsome husband's expensive gray flannel trousers and lean down to put her mouth — Hudson looked at Daphne then, and again she found herself blushing, terrified that he could read her thoughts. She looked down at her hands. Well, Claire probably didn't do that, she thought, because of her bad back.

The night seemed to go on forever. Now and then the others managed to say a few words, but mostly Claire held forth, while Hudson sat smiling benevolently at her. At midnight, Hudson opened a bottle of champagne and they all solemnly toasted the new year and each pair of spouses exchanged chaste kisses. *I've got to get out of here*, Daphne thought, *before I turn to stone.*

A few minutes after midnight, Laura surprised them all (even, if one could judge by the look on his face, Otto) by standing up and saying with a smile, "I'm so sorry, but we have to go now. We promised the baby-sitter we'd be home as soon after midnight as possible."

When Hudson and Claire didn't seem dismayed by this announcement, Daphne said, "I'm afraid we must be going along too," and rose.

Claire didn't get up — her back — but Hudson saw them to the door and handed out their coats and accepted their thanks for a lovely evening, and finally all four were out in the invigorating black cold of January 1, 1967. Daphne felt almost electrified by the change — movement, walking in the open air to the car, after sitting for so long without moving — cold air after the heat of the stuffy room; she felt vividly awake, and yearned for something *more* now, like someone who has awakened from a long sleep and is hungry, or wants to throw off the covers and rush eagerly into the day.

Daphne felt warm pressure on her arm, and there, wrapped in her black Persian-lamb coat (a present, Daphne would learn later, from Laura's wealthy German mother-in-law — and so *soft*), her dark hair falling around her face, her smile like a candle in the dark, was Laura, suddenly hugging Daphne to her. "Do

158

you believe her? Good God. Listen, you and Joe come to our house now," she whispered, and told Daphne the address.

In the car on the way to the Krafts', Joe and Daphne exploded with laughter about the horrible evening at the Jenningses', but as they pulled into the Krafts' driveway, Joe cautioned Daphne not to say too much; he wouldn't want any of his criticisms to get back to Hudson. And Hudson, he said again, was not like that at the college. He was enjoyable and took a great deal of interest in his colleagues and the younger faculty. He had heard that Claire had a reputation for being formal — and now they knew she deserved it.

It was late, though, and Daphne was tired, and the Krafts' house, at first glance, from the outside, disappointed Daphne, who had been expecting something — what? — *luscious*, after meeting Laura. The porch light illuminated a traditional commonplace split-level ranch house, the kind of house Daphne liked least in all the world. She thought they were so mediocre, and this house was in a little cul-de-sac of similar split-levels. It just didn't seem right to Daphne that an originally European college professor with a beautiful wife should live in a ranch house. Now the exhaustion of the whole late night came over her and for a moment she didn't think she could find the energy to get out of the car to go up to the brick-and-stucco building.

But the inside of the Krafts' house was a wonderful surprise. It was like a museum of modern art, except that it was comfortable. Everything was black, red, or white, except for the furniture, which was teak. The back wall of the living room was entirely glass, looking out over a forest, and hanging against the glass were prisms and multicolored sun disks and an amazing leaded-glass gargoyle that Laura said had come from the window of a ruined fifteenth-century German church. There were plenty of comfortable seats in the living room near the fire that Otto lit, and Daphne and Joe sank down into the plush receptive warmth of the long, deep black leather sofa.

While Otto walked the baby-sitter home, Laura brought out champagne and beautifully shaped pottery plates laden with Brie and Camembert and Edam cheese and salamis and sausages and small sweet pickles and olives and a liver pâté and a fish pâté and salty chips and sweet dark pumpernickel bread and speckled mustard. There were clever little plates and small knives and forks and spoons, and finally there was a large silver platter with eleven different kinds of elaborate cookies.

"My God," Daphne said, "were you

planning a party?"

"Oh" — Laura laughed — "no, not at all. Otto just enjoys eating and I love to cook. This is just stuff we have around. But of course for Christmas I always make lots of different cookies and breads."

It was a feast, and it was a delight to relax at last in this bright room, to laugh and drink a little too much champagne and talk and eat. Daphne and Joe stayed until four in the morning. Joe and Otto started talking college politics, college policies, and Laura moved close to Daphne, who sat with her shoes kicked off and her feet tucked under her. That night Daphne came under Laura's spell. Laura that night became her inspiration and teacher. She had never met anyone like Laura, who was so beautiful, and who touched people when she spoke to them, and was always touching herself while she talked, stroking her long hair or twirling a curl around her finger or slipping her hand just inside the neckline of her black silk blouse and gently, absentmindedly stroking her collarbone or turning the rings on her slender fingers. Daphne was envious of Laura's confidence about what was important in the world.

"Do you have any children?" she asked Daphne as she leaned up against the sofa. Strong traces of her German accent ornamented her speech, and this made her seem mysterious and cosmopolitan and exotic. Whenever she said "were," she pronounced it "wear": "We wear happy." Laughter always seemed to be underlying Laura's words, laughter or song, for her voice was lilting. Her husband's words plopped from his mouth, heavy pellets, each piece separate and weighty, but Laura's speech was music; it flowed and dipped and thrilled; it was sexual.

"No," Daphne said. She was going to say that she wasn't certain she even wanted children, but before she could speak, Laura leaned close to her and put her hand on Daphne's arm, imploring, almost caressing. Laura's hand was so soft and smooth and warm and her perfume was enchanting.

"Oh, but you *must* have children," Laura said. "Daphne, it is the most wonderful thing, you can't imagine! You must come up and see our little Hanno while he is sleeping. You will see what I mean — we must have children, in order to believe in heaven and innocence and trust and love and all the good things, all the *real* things, to offset all the grisly dribble our husbands deal with, with all their ghastly never-ending *words*." Laura rose and took Daphne's hand and pulled her up. "Come up with me, come, you'll see what I mean."

Daphne had her tall sliver of a champagne glass in one hand, and Laura had her glass in one hand, and, still holding hands, Laura pulled Daphne along through the house and up the stairs. The hallway was so marvelous with all its lithographs and black-and-white photos of the Kraft family at various places — Daphne glimpsed one as she passed in which all three seemed to be sitting on a beach completely naked — that only one fraction of her mind was able to point out that it had been years and years and years since she had held hands for so long a time with a woman. But Laura was both like a child, a childish best friend, and like some kind of fairy or witch or sorceress who was leading Daphne into sacred regions.

And it was a sacred region, for as Daphne stood over little Hanno's bed with Laura, still holding hands, she saw that what Laura had said was right. Here was what life was all about — the goodness of life, in any case. Here, on a small yellow wooden bed covered with what Laura called a yellow "puffy-puff," was an angelic-looking little child, a yellow-haired child with rosy cheeks, sleeping a pure and peaceful sleep. He was three years old. His room was gently illuminated by a glowing night-light of a little shepherd boy and two lambs. A brightly painted dappled rocking horse stood in one corner, and wooden soldiers, wooden trucks, fat furry teddy bears, lined the walls. A small yellow bookcase was filled with children's books and wooden puzzles. It was a lovely nursery, warm on this January night with the thick white carpet and the curtains pulled shut against the cold and dark. And the little boy lay there sleeping, no angles or sharpness, all softness and curves and peace.

Daphne realized that she was still holding hands with Laura, but it seemed appropriate somehow, for this was a moving moment for Daphne and it seemed to her that some kind of power and significance flowed like a warm current from her new friend into her own being. The little dark nursery was like a primeval cave, and Laura, standing so close to her that Daphne was embraced by her perfume, was the goddess of fertility and life and peace and domestic contentment. Here was the heart of the world, and Daphne came to know that profoundly, as any parent does when looking down on her sleeping child: here is the heart of the world.

After that night Daphne didn't let a day go by without at least talking to her friend on the phone. That night, after the two women tiptoed from Hanno's room, they went into the kitchen, ostensibly to brew coffee but really to talk about gynecological things: Laura's pregnancy, Daphne's kind of birth control, and when Laura began to describe in detail Hanno's birth (she had had natural childbirth and had nursed Hanno immediately), Daphne thought she hadn't come across anything as violently, passionately bloody and frighteningly allegorical since she had read Spenser's *Faerie Queene*. Something sprang up inside Daphne that night: an appetite for blood and gore and physicality that was related to sex but that was selfish and self-centered. Suddenly she could not get enough of hearing about being pregnant and having babies. Suddenly she understood that being a woman was a deliciously juicy and complicated and slightly underhanded thing.

They shared so much, so effortlessly. It was as if they were sisters. By Thanksgiving of that first year, Laura had become the dearest friend Daphne had ever had. Laura was just a few years older than Daphne, and a few years ahead of her — she had decorated her house, she had gotten to know people in the town, she had had a child. But it wasn't just that that made it seem natural for Laura to sweep Daphne off into real life; it was that Laura made ordinary life seem delicious, and Daphne wanted to learn to do that too.

Laura knew of the fabric mills near Greenfield where materials for draperies or pillows or clothes could be bought at amazingly low prices. And she knew which materials would last and which would fade or tear or stretch out of shape. Even though her taste in furnishings was modern, she seemed to know exactly the sort of thing that would go best in Daphne and Joe's house, which Daphne was slowly furnishing in pine antiques. Laura would put Hanno in his car seat in the back of their Mercedes (another gift from the wealthy mother-in-law) and stick a banana in his hand and drive Daphne up into Vermont, where they would spend the day looking in antique shops and secondhand stores. "Look," she would say to Daphne, pulling her over to a chest or dry sink that was layered and clotted and scarred with various coats of paint, "this is pine under here."

"Yes, but all the paint — " Daphne would begin, confused.

"Well, we strip the paint off!" Laura told her. "Silly. Haven't you ever stripped anything before? It's a terrible stinky job, but you find treasures underneath. And it's so much fun to stain it just the color you want, to polish it up."

Laura loved to sew; she helped Daphne choose materials, and helped her find patterns that were most becoming to her. It seemed to Daphne that Laura was brutally honest: "No," she would say in a dress store, "you don't look good in that. You have to be careful — big and white and freckled like you are — or you look like a peasant woman." Once, early that first summer, when they were in the dressing room of an enormous cut-rate clothing store in eastern New York State, trying on swimsuits, Laura put her arm around Daphne and pulled her so that they stood side by side staring at themselves in the wall-length mirror. "My!" Laura said. "Just think! If we had your breasts and my thighs, what a perfect woman we would be!" And she threw back her head and laughed.

Laura loved to cook. Nothing seemed formidable to her. The first night that the Krafts had the Millers — and the Jenningses and two other couples from the college — to dinner, Laura served, among other things, a succulent Beef Wellington. Daphne had never eaten Beef Wellington before, and thought it was the most fabulous thing she'd ever tasted. She asked Laura for the recipe, and the next day Laura brought it over — six typewritten pages of exacting notes.

"I can't do this!" Daphne wailed as Laura sat across from her in the kitchen, bouncing Hanno on her knee. "I can't stand around twisting mushrooms in a towel — six cups of mushrooms! That would take forever!"

"Oh, you are so American," Laura said.

"Everything must be quick and easy."

"How do you do it?" Daphne asked. "How could you have made this and taken care of Hanno too? It must have taken you all day."

"Oh, it took longer than that, of course," Laura said, smiling smugly. "These things do take time. But I make Hanno some play-dough so he is happy doing what Mommy is doing, and I put some Viennese waltzes on the stereo, and the house is full of music, and then it is a pleasant way to spend the afternoon."

Nothing seemed too much for Laura, nothing daunted her. She seemed capable of giving artistic attention to every dimension of everyday life. She dressed little Hanno, who was already a storybook child, in gray leather "lederhosen" with suspenders, and a thick pale blue sweater and exquisitely patterned socks she had knit herself. She crocheted an elaborate, dramatic black fringed shawl that, when wrapped around her shoulders, hung almost to the ground and made her look like a Gypsy, so sexual and exotic. Daphne admired it so much that one week later — just one week! — Laura presented Daphne with a shawl just like it, except in red, which Laura said would be better than black for Daphne's coloring. Daphne in her shawl looked mytho-logically beautiful, a princess, a queen, a sorceress. There was something so ancient and eternal about the way she and Laura looked, wrapped in those shawls, which swayed gently when they moved and enclosed their bodies in color as if in a cocoon from which they might emerge as changelings. Daphne had never had any piece of clothing she looked better in or loved more than that shawl — even now.

Laura made being a wife and mother seem luxurious. Over the weeks and months that Laura and Daphne talked, Daphne began to see why it was that Laura loved her daily life so much. Laura had been born in 1936. She had been a child during the war, not a baby, too young to appreciate what was happening, and not a teenager, when she would have been somehow involved, but a child of five and six and seven and eight, old enough to have some inkling of what was going on but no sense of control. She had lived in Hamburg, with her mother and father and sister Nikki. Her father was killed on the battlefield. Her sister was killed when a bomb fell on the city and Laura (then Hannelore) and her mother and Nikki were huddled in the basement of their house and the house from next door exploded into their basement, a section of wood falling onto Nikki's head. (Nikki was three years old.) Laura could remember walking down the streets of Hamburg, holding her mother's hand, saying, "Mother, I am hungry," and her mother saying, "There is no food, we have no food," and she could remember her mother quietly crying as she said that. She could remember chewing pages from books to still the pangs in her stomach. She was sent into the countryside to get away from the bombings, and also because country children were supposed to be better-fed since they lived on farms. But the farm was primitive and the outhouse smelled so foul that Laura secretly relieved herself in the bushes, and when the farmer discovered this, she was severely beaten. These were not atrocities she had lived through, but they were painful times, and the most heartbreaking, it seemed to her, was not that her father was sent to war and then was killed, for she had not known her father well, and not that her sister, whom she loved so much, had died, but that her mother would silently cry, standing outside a bakery window, because she could not buy bread for her one living daughter. Her mother had had everything taken from her.

"Now I have a child, and I know that if I can manage to keep my child's belly full every day, then my life is good," Laura told Daphne. Daphne listened, feeling guilty, for her own memories of childhood and the war years were so different. Her father had been an officer in the army, but he had never left the United States. Daphne and her mother had lived with Daphne's mother's parents in their huge Victorian house in upstate New York, and her grandfather had been adoring and talkative and they had had a wonderful time.

Now, from such different backgrounds, Daphne and Laura had met, and they had so much in common. They laughed at the same things, they enjoyed the same things, and most of all they found pleasure in each other's company. Finally it came about that Daphne realized she had entered into a conspiracy against her husband — a delicious, wicked, thrilling conspiracy — and her life was radiant with dimensions she hadn't thought of before.

It wasn't very far into their friendship before Daphne realized that Laura had been absolutely right: she should have a family, she did want children. But when she approached Joe about having a baby (they were still using birth control, or, rather, Daphne was — she was on the pill), he shocked her by saying adamantly, "No. Not yet."

When Daphne talked with Laura — the next day — she confided this to her friend, because she was very upset, she was hurt. But Laura surprised her by laughing. "Oh, of

171

course he said no! Don't you know that men are terrified of making babies? They don't think of a baby, a child, they only think of years and years of endless bills. And your husband and mine, these college professors, they think they can control everything, they think they can do everything in some kind of sensible order. They will wait until they are certain they will be able to pay for everything, the child's hospital bills all the way through the child's braces and to the college education, then they'll say, okay, let's have a baby, except that by then you are fifty-nine years old. No, you can't ask your husband for a baby, you have to sneak it out of him, which any woman can do. You just go off the pill sometime, and tell him that the doctor said you have to — and really, you know, it's not good to be on the pill for a long time, it messes up your ovaries. So sometime, *not* when you are in bed or making love, but when you are eating dinner and then he must rush off to a college function, when you know that he will be preoccupied, you tell him the doctor says you must stop taking the pill. But that you will use other kinds of birth control — foam is good for getting pregnant with. Or get a diaphragm and poke a little hole in it. But listen, you shouldn't do it just yet. He hasn't been teaching yet a year here. Give him a little more time to get settled, to feel secure."

Daphne listened with boundless admiration and, at first, a sense of guilt. To be plotting about something so serious as a child, which would, after all, not affect Laura but would completely change Joe's life! Even to be discussing something so private with someone other than Joe!

Sometimes Daphne feared she and Joe were really growing apart. Had been growing apart for four years — at the same time, of course, as they were also growing together. But when they met, they had both been submerged in English literature — reading it, teaching it, studying it, living in it. Then, for four years, Joe kept at it, gradually sinking deeper and deeper into his work, while Daphne bobbed up to the surface and looked around and got a glimpse of the rest of the world. They loved each other, but she had stopped being his compatriot; his country was English literature, while hers was, well, the entire rest of the world.

Before she met Laura, every time the phone rang in the evening it was for Joe, and whenever someone was late coming in, it was Joe, who had been asked for a beer by his students, for a drink by his colleagues. And in conversations at dinner parties she felt left out if she tried to join in a discussion about some fragment of the vast field of literature.

"I've always thought Dickinson was too heavy-handed with her symbolism," she might say, and before she could complete her thought or her sentence, the person listening (some poor professor who had gotten stuck next to her at a formal dinner table) would impatiently nod and look away and start a conversation elsewhere. What Daphne had to say now might be interesting — it might even be right — but it just didn't matter, because she was officially "just a wife," not an intellectual.

With Laura she suddenly felt she had joined, or formed, her own little private and very exclusive club. She needed a friend, a colleague of her own. Besides, Laura was such fun, and Daphne had forgotten how much fun she could have with a woman friend. The Millers and the Krafts grew accustomed to getting together for dinner once a week, usually at the Krafts' house so that Laura wouldn't have to get a baby-sitter for Hanno. Daphne would surreptitiously study Otto. Really, she knew so much about him, and such intimate things! — how his father, a wealthy industrialist, had never embraced his son even when Otto was small. Otto and his brothers and sisters had been raised by a nanny, and the closest his father ever came to

174

really touching his son was during his monthly inspections, when the nanny had the children bathed and shampooed and dressed in their finest, standing in a line in the nursery. Then Otto's father would walk along, examining and evaluating his children. He would always pinch the lower flesh of their upper arms. "This one needs more food," he would say to the nanny. Later, when the children were older, their father gave them brief mental inspections: "What is the capital of Greenland?" he would bark, and if they did not give the answer immediately, they were to be punished with a whipping in proportion to their flaw.

No wonder Otto was such a rigid man. Sometimes Daphne would think about and compare Otto's rigidity and Hudson's. It seemed to her that Hudson's carefulness always had the virtue of grace and elegance and lightness, like Hudson himself, a leanness about it, a slenderness, so that if he was rigid, it was like the string on a violin or an archer's bow — taut, but one could touch it, pluck it, one could make it sing or send an arrow soaring. Otto, in comparison, was heavy and earthbound. His rigidity was like a boulder, or like a cannonball that had already been fired and now lay, immobile, yet remained a kind of weaponry, still capable of violence.

No wonder he did not laugh easily, and when he did laugh, he sounded like a dog barking. He was handsome in a way, with his blazing blue eyes and that bald naked head. The baldness was aggressive; it seemed a kind of display. But he was not unkind. He was always pleasant to Daphne, and he did not intimidate Joe. Joe and Otto enjoyed getting together for dinner — there were always the college affairs to discuss, and then they both liked football. But Otto did love to follow rules to the letter, and according to Laura, even his lovemaking was scheduled. Daphne would never ever feel really comfortable with her best friend's husband.

Everything about Laura and her life and her husband, in the end, finally only made Daphne love Joe more. Joe was so romantic, such a wonderful lover, and he did feel as Daphne did, that what their lives were about was their love. No matter how busy he became, or how far from her he seemed to go during his days at the college, there were always a few nights a month when he came back to Daphne, came into Daphne, and went with Daphne back down under, into their submerged and secret deep liquid world. They curled around each other, pulled each other deeper with their legs and embracing arms, they took each other's breath, they made each other soaking wet. Joe and Daphne loved each other so passionately that one night of love could suffice them — even, still, exhaust them — for weeks.

She had had that with Joe. And she had had her friendship with Laura. Soon she had had her daughter. In those days, Daphne had had so much.

5

Jack was pleased with himself. He had had a good morning. After three weeks into the semester, he had just had three more students sign up for his class, which meant that the word was getting around that he was good. He had started off this Introduction to Neoclassic Literature course by having the students read Pope's self-satisfied mincing *An Essay on Man* ("One truth is clear, *Whatever is, is right*") while lecturing to them about the general conditions in the British Isles at that time: the lack of sanitation, the plagues and diseases, the absurdly unfair penal code, the contrast between the few very rich and the many chronically poor, the squalor, the illiteracy, and, for the women in his class, the complacent sexism — even Jonathan Swift had said, "A very little wit is valued in a woman, as we are pleased with a few words spoken plain by a parrot." If he had to teach this stuff, he wanted to get his students interested in it, even fascinated by it, and he had decided to do that by means of irony and rebellion — understanding one's tyrants.

This morning, before he had introduced Swift's *A Modest Proposal,* he had played on his cassette deck the rock group U2's song "Sunday, Bloody Sunday." It was easy to lead from there into a discussion of conditions in Ireland then and now; the music hooked the students and they *felt* the similarities of this age and the eighteenth century; so they would give this literature, this course, a chance. Hudson Jennings might not approve of his methods, but he couldn't object to the consequences; the students were reading the stuff, *all the way through,* and discussing it.

It was almost noon. Jack sat in his office trying to decide whether to eat there, while making notes on an essay he wanted to start work on, or whether to enjoy himself by going down to the cafeteria and getting a decent lunch and having some friendly conversation. Either way, he'd have a long walk. His office was located on the top floor of Peabody Hall, and the concession machines with their expensive cold sodas and stale sandwiches were in the basement, four flights down. Peabody Hall was a strange building, a building like Dorian Gray's face: the old awful part was hidden in the attic, while the first floor, which everyone saw, stayed beautiful. That was where the gracious faculty lounge was with its long windows and thick Oriental rugs and leather chairs and huge mahogany tables covered with current periodicals. Receptions were held there, in the Peabody Room, and it was also used as a refuge for the faculty during the day. Running the length and half the width of the building, it was so spacious that clusters of chairs and sofas were scattered around, with fresh coffee and hot tea kept in silver urns at one end of the room. It was a graceful room, and Jack went there often. The other half of the first floor was broken into two large lecture rooms and a grand foyer with brass plaques and oil paintings of former presidents of the college on the high walls. The second floor was given over to small classrooms. The third floor, which one always reached in a state of exhaustion, because the ceilings of the first two floors were so high, contained faculty offices. Hudson Jennings had an office with large windows and thick carpet near the top of the stairs. Jack's office was at the back of a warren of halls and offices; it had one high tiny window and no carpet. But it was *his* office, and he loved it.

He decided that because he deserved a reward for the way his class had gone this morning, he would go down all those stairs and out of the building and across to the cafeteria. He'd find a friendly face and clever conversation there — but suddenly he heard a commotion in the hallway. It sounded like Alexandra, screaming *"Bottle,"* but that couldn't be it.

Jack looked around the door and saw, to his amazement, Hudson Jennings leading Carey Ann, with Alexandra screaming in her arms. Carey Ann was extremely pale and her eyes were glazed so that she looked both blind and powerful.

"Here you are, my dear," Hudson said, ushering Carey Ann into Jack's office.

"Daddy!" Alexandra cried with delight, and reached out her arms to be taken and hugged. Jack was pleased by this, because it was flattering that his daughter was so thrilled to see him — and also because she had stopped screaming for her bottle.

"Your wife was having trouble finding your office," Hudson said.

Carey Ann turned her beautiful wide blue glassy gaze on Hudson and said, "Thank you so much."

"What a nice surprise," Jack said. He hadn't shown Carey Ann his office before — she hadn't wanted to take the time to come in and see it until she got more organized at home.

Hudson went off down the hall.

Carey Ann shut the door behind her so that the three Hamiltons were enclosed in Jack's tiny space.

"Oh, Jack," Carey Ann wailed, and tears began to shoot from her eyes. "Alexandra's been kicked out of play group!"

"What?" Jack asked.

Alexandra, knowing she was the subject of conversation, and possibly even aware that she was the source of her mother's tears, reached up a plump dimpled hand and gently stroked her father's cheek. "Prickles," she said.

"I want to die! I want to just die! I want to go home!" Carey Ann said. "I want to go back to Kansas."

"Oh, Carey Ann, oh, honey," Jack said, and tried to put his arm around her, consoling, but as he got close to her, his daughter leaned forward with both her little hands (her legs were anchored between Jack's arm and chest, her little bottom seated on his arm) and pushed her mother gently but firmly away.

"Go way," Alexandra said.

Carey Ann was crying so hard she didn't notice anything. Jack managed to pat her shoulder. "I hate everybody here," she was saying.

"Prickles," Alexandra said. She climbed up Jack's body so that her face was directly in front of his, blocking his view of Carey Ann. With both little fat hands she gently rubbed his face. "Daddy prickles."

How could anybody so cute be kicked out of a play group, for heaven's sake?, Jack thought as he nibbled on his daughter's fingers, making her giggle.

Carey Ann, ignored, began to talk loudly. She was actually kind of screaming: ". . . uptight New England *bitches!*"

Oh, God, Jack thought, for some of the other English and history teachers were in their offices on this floor now.

"Here," he said, pulling a heavy wooden office chair up to her. "Sit down, honey."

He sat down in his squeaky typing chair and found some felt-tip pens and blank white paper. "Here," he said to Alexandra, drawing a face on the paper, "Lexi draw picture!" He gave his daughter the pen. She looked at him suspiciously, knowing she was being bribed, but, kneeling on his lap, leaned across his desk and began to scribble.

"Now, Carey Ann," Jack said. "Start from the beginning. I want to hear exactly what happened."

Carey Ann was digging in her purse for some tissues. She blew her nose, then said, "Well, you know how Madeline Spencer called and asked if I wanted to join their play group. She's got little Zack, who is just Alexandra's age, and she had these four other friends who all had kids, and they said if I wanted to I could join their group and it seemed like such a good idea. Madeline seemed all right, in spite of her hair, once I got talking with her. We were going to meet three times a week, Mondays, Wednesdays, and Fridays, and leave all six kids together with two mommies to take care of them, and four mommies could be off, so each mommy could have two days off and one day on, and there'd always be two mommies together so we could talk and things. I really thought it was a neat idea." Carey Ann succumbed to another moment of sobbing.

"See, Daddy?" Alexandra said, taking her hands and pulling Jack's face toward her "picture," which was squiggles and swirls.

"That's *pretty*," Jack told his daughter. "Lexi draw another picture for Daddy." He gave her another sheet of white paper.

"So today was the first day, and we decided I would be one of the mommies to stay because Alexandra has never been left alone with a group of kids before and we thought she might feel more secure if I was there, and Madeline was the other mommy. And it started off just fine, we were at Madeline's house, she has this neat huge rec room just off the kitchen. And everything was okay for a while, but then Lexi wanted to go into the other rooms, you know how she likes to explore, and Madeline's rule was that the kids had to stay in the rec room or maybe go into the kitchen, but not into the rest of the house. Her rec room really is big and all, I don't know why Lexi didn't want to stay there and play with the other kids, but she kept trying to go into the dining room off the kitchen, and Madeline asked me not to let her go because she didn't want the other kids going off, her house would get messy, so I had to stop Alexandra, and she had one of her little temper tantrums."

Jack shuddered. He knew Alexandra's "little temper tantrums" well; they would have brought Attila the Hun to a screeching halt. He looked down at his daughter, who was drawing happily, intently, on white paper. He adjusted the pen in her plump hand and brought the pen in to the middle of the paper. "Stay on the paper, Lexi," he said, and kissed the top of her head.

"Then I got her settled down," Carey Ann was saying, "and it was sort of difficult, for if I paid any attention to the other kids, she got kind of jealous and sort of . . . I don't know, I mean she'd come tug on me or hit my legs or something. And I don't know why, but every time little Zack picked up a toy, Lexi wanted that toy, and she'd go grab it from him and say, 'Mine,' and I got embarrassed and tried to stop her, so she had another little tantrum. Madeline told me to just let her cry, and we tried to talk about it, but then Shelby Currier's baby had to have her diaper changed while Madeline was in the kitchen heating up Kathy Kelly's baby's bottle, and I had the little baby on the floor on a towel, and I was trying to change her diaper, and Alexandra came over and started pulling on me, saying, 'No! *My* mommy!' and I *tried* to explain it to her, that I had to change the baby's diaper, but Lexi started shoving the baby, trying to get her away from me, and then she picked up a play hammer and hit the baby in the face. She did it so fast I didn't even see it coming. Oh, God, Jack, that baby screamed, you never heard any baby scream like that, I thought she was killed. And her nose started bleeding, and Madeline was standing in the door with the warm bottle and she rushed over and grabbed the baby up and went off into the kitchen with it and put cold wet towels on its face, and when she came back she said, 'Alexandra ought to be spanked for that,' and I said, 'I've never spanked my little girl in my life and I never will,' so she said, 'Well, aren't you going to do *something* to punish her?' and I said, 'She didn't know what she was doing,' and Madeline said, 'She knew *exactly* what she was doing and if you aren't going to do something to teach her she was wrong, I don't believe you and she should stay in this play group.' So I stood up and took Alexandra in my arms and said, 'Well, all right, if that's how you feel about it,' and *she* said — oh, this is the worst part, because she stopped being angry and got all friendly and sympathetic, like she was sorry for me or something — 'Carey Ann, I really like you but you're harming your daughter. You don't discipline her at all. You're raising her to be so spoiled she's absolutely antisocial.' " Carey Ann broke off into another fit of sobbing.

Jack watched, feeling ill. Alexandra had stopped drawing and was staring at her mother, fascinated. She turned to stroke her father's face. "Prickles?" she asked hesitantly.

"And then what happened, honey?" Jack asked. Lexi turned back to her drawing.

"And then . . . and then," Carey Ann said, crying so hard she could scarcely speak, "and then I left."

Jack's stomach ached. He was baffled. Was his sweet lovely little girl some kind of bad seed? He didn't know what to do. He wanted to put his arms around his wife and pull her into his lap and hold her and soothe her, but

Alexandra always got upset if her parents did that sort of thing, and he wasn't certain just how much physical affection parents were supposed to demonstrate in front of their off-spring. But Carey Ann was truly more miserable than he'd ever seen her, and he'd seen her pretty miserable.

"You know," he said, musing, as if the thought were just occurring to him, "I think that somehow you and I have been doing the wrong things, honey. I think we've just been letting her get away with too much. Maybe we *should* start spanking her when she does something wrong."

"My parents never spanked me in my entire life!" Carey Ann said. "Never!"

"Well, my parents spanked me plenty, and I still know they love me," Jack said. "I'm not saying we should beat her. I'm just saying . . . oh, I don't know what I'm saying. Maybe we should go to the library and get a book on the subject."

"Oh, *books*," Carey Ann said, shooting him her you're-the-scum-of-the-earth look. "That's all you know about. That's all you can come up with, is books."

"Well, there are a lot of books on child rearing," Jack said. "I see them advertised in the newspapers' book sections. So there must be lots of parents like us who aren't sure just what to do. *You* read plenty of books about dieting and your thighs and all," he persisted. That was the wrong thing to say, he could tell. Carey Ann hated it if he mentioned her diets or her exercises to improve what she thought of as a terrible body (and what he thought of as heaven, the most beautiful thing on this planet). "Or we could go see a psychiatrist," he suggested.

"Jesus Christ, what do you think, Alexandra's *crazy?* Do you think *I'm* crazy?"

"No, no, no," Jack said, trying to calm his wife. "I guess I didn't mean a psychiatrist, I meant a counselor. Some expert who could give us advice on how to discipline Lexi."

But Carey Ann was really crying now, insulted by every single thing Jack had had to say in the last few minutes.

He looked down at Alexandra. First he saw her beautiful curling opalescent hair; then he saw that while he had been talking, she had taken the felt-tip pen and drawn squiggles and great sweeping spirals all over his desk blotter.

He physically recoiled, as if from a blow in the stomach. His desk blotter was more than just a functional piece; it had great sentimental value. Last Christmas, when they knew they were going to move back east, Carey Ann had surprised him on Christmas night by bringing out a pile of red- and green-foil-wrapped boxes, presents for him, presents she had not brought to the family gathering around the giant tree in the Skragses' living room, but had hidden, to be opened when Alexandra was in bed and just the two of them were alone together.

"I want you to know that these presents are from *me*," Carey Ann had said before she would let him open them, and she was blushing the entire time she gave them to him. "I mean, I didn't buy them with your money and I didn't buy them with my daddy's money."

"I'm not sure I understand, honey," Jack said.

"I mean I got a job for four weeks just before Christmas," Carey Ann said. "At Hall's. And you know my father doesn't own any of that store; he doesn't even know anybody who owns any of it. I got the job all by myself. In the perfume department. They always need extra help before Christmas."

"Carey Ann, that's great," Jack said, really touched, and touched even more by how serious Carey Ann was about this, and how intense.

He opened the first set of presents: it was a desk set consisting of blotter, leather pen cup, leather appointment book and address book with refill pages for the next few years, a little leather box full of loose-leaf notepaper, and a leather wastebasket. The leather was a wonderful chocolate brown, thick and fine, without any ornamentation, very masculine.

"That's for your study at home," Carey Ann told him. "Now open this set. It's for your office."

For just a moment Jack had felt a tingle of fear, for Carey Ann liked stationery with buttercups or elves or lambs on it, and she drew smiling faces on things and bought cards with rainbows and sunbeams on them for every imaginable occasion. What if the set she had bought for the office was in pale blue with gold trim or something?

But it wasn't — it was just like the other set, except that the leather was all a dark green that was almost black. It was very handsome, and he could tell it was very expensive. Carey Ann had probably spent nearly four hundred dollars for the two desk sets.

Jack had come close to crying that night. He had felt as sentimental and mushy and in love and blessed as he had the night he proposed to Carey Ann and she accepted. He had come to treasure his desk sets. This one had certainly classed up his standard hole of an office.

But now there were these indelible dark blue squiggles and swirls all over his desk blotter, on the thick felt and on the leather. The blotter was ruined.

Jack grabbed the pen from his daughter. "No!" he said. "I said to draw on the white paper, goddamn it!"

He didn't hurt Alexandra, but he had seldom spoken to her so sharply before, and the little girl jerked her head around to stare at him in amazement. Then she burst into wails. It was absolutely amazing how a child's face could be transformed in a flash like that, from something so innocent you could suddenly believe in angels, to something so crinkled up and red and blotchy and wide-mouthed and *loud* that you could suddenly — for sure — believe in devils.

For one pure moment that lifted itself up out of time and hung like a dewdrop above Jack's head, he hated his little girl. Well, maybe "hate" wasn't the right word. He thought he probably was losing his mind. Carey Ann was sobbing, Alexandra was screaming, his desk blotter looked like shit, and he didn't have any idea what to do now.

There was a knock on his door. Of course there was, of course someone would knock on his door *right now*.

"Here," Jack said, handing his crying daughter to his crying wife. God, he hoped it wasn't Hudson. It would be so embarrassing;

it would look like Jack was being cruel and abusive to his wife or child. He had gotten a good look at Claire and would bet money she had never cried or made a scene in her life.

It wasn't Hudson. It was a student, a girl in a baggy sweater. She stood outside Jack's office, sort of wincing with indecision.

"Mr. Hamilton?" she asked timidly. "Could I sign up for your neoclassic lit course? I'm sorry to bother you now, but this is the last date for late registration," she hurried to say.

"Sure, we've got room for one more," Jack said. While he took the form from her and signed it and told her what text to buy, she was busy looking anywhere but into his office, where the two other females seemed to have calmed down a little and were only sniffling.

"Thanks so much!" the girl said as she turned to leave. "I really can't wait to take your course!"

Jack nodded and smiled and then shut the door on her retreating figure. He turned to his wife. Carey Ann was now staring at him with a new look: suspicion? anger?

"Who was *that?*" she asked, her voice cold. Alexandra stared at her mother.

"Huh? That was just a student," Jack said. "I didn't get her name."

"Do all your students look like that?" Carey Ann asked.

"Well, no," Jack said, trying for some levity. "Some of them are men."

" 'I just can't wait to take your course,' " Carey Ann mimicked in a simpering high voice.

"What?" Jack asked.

"She probably wants to have an affair with you," Carey Ann said accusingly.

"Oh, yeah, right!" Jack yelled, losing his temper at last, going berserk. "I mean, I am such a sex object on this campus that they almost didn't hire me. I mean, no one wants to take my course because I'm a good teacher or anything, they just all want to get in my pants. The guys too — I mean, I'm such a hunk I turn straight guys gay at the sight of me." He caught himself finally; he was leaning over Carey Ann, yelling right into her face. She had started crying again, quietly, pathetically, the martyred wife.

"I'm sorry, Carey Ann," he said, and put his hand on her shoulder. Alexandra, who had been shocked into silence by his shouting, reached up her fat little hand and pushed his hand off her mother's shoulder.

"Go way," Alexandra said.

Jack went over and slumped down in his chair. He looked at his blotter, now a ruin, like his life. "I'm sorry, Carey Ann."

"You just don't understand," she said, digging in her purse for another handkerchief. "I used to be so popular and have a lot of friends and everybody liked me and thought I was pretty, and now here I am and I don't have any friends and no one to think I'm pretty, and you have these beautiful girls just crawling out of the woodwork to get to you and I can't even be in a little old play group and pretty soon you'll stop loving me."

"I'm not going to stop loving you." Jack sighed, thinking as he spoke that he halfway wished he could. "And everyone thinks you're pretty, you're the prettiest woman on the East Coast. Now let's settle down and talk about this sensibly," he said.

He had meant to be soothing, but before he could say another word, Carey Ann bristled, tossed her hair, and shot him a look that could kill. "Don't you patronize me!" she said. She was so mad now that she stood up and began to pace the tiny office, which was just barely big enough to pace in, especially since she still had Alexandra in her arms. "You want me to settle down and talk sensibly, which means you want me to just go on and act like nothing's wrong, and I won't. You think I'm being frivolous or childish or something, the way I've been upset since I've been here. Well, I want you to understand I'm *not* being frivolous or childish; I'm having a major problem with my life! I really am. Now, I love you and I know you love me, and we both love each other a whole lot, the same amount, but I was the one who had to give up something in order to spend my life with you. Why is that? Why weren't you the one to give up things? Who says that just because you have a Ph.D. in English you *have* to teach it? We could be living in Kansas City right now in a gorgeous house having a lot of fun. Or you wouldn't even have to go to work for Daddy. You could have kept teaching at the university there. You had friends there, you had students you liked. And I could still have had my friends and family and all the places I know and feel comfortable with, even if we were poor. You are just like a man! You want everything your way and if I'm not fitting into your little plans just perfectly, you think I'm not being *sensible!*"

Alexandra burst into a grin because with the word "sensible" her mother inadvertently spat on her face, which surprised Alexandra. Also, it was an interesting ride for the little girl, for each time Carey Ann got to the end of the room she turned so fast she whipped around, and pretty soon Alexandra got into the rhythm of it and hung her body out away from her mother's and grinned when the turn snapped her back against her mother. But Carey Ann's face was deadly serious.

"You want me to make friends right away — I know you do, and you don't even understand a thing about friendship. These women here are so stuck-up, they ask me where I'm from and I tell them I'm from Kansas and they get this kind of superior, very *amused* look on their faces like suddenly they know all about me and what they know is that I go around barefoot carrying slop to the hogs or feeding the chickens."

All at once Carey Ann ran out of energy and slumped back down in her chair. "You tell me to be sensible," she said in a softer voice. "What that means is that you want me to hurry up and make lots of friends and make the house look nice and be that mother out of *Leave It to Beaver*. I can't do that. I've got to go at my own pace. I've got to make my own friends. Just 'cause you and I are married doesn't mean we're going to like the same people. Like that Daphne Miller that you like so much. I can understand that you would like her 'cause she's been at the college for about a billion years and can tell you all about it. And she's so serene and all, like someone who never has had any problems. She just sort of goes floating and smiling through the universe like the old Queen of England, calmly talking to everyone, and I can see she'd be helpful for you to talk to. But if I'm going to have a friend it's got to be someone like me with some problems. If Madeline Spencer had said to me today, 'Carey Ann, you have the prettiest hair, I really envy you because I can't seem to get mine to do anything,' well, then it would have been easy for me to say to her, 'Madeline, I know Alexandra needs some discipline, but to be honest, I just don't know how to go about it.' Do you understand that at all, Jack?"

Alexandra had curled up in her mother's lap and was sucking her thumb. Jack wished he still sucked his. He had tried to pay attention to his wife and understand her, but sometimes her logic seemed unique to the point of nuttiness. It was the most he could do to say, "Look, Carey Ann, we're both strung-out. We've got a lot to talk about, but we can't solve everything right this instant. I'm starving. Let's go over to the student union and have some lunch. Alexandra will love the french fries." He held up his hand to forestall another scream. "I'm not trying to get out of discussing all this. I'm just hungry and I think I'll be able to talk about it all better after I've eaten."

"All right," Carey Ann said. She stood up, wiping her eyes.

The history department was also in Peabody Hall. The history-faculty offices and secretarial cells were on the third floor, along the south side; the English department ran along the north. In between was the huge warm thrumming Xerox room with its massive compliant machines. Jack was on his way at four o'clock to find Daphne's office, but as he passed by the Xerox room he caught sight of his friend bent over a machine.

"Hi!" he called, and stepped inside.

"Oh!" Daphne jumped, looking over her shoulder.

"I didn't mean to scare you," he apologized.

"I know you didn't." She laughed. "You just can't hear anything when the machine's going. Besides, you caught me with my shoes off."

Jack looked down; so he had. Daphne's brown leather shoes lay on their sides, their long heels pointed at each other, on either side of her stockinged feet.

"Come over here and talk to me," Daphne ordered. "I've got to get this paper copied for Fred. He needs it for some journal." She leaned close to Jack as he approached. "It is so boring," she said through her teeth. "The paper, I mean. I had to type it."

Jack went around to the other side of the Xerox machine. Daphne had a nice rhythm going: she raised the lid, picked up a sheet of paper, put another down, shut the lid, put the paper in a pile, and picked up a new sheet of paper from another pile. The machine hummed and clicked and stuck out a tongue of copied paper into its tray. He watched for a while, admiring her precision and organization. Her movements were almost hypnotic. She was like the machine — efficient, smooth — but unlike the machine with her grace. Next to the machine she seemed very female and curvaceous. Her breasts were right at the level of the lid, right in his line of vision as he watched her work.

"I have a favor to ask you," he said, shaking away his thoughts. When Daphne looked at him questioningly, he went on, "I wonder if you would baby-sit for us tonight." He held up a hand, forestalling any comment she would make. "I hope this isn't an insult," he said. "I mean, I know it's an imposition, and I know you're not a baby-sitter. But I've been trying all afternoon and I can't find anyone who can come on such short notice. Hank Petrie gave me some names, but they're all high-school girls who have to study for tests. And Pauline White gave me a name, but that woman already had plans."

Daphne just looked at him, a funny smile on her face.

"I guess it's kind of an emergency," Jack

went on. "To tell the truth, I'm a little desperate. Carey Ann is having a difficult time adjusting to the move and I need to have a long, uninterrupted talk with her. It's hard to talk with Alexandra around."

"Did Carey Ann get on with any of those women I introduced her to at the party?" Daphne asked.

"Well . . . " Jack hesitated, not certain how much to say. He didn't want to betray Carey Ann; he didn't know, after all, who might be good friends of Daphne's — she did seem to know everyone — and he didn't want to say anything he would mind having repeated.

With a sudden little flurry, Daphne stopped copying, piled up the papers, and flicked a button on the Xerox machine. Silence fell around them.

"Sure I'll baby-sit," she said. Her cheeks were flushed from the warmth of the machine. "What time would you like me to come down?"

She was so easy!, Jack thought. Daphne was so easy and pleasant, and on his side. Somehow she had learned the trick of taking the world in stride. And she had such good legs — he watched her step back into her high heels.

"God, this is really good of you," Jack said. "You'll have to let us do something for you sometime. I really appreciate this."

"We country folk have to stick together," Daphne said, smiling. "Don't worry about it. I'm sure sometime this winter I'll get sick and ask you or Carey Ann to get me some medicine, something like that. What time do you need me?"

"Six-thirty?" Jack asked. "Is that too early? We all have to get up early tomorrow, so we should make it an early night."

"Six-thirty is fine."

Carey Ann was on the floor with Alexandra, helping her put huge wooden pieces into a puzzle that would soon be a rabbit. Alexandra jumped up and ran to Jack as soon as he came in the door.

"We're going out to dinner. I've got a baby-sitter!" Jack said, picking his daughter up and whirling her above his head. "Daphne Miller's going to come down."

He was grinning up at Alexandra, so he couldn't see Carey Ann's reaction to this news — he wasn't sure he wanted to see it. She didn't say anything.

"I couldn't find anyone else," he went on. "I got some names from Hank Petrie — he's in English too, but his kids are older, but not old enough to baby-sit. They're all high-school girls who will come on weekends but not on weeknights. It'll be good having Daphne — I won't have a long drive picking her up and taking her home."

"It's nice of her," Carey Ann said slowly. "After working all day and all."

"She's coming at six-thirty. So go put on your dancing clothes, mama!" Jack made squeaky kisses on Lexi's tummy.

The phone rang.

"I'll get it," Carey Ann said.

Jack carried his daughter into the living room and sank down onto the floor with her. She was having a giggling fit. He lay on his back, drew his knees to his chest, and put Alexandra on his legs, bum against the shelf of his feet. He held on to her hands and bounced his legs, and Alexandra laughed with pleasure.

"Yes, this is she," Carey Ann was saying. "Oh, yes. Oh."

Jack paused in his bouncing for a moment, trying to hear the conversation, trying to figure out who was on the other end of the line. But Alexandra screamed, *"Go,* horsie!" He bounced his legs again. He hoped it wasn't Daphne, backing out.

He bounced Lexi till his legs grew tired, then lifted her above his head and turned her into an airplane. Finally he said, "Daddy's tired," and let her down onto his chest and stomach. He hugged her. She snuggled against him. They both caught their breaths. Carey Ann hung up the phone in the kitchen and came into the living room. She sank down onto the sofa like someone who'd just been turned into jelly. There were tears in her eyes. Oh, no, now what?, Jack thought, his heart sinking.

"Oh, Jack," Carey Ann said. "You'll never guess. Oh, I'm so happy." She smiled radiantly.

"What?" Jack said. He sat up, bringing Lexi up with him. She crawled off his lap and walked over to her mother.

"That was Shelby Currier," Carey Ann said. "You know, the mother of the little baby that Alexandra hit today? Well, you won't believe this, but she called to tell me not to worry about it. She said she knew I probably felt awful about it, because she has a little boy — Aaron, he's four, he's in preschool — and when he was two, the same sort of thing happened to them. Another little boy pretended to shoot at him with a toy gun, and Aaron said, 'Don't you shoot me!' and picked up a wooden block and threw it and hit the little boy in the face. Made him have a terrible nosebleed. Shelby wanted to die. And the other mother was really awful about it, acted like Aaron was a psychopath or something. Oh, Jack, Shelby's so *nice*. Jack, she belongs to this other group. It's a group of young mothers who get together one night a week just to talk about their kids and their problems. Each week they meet at someone's house, and they have a theme, like thumb-sucking or discipline or sibling rivalry, and it's at her house tonight and she wants me to come. Oh, Jack, would you mind if I didn't go out to dinner with you tonight? I mean, I love you, but . . . "

Jack grinned at his wife. "I love you, Carey Ann. Even if you prefer someone else to me."

"Oh, Jack!" She grinned, then jumped up. "What shall I wear?"

Carey Ann had just driven off in her white Mustang convertible and Jack was still standing in the doorway with Alexandra waving in his arms — her entire arm going back and forth like a windshield wiper — when Daphne Miller came walking down the dirt road and into their yard. She was wearing jeans and a sweatshirt and sneakers.

"Oh, God!" Jack said. "I forgot to call you. We had a change in plans. Well, listen, come on in anyway. Have a drink with me. The least I can do is give you a drink."

Daphne smiled. "All right. It will give me a chance to get to know your daughter better. In case you ever need me to baby-sit again, she'll be more comfortable with someone she's familiar with."

Jack sat Alexandra on the kitchen counter and gave her a slice of lime to entertain her while he fixed vodka tonics. He was suddenly happy — this miracle had happened for Carey Ann, and now he had a pleasant adult to talk to while he baby-sat his daughter, whom he adored, but who could get a little boring over the course of an evening. He told Daphne where his wife had gone.

"I'm so glad," Daphne said, taking her drink. She followed Jack into the living room and sat down with him and Alexandra on the floor. "Shelby Currier's very nice," she said. "You know, she used to be a model. She married Watson Currier, who must be the homeliest man on the Lord's earth, and he's a chemistry prof and *shy!* The two of them couldn't be more different. It's always a mystery when two people choose each other, isn't it? But Shelby is just as happy as a clam."

"Well, I'm relieved," Jack said. He told Daphne about the play-group incident, using gestures and euphemisms and disguised language so that Alexandra wouldn't know they were talking about her.

"Oh, it's the hardest thing to move into a new town," Daphne said. "I know. When I first moved here, I was a young faculty wife just like Carey Ann. The first semester, all I did was look at wallpaper books and paint the kitchen." She laughed. "It's a wonder Joe didn't leave me then," she said. "He'd come home from work and I'd have about seventeen billion wallpaper patterns for him to look at, all marked in the book with strips of paper."

She laughed, and suddenly spread her legs out in a V from her body. She grabbed a ball and held it at her crotch, then rolled it toward Alexandra, who was now sitting that way. "Now, roll it to Daddy and Daddy will roll it to Daphne," she said. "Watch out for your drink," she told Jack as he arranged himself for the game.

Alexandra loved the game. Jack and Daphne talked — interrupting themselves constantly to pay attention to Lexi — and after a while Jack made them each another drink and they rolled the ball in the reverse direction. The living-room window gleamed, a wall of light. After a while Daphne said, "I love it when it's just like this — not quite dark, but not daylight either. It makes the air seem so gentle." They decided to go out for a little walk. Jack zipped a sweatshirt onto Lexi and stuck her fat feet into their sneakers. Then, Jack holding one of the child's hands, Daphne the other, the three of them walked down the dirt road toward Daphne's house. The tunnel of trees was black. They could hear Dickens barking.

"Let's turn around and go back before he has a heart attack," Daphne said, and they did. "Hear the birds, Lexi? They're calling good-night to you."

It seemed perfectly natural for Daphne to fix them another drink while Jack changed Lexi's diaper and put her in her sleepers. They were talking about the English department now, and about Hudson, and about different writers. It was a pure relief to Jack to say some things to someone who understood — who knew what college departments were like, what kind of squabbling and rivalries and games went on.

"I'll be right back," he said, and went up the stairs and carefully lowered his sleeping daughter into her crib. He was surprised, when he came back down the stairs, to see that Daphne was crying. He couldn't imagine what had happened. It always amazed him how much women cried, and how easily.

"I'm so sorry," Daphne said. "Forgive me. I just . . . it was just seeing you like that with your daughter. The way you held her and looked down at her. You love her so much."

To Jack's dismay, Daphne bent over and crossed her arms on her lap and sobbed into them. He sat down on the sofa next to her, moving cautiously.

"I guess all fathers aren't like that, huh?" he said. He didn't want to probe, but he didn't want to be aloof, either.

"Cynthia's father wasn't," Daphne said. "Oh, Alexandra's a lucky little girl!" She raised her head and wiped her eyes. "I'm getting maudlin. I'd better go."

"No, no, finish your drink. Tell me about Cynthia's father." Jack sat at the other end of the sofa, looking at Daphne.

"Joe never wanted children," Daphne said. "He was always so wrapped up in his work. While I . . . I hadn't thought of having children, but all of a sudden this need grew right out of me. For a long time I tried to stifle it, thinking I could cajole Joe into having children. I had this very good friend, my best friend in those days, and she had the most beautiful little boy. While I was thinking about getting pregnant, Laura got pregnant for the second time. She was so thrilled, and I was so happy for her — but so jealous as I watched her growing bigger. And she loved being pregnant and loved talking about it." Daphne stopped to sip her drink.

"That summer Laura and her husband went to their house on the Vineyard and Joe and I went down to spend a week with them. We had a wonderful time. We biked everywhere, swam — Laura and Otto swam naked when they could, they said they always went to nude beaches in Germany. That seemed so exciting and . . . oh, chic, to Joe and me, so deliciously wicked. The Krafts were fascinating. We all swam in the ocean and read books and ate enormous amounts of food."

Daphne scrutinized Jack. "Why am I telling you all this?" she asked, and without waiting for his answer, went on: "Are you sure you want to hear all this? I don't know why I'm thinking about it all now."

"Go on," Jack said.

"One afternoon we went out for a sail in Otto's boat. Just the four adults; we left Hanno with a sitter. It was a nice big boat, with a cabin with a head and a galley and room to sleep six. It was the most beautiful summer afternoon — there was just enough wind to make us skip right along, yet it wasn't too choppy. We'd been sailing for perhaps an hour. Suddenly Laura made this sort of grunting sound — so impolite, you know, I laughed with embarrassment for her, and she sat up all of a sudden and said something in German. Then she got up and went down below. I followed her. She went into the head. I stood by the door. 'Tell Otto to head back to shore,' she said. 'Tell him he must hurry.'"

Daphne looked down into her drink. "She was losing the baby. She came out and lay on a bunk and I put pillows and towels under her bottom to elevate her, to stop the bleeding. But it didn't help. By the time we got to shore, she was holding my hand and crying so terribly and writhing. She was in such pain. She thought she was going to die. I thought she was going to die. And she said . . . Laura said" — Daphne was crying a little now — "she kept saying, 'Daphne, don't let this scare you. You must have children. Even if I die this way, don't be afraid. It's a fluke. It won't happen to you. You must have children. That is what life is all about.'

"She didn't die. We got her to the hospital, and she didn't die. Though of course the baby did." Daphne looked up at Jack, her eyes blazing. "Have you ever sat with someone while they are dying?" she asked. "It's an amazing thing. You feel so intense. You feel you are at the center of the universe. You feel so important — and yet you have no power. You think you will do anything, unimaginable things, to keep this person you love alive.

"I would have had children even if I hadn't met Laura, of course," Daphne said, her voice growing lighter. "But that was a crucial moment in my life. So — what I'm trying to *get* to — I went ahead and got pregnant without Joe's consent. Without his knowledge, actually. It's not unusual, you know. Since then I've met lots of women who have sort of sneaked their children into this world. But I assumed that Joe would love his child, once he saw her, held her."

Daphne seemed very tired all at once. She looked into her empty glass. The living room was so dark that Jack, at the other end of the sofa, could hardly see her. "But he didn't," she said. "My husband didn't love his daughter. He didn't love her at all. That's why I was crying when I saw you holding Alexandra that way, rocking her that way. It, um, made me long for something I never had. I'm sorry I got so emotional on you. It must have been all these drinks. I really do apologize."

Jack moved down the sofa and put his arm around Daphne. "Don't apologize," he said. "Please don't apologize. I'm glad you told me. I'm glad you could tell me."

Then, to his surprise, he took Daphne's face in his hand, and, meaning simply to get her to meet his eyes so that she could read his sincerity, he began to kiss her. "It's all right," he kept saying, kissing her cheeks and her forehead and her chin, and then her mouth. She was trembling — from her crying, he thought — and she sat with her hands docilely in her lap. So it at first was not a matter of desire, but a matter of consolation. But to his surprise, he kept kissing her — God, she was so soft, her

212

limbs were soft, endlessly soft, and he kept saying, "It's all right. It's all right."

When he kissed her for a very long time on her mouth, she put her hands up against his chest as if to push him away, but she did not push him away. Their kissing turned into something very different from consolation, something flew out of their depths, like a bird flushed from the underbrush, flashing up into the air, something like a bird, with a life of its own, and they could kill it or let it live, the decision was theirs, but at first they reacted with their instincts, and they let it live. It was life, as all love is life, like a bird fighting to survive, to fly and be beautiful and have its own way for a while. Jack's hands were everywhere on Daphne's body, all the places he had wanted them to be, against the warm plump freckled skin, the full breasts, the rounded limbs.

He pulled up her sweatshirt. He wanted to see her breasts.

Daphne twisted away from him. She stood up and pulled her sweatshirt down. It was so dark they could not see each other except for their outlines, and the gleam of their wet mouths and eyes. Yet their breathing was so heavy they could almost see it; their panting was heavy and alive, like an animal roused in the darkness.

"We can't do this," Daphne said. "We can't

ever do this again. We must never do this again."

Then, stumbling a bit against the furniture in the dark room, she went through the living room to the front door, opened it, and was gone.

Jack sat in the dark for a long time, thinking, wondering what on earth he'd been doing. He sank his head in his hands.

About nine-thirty he got up and turned on some lights. He washed up the glasses and put away some of Lexi's toys. He thought, as he worked, how the toys were false — gave a false view of the world. For there was the wooden puzzle, and all the pieces fitted together to make a completed picture of a rabbit with a blue bow around its neck and a little wicker basket full of colored eggs in its paw. There was the wooden box with shapes cut into the lid — a three-dimensional X, a square, a circle, an oval, a triangle. Each piece perfectly fitting through its own hole, and absolutely *not* fitting through any other. The rock-a-stack, where colored plastic rings like inner tubes for dolls fit onto a yellow plastic pole, the largest at the bottom, the smallest at the top. There was no ambiguity in these toys, no duality, no confusion. Was it right to teach a child that the world was structured so clearly, that each thing had its place and only one place, that two contradictory things couldn't exist simultaneously?

Carey Ann came in the door like a teenager in love for the first time. She was glowing. She took Jack by the hands and pulled him over to the sofa and made him sit down and listen to her. She had had a wonderful time. She had made friends, she had stayed after everyone else left and had a long serious talk with Shelby Currier — Shelby used to be a model and they had so much in common, so much to talk about. Jack listened to his wife, smiling at her eager happiness. He had looked in the mirror about eighty times before she came home, checking to see if anything *showed*, if there would be any way for Carey Ann to tell that he had been kissing someone else. As far as he could tell, his face looked just the same. At any rate, Carey Ann was so fired up about her new friends, she probably wouldn't have noticed if a giant purple wart had grown on the end of his nose during the evening. She was going to try the play group again. And tomorrow she and Shelby were going to spend the afternoon at the park; Shelby had such good, sensible ideas about disciplining kids.

"Shelby says we've got to stop letting Lexi sleep with us. We've got to make her spend

215

the whole night in her own bed, in her own room. She said we should be really firm about it. We can explain it to Lexi very *calmly*, and every time she crawls in bed with us, we just firmly put her back in her own bed and tell her we'll see her in the morning. *And* she says that if she keeps crawling into our bed and doesn't stay in hers, we should lock the door from the outside, so she can't come into our room or leave her room. And she says that Lexi will cry and cry and cry enough to break our hearts, but that we can't give in. She's got to learn to sleep all night through in her own bed. That way we'll all get a full night's sleep and I won't be so wiped out all the time. She was telling me how hard it is with strong-willed babies, how with Aaron, when he was two, she couldn't get him to stop grabbing things off the shelves in the grocery store. She spanked his hands — that didn't work. She tried reasoning with him — that didn't work. Sometimes when she took things from him to put back on the shelves, he screamed with anger and people looked at her funny. So she did what she read in an early-childhood-behavior book — she told him that if he did it again, she'd put him in the car and leave him there while she shopped. So he grabbed something, and she left her cart right there in the aisle and carried this screaming little boy out to the car and put him in his car seat and locked all the doors, but left the window down for air — it was fall, it wasn't too hot or too cold — and then she went back into the grocery store. She said you could hear Aaron screaming all over the parking lot. She said when she walked away from that car, other people in the lot looked at her like she was the devil incarnate. She heard people talking about it in the grocery store, how some mother had left a poor little baby alone in a car. She said she was shaking so hard she was nearly in tears, and of course she couldn't really think about her groceries. She was afraid that someone would kidnap Aaron, or that he'd hurt himself in the car somehow, or that he'd choke to death crying, or any of those things. But she got her groceries, and when she got out to the car, Aaron was still crying like his heart was breaking — he was frightened, he'd gone all red and white. Some ladies were carrying their groceries to a car and one fat old bat said to Shelby, 'You should be ashamed of yourself. What kind of mother are you?' She felt like a monster. Aaron was so mad at her he screamed all the way home. Shelby was so mad at him she was afraid she'd hurt him. She wanted to shake him. So she took him in and put him in his crib, then brought in the groceries.

By the time she had unpacked them, he had fallen asleep with his skin all blotchy and his breath coming in little whimpers and he was sucking his thumb and stroking his blanket for comfort, and she lay down on the floor next to the crib and felt like the worst mother in the universe. And Aaron wasn't perfect after that in the store, but he was a lot better. If she threatened to take him out to the car, he straightened right up, just because of that one time. Oh, God, Jack, it feels so good to talk to someone about all this!"

It was almost midnight before Carey Ann had cooled down enough to go to bed. Jack came out of the bathroom and had a nice surprise — she was under the sheets without a nightgown on. He couldn't remember the last time she had come to bed that way, signaling that she wanted him. Seeing Carey Ann waiting in bed for him naked that way was like seeing the sun coming up after a night lost in a swamp. He could find his way again. He got in bed with his wife and began to kiss her and stroke her and touch her. He was nearly nuts with desire for her, and for the first time in months she was just as nuts with desire for him. "Oh Jack oh Jack oh Jack," she kept saying, and she nuzzled and whimpered and pressed against him and kissed him a million times.

"Daddy?"

He was just about to enter Carey Ann when he heard his daughter's voice right at his elbow. He jerked his head around so fast his neck cracked.

"Mommy?" Alexandra said, crawling up on the bed toward her mother.

Jack leaned over and switched on the light, carefully holding the sheet against him so he wouldn't give his daughter some kind of trauma. He grinned at Carey Ann. "I'm not exactly in shape to get out of bed at this moment," he said.

Carey Ann stood up. She took Alexandra in her arms. "Lexi sleep in Lexi's bed," she said, heading for the baby's room.

"*No!*" Alexandra yelled. "Lexi sleep with Mommy!"

Jack heard Carey Ann speaking in a reasonable tone of voice. "From now on, Lexi sleeps all night in her own bed. Mommy and Daddy sleep all night in their bed. We have to get a good sleep or we get too tired. Here, Lexi has her bunny to cuddle."

Jack could hear Lexi trying to scramble out of her crib. She was screaming at the top of her lungs. "*Lexi sleep with Mommy!*" After a while she changed: "*Daddy! Lexi want Daddy!*"

Carey Ann was shuffling around out in the

hall. When she came back into the bedroom, she was breathing fast, but for a different reason. "I've shut her in her room," she said. "I tied one of my scarves to the doorknob and then to the stair banister — Lexi won't be able to pull it open. And the other door locks in the bathroom."

She sat down on the bed next to Jack. For a while they both just sat there listening to Alexandra scream. "Do you think we're doing the right thing?" Carey Ann asked Jack.

"I do," Jack told her. "I really do. I think it's probably about time we did this."

"I don't think she can hurt herself in there, do you?" Carey Ann asked.

"I'm sure she can't."

Jack and Carey Ann sat side by side, naked, on the bed, listening to their daughter scream. It was amazing how loud she could be, and how persistent. Fire departments and burglar-alarm companies ought to tape-record babies screaming, Jack thought; it would be much more effective than any artificial sound. Jack's hair was practically standing on end. An anger was billowing in him, a desire to hit something. Carey Ann was turning white and shriveling down into the bedclothes. She looked sick at her stomach.

"Isn't she ever going to stop?" she asked Jack.

The room seemed to be filling with the color red. Alexandra was stopping now and then to gulp more breath — then she screamed some more. Jack's penis had crawled nearly up inside his body to get away from the noise. He felt like a monster.

He felt even worse, a few minutes later, when Alexandra's crying changed from angry screaming to pitiful whimpering. "Dad-dy," she was saying to herself. "Mom-my." They could envision her lying in her bed, lonely, bereft, betrayed, unloved, confused — traumatized? Were they ruining their little girl for life?

Then: silence. But it was not soothing. It was terrifying.

"Maybe she's dying," Carey Ann said. "Maybe she's stopped breathing. Maybe she's choked to death."

"Maybe she fell asleep," Jack said.

"Don't be cruel," Carey Ann said. "This is the first time we've ever made her stay in her room."

"And it worked," Jack said. "You were strong, Carey Ann."

"I've got to go check her," Carey Ann said. "I've got to be sure she's okay."

"Something tells me this is not a good idea," Jack said.

But Carey Ann was up and gone — through

221

the bathroom into the baby's room.

As soon as she opened the door, Lexi, who had been lying in her crib sucking her thumb, jumped up. *"Mommy!"* she screamed.

"Lexi go to sleep now," Carey Ann said, shutting the door fast and locking it.

Alexandra began to scream full blast again.

Carey Ann and Jack sat in bed waiting for the screaming to stop. When it finally did, Carey Ann looked at Jack. He shook his head at his wife. So she did not go check on the baby again. They turned off the light and slid down between the sheets. Jack felt as if he'd just climbed out of a Cuisinart. He was both exhausted and jazzed-up. He turned to Carey Ann, wrapped his arms around her.

"I can't now," Carey Ann said. "Not now. I'm sorry. I just don't have any energy for it. I can't get in the mood. I feel like crying. I feel like a person who's left a puppy out in the cold."

You are leaving me out in the cold, Jack said to his wife, but only in his mind. He turned on his side and tried to go to sleep. This is a start, he reminded himself. Marriage is long, and we've made one change. This is a start.

WINTER

6

Cynthia came home for Christmas vacation.

When she was about twelve, she had started tearing the skin off her fingers. It was a terrible habit, a disgusting one, and seemed to indicate deep problems. She would start somewhere around the fingernail, and finding a tiny sliver of loose skin, would peel the skin down toward the knuckle. Some days all the fingers of her hands were an angry, naked, injured red.

Daphne had tried everything to get Cynthia to stop. First she had just ordered her to *stop doing that*. So Cynthia stopped doing it — in front of her mother. But at night, when they were eating or watching TV together, Daphne would look over and see her daughter's injured hands. Then she tried to bribe her — Cynthia was still young enough to play with Barbie dolls, and complained often that she had three Barbies but only one Ken, so she had to keep killing one Barbie's boyfriend off so he could be with another, or make him date all the Barbies at once and even commit bigamy. Daphne told Cynthia that if she would stop tearing her skin, she would buy Cynthia two more Ken dolls. But even though, over the next few weeks, Cynthia made a valiant attempt, she could not stop. So Daphne threatened Cynthia with Cynthia's worst punishment — being grounded so she could not spend the night with her friends or have them over for the night. Even that did not work. Cynthia cried grievously, but she could not seem to help herself.

"All the girls at school do it, Mom. We just get bored."

Daphne went to see Cynthia's teacher. He reassured her that this was just a phase that Cynthia was going through, that indeed many of the girls did do it, that it was often a sign of boredom. And Cynthia was so bright — but so bored with many academic subjects — that it was not surprising that she tore at her skin. Preadolescents and adolescents often had many revolting little habits, the teacher said; adolescents all sucked their hair or chewed their nails or, if they were unfortunate enough to have zits, sat all day in class rubbing them. You got used to this sort of stuff as a teacher, and it wasn't a sign of psychological disturbance or unhappiness.

So Daphne learned to ignore this. She said nothing more to her daughter about it. When Cynthia was twelve and thirteen, she used to wear Band-Aids to school, and when they ran out of Band-Aids, she wrapped Scotch tape around her fingers. Then she sat at school and tore at the tape, tore it in shreds.

She also used to sit, watching TV by herself, and coat her fingers with Elmer's glue. After it had dried like a second very white skin, she would carefully peel it off. Little curls of dried white glue would lie around on the carpet like hundreds of fingernails.

When Cynthia reached fourteen, she spent more time on her hair and clothes and general hygiene. She didn't peel her skin quite so much — she painted her nails, and peeled that. She painted them almost every night with two or three coats of thick oily paint, and when she came home from school the next day, her nails would be almost bare, with only a few shreds of color left. And she still, now and then, tore her skin.

She was doing so well in school, and then she was the lead in the high-school play even though she was a sophomore, and she was so happy and popular and outgoing that all of Daphne's friends agreed that Cynthia's habit was not the sign of a deep-rooted problem. Pauline White said that when she was a teenager she used to pull her eyelashes out, one by one, and study them for a long time, how the root end was white, how some were longer and thicker than others. Daphne tried not to worry. But she secretly thought: Cynthia peels her skin, tears at herself, *mutilates* herself, because her father doesn't love her and never pays any attention to her.

And perhaps she had been right. For Cynthia was still peeling her fingers when she left for California and her father, and now here she was home on vacation, and her fingers were whole and perfect.

When Cynthia had stepped off the plane, Daphne had gasped. Cynthia was so beautiful. And she looked so grown-up, so terribly sophisticated. Her thick blond hair was cut almost punk, very short and slicked back behind her ears and up at her forehead, and she wore long dangling earrings and lots of eye makeup — put on subtly, put on with the hand of an artist. She had lost a great deal of weight. She had gotten taller in the seven months she had been away, but she had also lost a lot of weight.

"Cynthia," Daphne asked, keeping her voice casual, "are you anorectic?"

Cynthia smiled. "No, Mother. We just eat lots of fruits and vegetables out there."

Gone were the loose and flapping clothes of yesteryear; Cynthia now wore skintight toreador pants with tight long sweaters cinched at the waist. Cyn was dressed rather like Daphne had been as a teenager in the fifties, but Daphne knew better than to say so.

Clothes. With girl children it was never simple. Two years ago, when David died, Daphne had reacted to his death by gaining weight. She almost didn't know how she did it — she didn't pig out or eat obscene amounts. But she was always so tired, and normal life seemed to require such vast amounts of energy that she had to keep eating this and that simply to find the power to get through each day. She had been numbed by David's death — a loss of yet another person whom she loved and who loved her — and she couldn't find the strength to diet, or the will to care, for a while, what she looked like. With David gone, really what did it matter what she looked like? She was certainly not too fat to work the word processor or the type-writers. Oh, she wasn't even really *fat*, just heavier than normal.

That February, when Cynthia rushed into the house from school, wild with joy, to tell her mother she had been cast as the lead in the spring school musical, *West Side Story*, Daphne was thrilled and proud. She was usually terribly careful about money, she had to be, but that night, seeing how her enthusiasm buoyed up her daughter, she called Pauline and Douglas White and four of Cynthia's best friends and took them all out to the most expensive restaurant in town for dinner. She had them all come to the house early, for champagne, which she rushed out to buy and which she let Cynthia and her friends drink (it was a Friday night, and she did not let them drink too much).

It had been a grand celebration, a perfect one, absolutely on the spur of the moment; Pauline had put her casserole in the freezer, because Daphne had insisted that everyone had to celebrate that very night, the night that her daughter had been chosen over all the juniors and seniors for the lead. Everyone toasted Cynthia, who was rosy with happiness, and when the evening was over, Cynthia had come into her mother's room, in her nightgown, and embraced Daphne.

"Thank you, Moochie," she said. "That was the nicest party in the whole world."

"You deserved it, Coochie," Daphne replied, hugging her back.

Daphne had gladly driven Cynthia out to the high school for rehearsals and gone again much later to drive the other actors and Cynthia home. She did this over and over. She drove Cynthia out opening night and dropped her off an hour before the performance, then went home to dress for the play and the reception afterward. She had taken Cynthia shopping and let her buy the dress she wanted for the reception — Cynthia chose a slinky black thing that was probably too old for her, but when she put it on, the dress looked appropriate. Cynthia looked ravishing. The dress was too expensive, just as the party had been — but then, Daphne said, sometimes you just had to go a little crazy, especially at times like that.

The play went off splendidly. Cynthia was queen for the night. At the party afterward, Daphne stood in a corner talking with other parents and wondering if what everyone said was true, that Cynthia had special talent, that she could be an actress, that she was magnetic onstage, that she was the real thing. She watched her sixteen-year-old daughter slinking around in the black dress with enormous amounts of makeup on and her hair dyed black for the play. "I made her!" Daphne wanted to yell at people. "I made that child in my body."

The high school was about five miles out of town, set among fields. When the reception for opening night ended and everyone piled into cars and drove out of the highschool parking lot, Daphne and Cynthia were finally alone together in the car.

"Cynthia, you were wonderful," Daphne said.

Cynthia burst into tears. "Mother, how could you!"

Daphne looked over at her daughter. "What?"

"How could you have worn that old-fashioned old dress! To my play! And my reception! I wanted to *die* when I saw you."

Daphne stared down at her lap in amazement. It was true that over the past few years she had bought many more clothes for her daughter than for herself — that was only logical; Cynthia kept growing out of her clothes and needed new ones. And she cared so much about what she wore and how she looked. And Daphne had a closet full of dresses and shoes she had accumulated over the years. Well, with all the weight she had gained recently, she had bought a few new things for comfort, but she could still squeeze into her old clothes.

She thought she had looked fine for the reception. She had found, at the back of her closet, an old Indian cotton dress, in all shades of purple, with quilted cuffs and bodice, and little mirrors and embroidery all over. It fell full from the bodice and floated loosely down to her mid-calf. It made her hair look very black and her eyes look very blue, and, Daphne thought, it hid her excess weight well.

"I don't understand," she said to Cynthia. "To what are you objecting?"

"To that dress!" Cynthia answered, nearly shouting. "Oh, Mother, how could you do this to me?"

Daphne was quiet in response. In the past few years Cynthia had become more and more critical of her mother, sometimes with reason, but this seemed beyond the bounds.

"It is a perfectly beautiful dress," Daphne finally said.

"It is so out-of-date!" Cynthia said. "*No* one wears dresses like that anymore! Have you ever seen anyone wearing a dress like that in the past trillion years?"

Daphne took a deep breath. "I think it's a shame to ruin your opening night, your success, with this kind of discussion."

"Oh, Mom," Cynthia wailed, "don't you understand? How can I feel successful when you're going around like a . . . a bag lady? What are you trying to do, announce to the world how you give everything to your daughter? That I'm some spoiled little brat and you're the martyr of the century?" After a deep pause for breath, Cynthia said, "You would have bought a new dress if David were still alive."

Daphne drove in silence, trying to interpret this newest message from her daughter. She had wondered how much Cynthia missed David, how much she mourned him. On the one hand, David had been her mother's friend, and Cynthia was so involved with her peer group that David had been only a tiny dim star orbiting the periphery of Cynthia's life. But, on the other hand, David had been the grown-up man in Cynthia's life, out there at the edge of it all, circling, always in sight, someone who gave limits and boundaries to Cynthia as she exploded into womanhood, someone who, with Daphne, provided a sense of safety.

In any case, David had been Cynthia's only "male role model," that precious necessity that psychologists and elementary-school teachers liked to terrify divorced mothers with. Daphne had known David for twelve years, and had "gone with" him for eight, ever since Cynthia had been six. Daphne thought that David had come to love Cynthia, and she him. His devotion was great; he attended all her events, brought her birthday presents and Christmas presents, played soft-ball and tennis with her, and he never let her see him in his nasty drunken states. Well,

Daphne had had a hand in that. She had worked very hard to protect Cynthia from the knowledge of David's alcoholism. How could it be explained to a child? There were times when David, kind, gentle David, suddenly staggered and fell down, or cursed or spoke obscenely, or roared and smashed things, or blacked out, slumping, slobbering, in any corner of the room. David carried a monster within him who could erupt at any moment, and Daphne was always on guard, keeping that monster from Cynthia's sight. She refused David's repeated offers of marriage because of his drinking, and when Cynthia asked, as she occasionally did, why Daphne and David didn't marry, Daphne answered her daughter vaguely, "Oh, it's just not the right time," or, "Maybe someday, but we like things the way they are now." And Cynthia had seemed content with that.

Daphne had not been able to protect Cynthia from grief when David died. For that, only time brought relief. Even so, for months Cynthia would occasionally, out of the blue, burst into tears and tell Daphne that she missed David. He had been the closest thing to a father she had had.

But more than a year had passed. Perhaps Cynthia was caught, at some point in the whirlwind of her adolescent emotions, missing David, saddened that he wasn't there tonight to see her great success. But Daphne thought there was something else, something more, and it had to do with money.

Daphne always had to be very careful with money. There was never enough. Joe regularly sent the monthly child support, but never any extras, and college secretaries did not make a huge amount. Each year Daphne tried to save some money for college for Cynthia, and some for a vacation — this summer, she had carefully explained to Cynthia, there would not be a vacation as such. They would not be able to go away for a week or two to the Vineyard or Maine. She did not go into detail about this; she did not tell Cynthia that there would be no vacation because Cynthia's clothes this year, which Cyn had wanted so desperately, and because the celebration dinner Daphne had given when Cynthia was told she had the lead, and because even the huge bouquet of flowers Daphne had had sent to the dressing room for Cynthia's opening night had nibbled away all the money for a trip. Perhaps they would go into Boston for a few days and do the museums and Quincy Market. And after all, they were living in Massachusetts, where people from other states came for their vacations. Cynthia hadn't seemed bothered by this. She had even decided that she would try to get a full-time job, baby-sitting, if nothing else, so that she could seriously add to her savings account. For Cynthia had always worked too, baby-sitting, to help pay for her clothes, the movies, the school trips; she had always worked good-heartedly and without complaint.

But did Daphne? Always work good-heartedly and without complaint?

Well . . . usually. There had been times in earlier years when Daphne, exhausted with a sick child and sick herself, had complained a lot. Had wept. There had been times when Cynthia would beg for a box of expensive cookies and Daphne would snap, "Look, we hardly have enough money for milk." But this past semester Daphne had not even mentioned money. She had wanted Cynthia to have a wonderful semester, free of worries, so she could concentrate on school and the play. Really, Cynthia's criticism was, Daphne decided, unjust.

When they went into their house, Daphne said, "Sit down and talk to me a minute, Cyn," and turned on the living-room lights. Dickens waddled over and laid his head in Cynthia's lap, and automatically she opened her hands so he could lick them. Fred, the cat, had died of old age not long after David's death. "Cynthia, what is all this really about?" she asked.

Cynthia looked at her mother and burst into tears. "I don't know," she said. "Oh, Mom, I'm sorry. I love you so much. I really do love you so much. I don't know why I get so mad at you. I don't know why. Sometimes just the sight of you irritates me so much I could scream! But I really love you! Do you think I'm crazy? Do you think I should see a shrink?"

Daphne went over to sit next to her daughter. She put her arm around her. "I think you're a teenager." she said, smiling. "I think you're just a normal teenager. Now," she said, "can we have some cocoa and talk about the play? God, Cynthia, you were divine! How do you think it went?"

Then they were okay again. They went into the kitchen and sat up late talking — Cynthia talking, reliving every moment, while Daphne listened, entranced.

The day after opening night, Daphne had found in the mail a letter from California, addressed to Cynthia, from Joe. Daphne held the letter in her hand as if it were a ticking bomb, which in a way it was. Joe had not written to his daughter in all these years, not so much as one birthday note. So what was this? She wanted to tear the letter open and read it herself, but it was addressed to Cynthia, and Cynthia was out. She waited, heart thudding as if she were in a race. As if a war had been declared.

For those few moments in her life, Daphne had no dignity. In the late afternoon she hung around the front hall, pretending to pick dead leaves out of the Christmas-cactus pot, waiting for Cynthia to come in the front door and find the letter waiting, where all mail waited, on the front-hall table. Like a jealous lover, she smiled and spied, watching Cynthia's face when Cyn came breezing in the front door that afternoon.

"Hi, Mom!" Cyn said, and immediately her eyes went to the table — so she had been expecting this! — and she tossed her books on the hall chair and grabbed up the letter. Daphne, kneeling over her Christmas cactus, heart knocking away inside her, watched eagerness . . . amazement . . . *ecstasy* spread across her daughter's face.

"What is it?" she asked before Cynthia had even finished reading the letter. She was insane with curiosity.

"Daddy's coming to see me in the play!" Cynthia said. "Oh, *wow*, he's flying all this way just to see me in the play!" She twirled around the room as if waltz music were filling the air.

Daphne rose gingerly, as if in the last few seconds she had aged fifty years and all her bones were so brittle that one slight touch would break them. "How did he know about the play?" she asked.

Cynthia stopped her twirling. She looked at her mother defiantly. "I wrote to him," she said. "I found his address in your address book and I wrote to him and told him about the play and sent a picture of myself and told him that now I was an interesting person, he might want to get to know me. I invited him to come see the play." Her joy overwhelmed her defiance. "And he's really coming!" she whooped.

"But, Cynthia. Why didn't you tell me?"

"Tell you what?" Cynthia asked, eyes wide, moronic.

"Why didn't you tell me you had written to your father?"

Cynthia shrugged. "I don't know. I guess I didn't think you'd mind. I didn't think he'd write me back, I guess."

Mother and daughter looked at each other.

"I never have tried to keep you from your father," Daphne said evenly. "I've always made attempts — "

"*Mom.*" Cynthia bugged her eyes out at Daphne. Then, obviously trying to control herself, she said with ultimate patience, "I know you've tried with Dad. But now I thought I should try. This isn't about you and Dad, Mom. This is about me and Dad." She looked down at the letter, and in spite of herself, her joy came rippling out of her, brightening her face with radiance. "I've got to go call Donna!"

She raced from the room and into the kitchen. Daphne sat in the still eye of the storm and listened to her daughter dial the phone. "Donna!" she screamed. "Guess what! My *father's* coming to see me in the play! He's going to fly all the way from California!"

There were holes in several of Daphne's underpants, and suddenly she felt a strong desire to mend them right away. She went to her room, took out her sewing kit, and set to work, stabbing and yanking the thread through like a madwoman. She had tried. God, this was a slap in the face, it was Joe saying, "Cynthia, I'll have something to do with you as long as your mother isn't involved," but why should Joe act as if Daphne were the poisonous one? Daphne had always been the one who tried. There had been hate in her heart, but she had kept it hidden, or released it in tearful outbursts only when alone or with Pauline and Douglas. When Joe remarried and moved to California, Daphne had tried to

241

keep him interested and informed about their daughter. Cynthia had been only two when he left, just a baby. Every four months or so for the first few years, Daphne had sent Joe current photos of Cynthia as she progressed from a toddler to a kindergartener with braids and a bike. She sent neutral, polite letters about Cynthia's ballet or piano lessons, friends, school activities, along with copies of Cynthia's report cards.

Not once had there been any response. She might as well have sent it all into a black hole. Once a month she did receive the court-decreed child-support payment in a plain white envelope, but never any personal word, never any questions or suggestions or congratulations. It was as if Joe were paying a utility bill, or income tax, a legal necessity, nothing else.

Bizarre. Joe had been the one who had had the affair, but he had been furious when Daphne wanted a divorce. He would never forgive her for not forgiving him. And perhaps that was just. But that he would take his anger out on his daughter, that he would have such a total lack of interest in Cynthia — that was bizarre.

When Cynthia had been very little, Daphne sent her bright funny Christmas cards and birthday cards and presents and signed them "Love, Daddy." But when she was eight, Cynthia seemed too intelligent for such a charade, and who was this "daddy," anyway, who communicated only twice a year? Very carefully Daphne explained that Daddy had gone away to live in California so he could teach there and that he was very busy and forgot about holidays. Later, when Cynthia was older, Daphne made Joe out to be a sort of absentminded-professor type. "It has nothing to do with you, sweetie," she said. "It's not that your father doesn't love you. He doesn't know you. He's just too wrapped up in his work. Some men are just that way."

What else was Daphne to say? That Joe was cold, egocentric, reprehensibly unloving? Psychologists warned: Don't criticize the other parent; the child knows that parent is in her somehow and she will come to hate herself. Daphne had tried to protect Cynthia. She had tried to remain neutral always. She had never ranted, raved, hurled insults about Joe — within Cynthia's range of hearing.

Now Daphne pricked her finger with the needle and blood spotted the white cotton underpants right at the elastic waist. What she wanted to do right now was to grab that cloth and tear it. She wanted to hear the material shredding, she wanted to feel destruction, the power of ravage. But after all, Cynthia had said a true thing: this was not about Daphne and Joe, this was about Cynthia and Joe. If

Daphne could only hang on to her sense and stand back, if she could only control her jealousy and fears, then perhaps Cynthia would have a father in her life.

And wasn't that what Daphne wanted for Cynthia?

Joe called Cynthia that evening to tell her his plans. Cyn answered the phone — it was infinitely odd to Daphne to hear her daughter say casually, "Oh, hi, Dad."

Daphne waited for Cynthia to call her to the phone — wouldn't Joe want to check plans with Daphne, ask her for information? After a few minutes she could stand it no longer.

"Tell your father I can pick him up at the airport if he'd like," she said.

"He says thanks, but he'll rent a car in Boston," Cynthia relayed. "Okay, see you then," she said to her father. Hanging up the phone, she turned to Daphne with the face of a woman in love. "Mom, he's got such a nice voice!"

"Mmm," Daphne said, trying to sound noncommittal. "What are his plans?"

"He's going to fly to Boston, rent a car, stay at the Westhampton Inn, and see the play on Saturday night. He wants to take me out to brunch on Sunday morning, then he's got to fly back to California."

"Quick trip," Daphne said, smiling, heart thudding. Thank God he's not staying, she thought. This will be over before I know it.

That Saturday night she did not see Joe; she did not attend the play, but went to the Whites' to drink and be obsessed. Sunday morning, though, it was she who opened the door to Joe's knock.

There he stood, on her doorstep, her ex-husband, the man who had changed her life, the man who had married her, impregnated her, wrapped himself around her, and betrayed her. He was bald, and that sign of age made her happy, but he was slim and tanned and he must have been wearing contacts; she knew he needed glasses. With that tan, without the familiar blond hair and glasses, she would not have recognized him if she had passed him on the street.

Joe stood on her doorstep, and Daphne found herself smiling an absurdly friendly smile: if she met him now, she would not find him attractive! He seemed like a pleasant man, but so nondescript. She felt no yank of desire. Her heart floated out of her like a balloon.

"Hi, Joe. Cynthia's just coming. Would you like to come in?"

"Here I am!" Cynthia called, rushing down the stairs, swinging her purse. "Hi, Dad. See ya, Mom."

Joe nodded at Daphne and smiled with his mouth, but his eyes stayed cold. He put his arm around his daughter's shoulder and led her to his rented car. Daphne stood in the doorway watching them walk away. The only thing Joe had said to her was, "Hello." After all these years. Not even a "How are you, Daphne?" If she read his expression correctly, then Joe still hated her. But why? She was the one who should hate him. Certainly at the moment she had feared him.

And she had been right to do so.

When Cynthia came home from brunch with Joe, she told Daphne that her father had invited her to live with him and his wife in California, and Cynthia had accepted his invitation. Daphne stood in her sunny living room on that clear spring morning and felt her blood turn to venom.

" . . . and I think it will really be good for me," Cynthia was saying earnestly. "It will broaden my horizons. I'll be able to see what a completely different part of the United States is like and get to understand a different culture."

Daphne looked at her child and thought: I hate you. You are a stranger. You are a monster. You are an ungrateful, spoiled little bitch.

"Don't look at me that way, Mom. *Mom*, I

knew you'd be this way. Mom, come on. Dad lives in California, he lives near *Hollywood*. He's going to give me a car. He says he's really proud of me, Mom, and he wants to help me be an actress, he thinks he really could help me and I really could be an actress. You're always complaining about how we never have enough money and you never have any help, and now here I'm going to be getting some help, which will help you — I mean, you'll be able to spend some money on yourself for a while. . . . "

"I can't believe you chose to live with your father instead of with me," Daphne said. The words were choking her. Her grief was choking her.

"Mom, it's just for a year. Like I've lived with you for sixteen years, right? I mean, Dad has paid child support all along, and he deserves a turn, right?"

"But how could you accept his invitation without discussing it with me? Don't you care what I think? How I feel?"

Cynthia looked down at her feet. "I guess I was so surprised and excited I just accepted right away at once." She looked up at Daphne. "Mom, I've never even seen California. I've never even seen anywhere."

"Don't you know how much I'll miss you, Cynthia?" Daphne said, keeping her voice gentle but not letting it break.

"Well, I'll miss you too."

Daphne looked at her beloved only child and thought: I hate you as I have never hated anyone else in my life. I hate you enough to hurt you. I want to hurt you as much as you are hurting me.

"Oh," Daphne said. "Cynthia." With great and agonizing control, she walked past her daughter. She grabbed up her purse where she had left it on the hall table and went out the front door. She got in her car and drove off down the street. She drove around for almost an hour before she went to Pauline's house. When she stood on Pauline's doorstep, knocking on the door, her eyes were so swollen from crying that she could scarcely see through the puffed and painful lids.

"Oh, God . . . oh, sweet Jesus God," Pauline said when Daphne told her the news, and hugged Daphne and then made her sit down and drink quantities of Scotch.

"You can't blame her, you can't blame her," Pauline had said. "Every girl wants her father to love her — to adore her. Daphne, you have to let her go."

It had not even occurred to Daphne not to let Cynthia go. She would never stop Cynthia from going. But that Cynthia had not even hesitated when asked!

"My whole life has been devoted to raising that child."

"Maybe Cynthia is aware of that." Pauline used this cruel observation as a form of surgery, as a means of healing, like cauterizing a wound. "Maybe she thinks it's time you devoted some of your life to yourself."

"Oh, come on!" Daphne exploded. "It wasn't like that, and you know it! I didn't *sacrifice* my life to hers! I had a good time, I had fun — I had David."

"Well," Pauline said calmly, "in any case, Cynthia was destined to leave home soon. In two years she has to go off to college. If you had the money, you would have sent her to some kind of camp. Or prep school. It's time for Cynthia to go. It's time for you to move on too."

Daphne wanted to hiss and spit at her friend. She wanted to coil up in a long rope of frenzied muscles and strike out at Pauline, flicking at her with her venomous tongue. That was the night the snake came to live inside her, coiling deep in her abdomen, that subtle eager creature that lifted its diamond-shaped head, its glittering eyes, and smiled its evil sneaking smile whenever Daphne thought of her daughter. Or her ex-husband. Or any number of other things. It accompanied Daphne everywhere she went, even in her sleep.

When Daphne finally went back home, she found that Cynthia had eaten dinner and done all the dishes and cleaned the kitchen. She was already asleep in her room, at nine o'clock. Or pretending to be. Between the evening of her announcement and the middle of June when she left for California, Daphne and Cynthia said perhaps eighty-three words to each other, most of them repetitive and mundane: "Will you be home for dinner?" "Did you give Dickens his walk?" They did not discuss Cynthia's decision again. Clearly Cyn did not want to know about Daphne's thoughts — or feelings — on the matter. Cynthia was ostentatiously polite and helpful around the house, always making her bed and doing her chores without being asked, as if heading off any explosion that could lead to a discussion. Daphne was polite in return. She would not let Cynthia see how much she was hurting her. She drove around with a realtor, looking for a house she could afford, put a down payment on the Plover cottage, cleaned out the home she had shared with Cynthia for fourteen years and held a mammoth tag sale, sold the huge grand piano that had been her mother's, found the dilapidated baby grand, and began sewing curtains for the new house, where she would move at the end of the summer. She acted as if she were excited about her future too.

But in a flash, while Daphne still didn't believe it would happen, Cynthia was gone. The house was empty. Her clothes and treasures were packed and sent off, and her bedroom, which had been cluttered with the signs of a happy active life, sat in the midst of Daphne's house as still and tidy as a room in a museum. Daphne wanted to set the house on fire and let it burn down around her.

One good thing: she had lost all the weight she had gained after David's death. For a long while after Cynthia left her, she had no appetite. Wasn't that odd? When David had died, she ate and ate; when Cynthia left, she could not swallow. Daphne didn't know what it meant; she did not care to know. She was relieved when she could finally move into the cottage, leaving behind the house where she had lived so much of her life with her darling daughter.

After the night when Jack had kissed Daphne — and she had kissed him back — he had caught up with her in the college parking lot and awkwardly apologized.

"I'm so sorry," he had said. "I don't know what came over me."

"It's all right," Daphne had said. She had been so exhausted that she had held on to her

251

car door in order not to sink onto the ground. She had spent the night, after Jack's kiss, wide-awake, thinking — and longing. Not just for Jack, perhaps, but for someone. She had longed to be in a lover's arms.

Jack had mistaken her pallor and gravity for censure. "I've been so stressed-out and confused lately," he said. "Carey Ann and I . . . well, this has been a rough spot in our marriage. The move, I mean."

"I understand," Daphne had said. If she had had the energy, she would have been touched by Jack's agitation and misery; she thought he was feeling guiltier than he should. She was older than he was and knew that often, with friends, the sexual undercurrent broke through the dam of propriety. People were always going around mending their dams, tamping back sex.

"I love my wife," Jack said. "I really love her. I've always intended to be faithful to her. I still do. I don't know what came over me." He was sincerely baffled.

"It's just that I'm so irresistibly attractive," Daphne said, grinning, trying to break the tension between them. She did not want to lose his friendship. She liked him too much. "Who could blame you?"

Jack laughed gratefully. "Well, you *are* attractive," he said gallantly. "But I promise

252

to control myself in the future."

Daphne held out her hand. "Let's be friends," she said.

He shook her hand. "Friends," he answered.

Over the past three months, Daphne and Jack had become real friends. Daphne needed him as a friend. With so many people gone from her life, and as winter set in, she felt gradually more isolated in her little house at the dead end of the road. Few people read as much as Daphne did, and Jack was a reader. They had an endless supply of things to talk about. Sometimes Daphne would put down a book and want nothing more than to call Jack to talk to him about it.

Jack needed Daphne, and she knew that. As the semester wore on, it became clear that Jack and Hudson Jennings were having difficulties settling into a comfortable relationship with each other. Daphne was caught in the middle. She kept trying to explain one man to the other. Jack was adored by the students, and now he ate his lunch every day in the cafeteria at a table packed with students — some weren't even in his class — and they talked about everything. He never thought to sit with the faculty members, and when Daphne suggested that it might be politic to do so now and then, Jack said, "But the students are more interesting. And I'm a teacher!"

He *was* a teacher, and that became the focal point of their friendship. He was teaching, in addition to neoclassic lit, three sections of freshman English. He found it a challenge teaching grammar and punctuation to college students who still didn't "get" it. Sometimes even very brilliant students would have trouble with the basics of sentence structure, while students who were struggling in everything else took instantly to grammar. He almost believed it was genetic, chemical, that there was something physical in the brain that ruled one's disposition toward language.

Daphne had dug out the old files and lesson plans she had used when she taught freshman English so long ago at U. Mass., and some nights she sat with Jack at his dining-room table, talking about teaching. For Daphne this was as delicious as talking about old lovers with a friend. The pleasures of the classroom! The glory when a student finally got it right!

They had plenty of time to talk, because Carey Ann had become seriously interested in early-childhood learning. Once she had discovered that there were definite things one could do to try to shape a child's behavior, she attacked the subject with the zeal of a religious convert. She attended her group one night a week, and sat in on a class in early-childhood behavior at a community college two nights a week. She was too late to enroll for credit, but she hoped to start working for a master's the next semester.

So three nights a week Carey Ann was out, leaving Jack to baby-sit. Alexandra went to bed at nine o'clock now, and after a month of major war and minor skirmishes and a few more weeks of creative rebellions, she had settled down nicely. Most nights Jack used the quiet for work, but about once a week he invited Daphne down and they would talk about everything — his classes, Hudson, her classes of long ago, the newest novels. Everything, really, but Jack's marriage. He told Daphne that Carey Ann was happy now, that she had friends, that she loved her night classes. He could see his wife changing before his eyes — as if she were one of his students. He was happy because Carey Ann was happy; a burden had lifted. He was changing too; he was learning that he could do only so much to help his wife and daughter be happy — no matter how hard he worked to protect them, to provide an all-encompassing shelter for them. Life would still find a way to sneak through and wham them, disorient them, discomfort them. Happiness and exhilaration could come to them totally independent of him, too. Jack did not know why this surprised him. After all, he needed his teaching, his work, to make him happy. Carey Ann and Alexandra, in all their amazing beauty, were necessary to him, but he needed his work too.

Sometimes, when Carey Ann got involved in a long telephone conversation with a friend, talking about her course work or her teacher or a rough spot with Alexandra or about food or her period or even a recent argument with Jack, Jack would freeze where he was, listening to his wife with a mixture of satisfaction and irritation. In Kansas City she had spent hours on the phone, and now she was doing it again. He could remember his sister doing it, and his mother. Women channeled the chaos of life into the telephone and came away at peace, as if in the process they had transformed and ordered and tidied up their corner of the universe. He envied Carey Ann the rich pleasure she got from talking on the phone — sometimes her voice was so rich and intimate she sounded almost sexual. He was glad she now had good friends to talk to and good things to talk about. But sometimes he felt left out and sometimes he felt intruded upon, and diminished, as if his wife, with her words, was paring him down, tidying him up, turning him into something much less complex than he really was.

From these telephone conversations he learned that Carey Ann truly did not mind that he spent time with Daphne, that he had drinks with her when Carey Ann was in class, that he spent hours talking to her. According to Carey Ann, Daphne was "as old as the moon." Sometimes Carey Ann spoke of Daphne with smug pity — she felt so sorry for the older woman because her daughter had left her. Once Carey Ann had spent almost an hour discussing with a friend all the things Daphne might have done to cause Cynthia to leave her for her father. For that was the great mystery — why the girl had left her mother. What had the mother done to cause it? What terrible monstrous flaw was Daphne hiding, what cruel or crazy thing had Daphne done? Had she secretly abused her daughter somehow, verbally if not physically? Surely Daphne had done *something* wrong, something really dreadful. Carey Ann knew that her own daughter would never choose to leave her; they were so close, they needed each other so much, Alexandra was her sunshine, as Carey Ann was her daughter's. Well, they would never know about Cynthia and Daphne, they would always wonder. Carey Ann would always be suspicious of Daphne, but she was proud of herself for understanding Jack's friendship with Daphne. It made

257

her feel *mature,* that she could be relaxed with Jack liking a woman that she herself did not like.

When Cynthia wrote to her mother — for she did write once a month from California (and Daphne wrote to her daughter once a week, at least, having so many things to tell her, missing her so much, wanting Cynthia to know she was loved even though she had chosen to leave) — that she would like to come home for the three weeks of Christmas vacation, Daphne had felt elated. She had spent every extra moment fixing up the attic bedroom, which until then she had left in a general mess. She had dug the box of Cynthia's old toys out of the storage room and lugged it up to the attic and left it there, casually, half-opened, in the corner, in case Cynthia wanted to look at them for sentimental reasons.

Now it was Christmastime, and here Cynthia was, sitting on the floor with Baby Betsy, the doll she had had since she was four. She was playing dolls with Alexandra, who was enchanted by Baby Betsy and was intently watching Cynthia change its clothes, so that she could learn how to do it too.

With just four days left before Christmas, Daphne, in a spurt of mushy Christmas neighborliness, had invited the three Hamiltons for dinner. Her house was too small to hold a bigger party, although she was going to have some people in for champagne and dessert on Christmas night. But Carey Ann and Alexandra were leaving on Christmas Day to fly back to Kansas City to spend some of the holiday with her family and friends. Jack would remain at home to use the vacation time to write an essay on twentieth-century writers for an international journal.

This holiday night the Hamiltons and Millers were gathered together with good cheer. Tonight Daphne was wearing a red velvet lounging robe and heavy dangling gold earrings, giving her the majestic look of a Greek oracle or goddess, of warmth perhaps, of comfort. Certainly she had made them all comfortable tonight: a sparkling fire, candles flickering, a British boys' choir softly heralding them from the stereo. They had just finished their apple pie laced with cinnamon, and were sipping the rest of their champagne. Jack was cozily ensconced on the sofa, Carey Ann nestled against one arm, Daphne leaning near the other, as the three adults looked at old photo albums of Cynthia as a child. On the floor, Cynthia was still enchanting Alexandra with her old doll. When a switch on her back was flicked on, Baby Betsy "crawled" across the floor in stiff, robotlike jerks. Now

Cynthia had put Baby Betsy on her stomach and, lifting a hatchway in the doll's rear end, exposed two huge batteries that lay inside the doll like electric intestines.

Daphne laughed. "Is that disgusting or what?" she said.

"Mom!" Cynthia protested. "This was my favorite doll!"

"I know, sweetie," Daphne said. "I never could understand it. I always preferred those soft cuddly dolls. This doll is hard plastic; it's like cuddling a kettle."

"But it crawls, like a real baby!" Cynthia said. She put the batteries back in the baby's bum, latched the lid, and held it against her protectively, as if it were a real child. She smoothed its hair — what was left of its hair. The doll had had so much attention over the years that it showed signs of wear and tear — hair gone, eyelashes missing, an overall look of grime coating its plastic skin.

Cynthia handed the doll to Alexandra, who turned it on. Automatically the doll's arms and legs started flailing in the air, and it whacked Alexandra in the face. Alexandra dropped the doll, startled. Her face scrunched up and her mouth opened to let out a wail. Quickly Cynthia flicked off the doll and handed it back to Alexandra. "There," she said. "She's quiet now. Let's go up to my room and see what else I've got that you'd be interested in. My old stuffed animals are still up there." She took Alexandra's hand and led her off.

"What a nice girl she is," Carey Ann said as they heard the two daughters slowly making their way up the steep attic stairs. "She's so good with Lexi."

"Look," Daphne said. She pointed to a photo: Cynthia at four, at Christmas, with the brand-new Baby Betsy in her arms. The little girl in the picture had long ringlets of white-blond hair, and rosy pudgy cheeks, and plump elbows and knees, and she was wearing a dress Daphne had made for her, a long dress of white velveteen with pink bows and ribbons and lace everywhere. Cynthia looked like a doll herself, or like a sculpture made from candy.

"It's hard to believe," Jack said. "Hard to believe that Cynthia was ever that small."

"I know," Daphne said: "She's so terribly grown-up these days." She ran her finger over the picture of her young daughter, as if she could actually feel Cynthia as a child again. "Those were the sweetest days," she said. Without realizing it, she almost crooned the words. "I sang her lullabies every night of her life until she was five. 'Sweet and Low.' The old Brahms favorite. A southern thing my

261

mother used to sing to me. I think some of the happiest moments I've ever lived were spent rocking Cynthia in my arms in her dark bedroom, with the little shepherdess night-light glowing nearby. Everything seemed so good then, so safe. It was almost as if *I* were being held in someone's arms." For a moment all three adults sat in silence, remembering, staring deep into the fireplace, where the solid logs that had once been branches, trees, now smoked and flared, spinning before their very eyes from wood into smoke and ashes and into golden heat, rushing light.

The sound of thumping brought them back into the present. *Thud thud thud thud,* and here came Cynthia into the room with Alexandra toddling along behind her as fast as her fat baby legs would take her. Cynthia had brought down the cardboard box full of stuffed animals, dolls, dress-up clothes, all the very favorite old toys, all the things that she had insisted not be part of the various tag sales and toss-outs in the past sixteen years of her life.

"Look!" Cynthia said, grinning. She knelt on the floor and began to take things out and hand them to the enchanted Alexandra. "See this teddy bear? This furry thing — look, it's a hand puppet." She slipped it on and the green caterpillar began to writhe over to tickle

Alexandra under the chin. "And oh, here's my Alice!" she said, taking out an expensive Alice in Wonderland doll in a blue dress with a white apron. Cynthia looked at her mother. "I'm giving all these to Alexandra," she said.

"Oh!" Carey Ann exclaimed, enraptured, and fell on the floor next to the box to join in the discovery of the treasures. "Look, Lexi, a kitty!"

Jack saw Daphne's body tense. But still she smiled, and her voice was light. "Really, Cynthia, are you sure you want to?" she said. "I mean, it's sweet of you, but all these things — your favorites . . ."

"Oh, Mother, don't be sappy," Cynthia said. "I loved these things once, but that was when I was little. They mean nothing to me now, and they just clutter up your house."

Daphne rose and went over to stab the brass poker around in the fire. When she straightened up and looked back at her daughter her face was flushed from the heat. "I don't mind having them around. I like them. They have memories for me too. And I thought you might want to save them for your children."

Cynthia was sitting on her knees, and now she leaned back on her arms, looking up at her mother. "Oh, Mother, I'm not going to have *children* for a million years," she said.

"Give me a break. I mean, really."

Daphne was moving around the room, taking up the champagne bottle, filling the glasses. Carey Ann and Alexandra were having an orgy in the toy box.

"You never know," Daphne said. "You might fall in love in college. Girls are changing, things are changing. People are having babies young again. In their twenties."

"Not this girl," Cynthia said. "*I'm* not getting married. I'm not having babies when I'm in my twenties. Uggh!" She shuddered in her extreme distaste. She was very beautiful, so blond, her skin as sleek as an otter's, her eyes clear. She was precocious and sexual and she had her own powers now and knew it.

Daphne could not look away. Her daughter was the most beautiful thing in the world.

"Oh, Mom, I might as well tell you now," Cynthia said. She stood up all of a sudden and brushed at her skirt, although nothing was there. She tossed her head and gave her mother a defiant look. "Dad's on sabbatical next year. He's going to teach in England. I'm going to go too. I'm going to see if I can get into the Royal Academy of Dramatic Arts. If not, I'll try any other acting school."

Daphne thought: In all the fairy tales, it is the old woman who is the bad one, it is the old woman who is the witch that traps Rapunzel in the tower, that gives Snow White the poisoned apple, that tries to turn Cinderella into a kitchen slave, and now I know why. And for a split second she felt herself transforming right there in the living room, she felt her fingers contracting into gnarled and twisted claws, her nose growing long and sharp and wart-covered, her chin curving up to meet her nose, her back humping over. She was a hag. She was a hideous old hag, a cackling evil thing.

Why tell me this now?, Daphne thought, and immediately answered herself. Because she thinks the Hamiltons will provide protection. I won't freak out at her in front of them.

All these thoughts flung themselves through Daphne's head like a throng of birds, flashing through, now here, now gone. She was left standing with a glass of champagne in one hand and a bottle of champagne in the other. She felt such grief at this casual announcement of her daughter's that she knew she could crush the bottle back into sand in her hands.

"How wonderful for you, Cyn," she said. "I've always wanted to live in England. How splendid that you'll have the opportunity." She poured champagne and drank. She crossed the room and curled up in a chair. "If you take a battery from Baby Betsy and put it in the monkey's back, it will beat the drums," she told Carey Ann and Alexandra. She was as normal as oatmeal, except she had forgotten to set the champagne bottle down and was holding it, unwittingly, in her right hand.

Cynthia blinked at her mother's under-stated response. She sank down onto the floor and helped Carey Ann with the electric monkey. So much of its fur had worn away, it looked sick. "Well, I may not get into RADA," she said. "And it isn't *certain* that Dad'll go to England. But pretty certain."

"Have you been to England?" Daphne asked Jack brightly. So brightly. She was like a faculty wife at a tea party.

So on they talked. They made conversation for almost another hour, until Lexi began to show signs of exhaustion. To her great delight, when the time came to go, Jack put all the dolls and animals back in the huge cardboard box, then put his daughter in on top of them all. She clapped her hands and giggled with glee. Jack staggered out the door and down the road, lugging his daughter and her new box of loot. Carey Ann followed, calling good-night.

It was a clear cold night, no wind. Daphne shut the door against the fresh frosty air and turned briskly back to the house. "That was fun, wasn't it?" she said. Without waiting for an answer, she began to bustle. Dishes off the table and into the kitchen, glasses off the floor, bustle, bustle, while her daughter trailed along behind, making attempts to help. Actually Cynthia got in the way more than anything. Daphne was so quick at grabbing up everything, it seemed she had fourteen hands. Daphne's face was set in a pleasant sort of look but her eyes were deep and glazed. She turned to put the apple pie in the refrigerator just at the moment Cynthia moved to put the butter there.

"Let's leave these dishes till morning," Daphne said. "I'd like to sit and relax by the fire for a while." She wandered back into the living room, where she grabbed up the half-full bottle of champagne by its neck and plunked down, not on the sofa, but in front of it, leaning back against it so that she could stretch her feet out and warm them at the fire. Still her face was frozen.

Cynthia sat down on the floor next to her mother, her back to the fire. "Mom," she said intently, and then was quiet for a while, as if she had just explained everything. Finally she began again. "I hope you understand. About my going to England. I mean, this might be my only chance in my entire life."

"Well, of course I understand, dear. Whatever did I say that made you think differently?" Daphne said, giving her daughter a cocktail-party smile.

"Mom." Cynthia sighed. "I knew you would do this. I knew you would. Mother, I'm not leaving *you*. I'm not choosing Dad. I'm choosing England, I'm choosing excitement, possibilities, things I just couldn't have if I stayed here. Oh, Mom, come on."

Daphne cocked her head, bright as an innocent, stupid little bird. Her heavy earrings swung against her face. "Why, Cynthia, I haven't said one thing against it. I'm delighted for you, dear!"

Cynthia banged her feet on the floor in exasperation, something she hadn't done since she was five. "Stop it!" she yelled. "Just stop it, Mom! I know you. I *know* what you're thinking."

Then Cynthia saw the anger flash up in her mother's eyes as brilliantly as the fire behind her, and fade as quickly as it had come.

"Cynthia," Daphne said, "I do mean it. I really am delighted for you. I'm only tired, dear — this dinner party was a lot more work than I'm used to these days." Her voice was very gentle.

"You miss David, don't you?" Cynthia asked. There was something about her mother's face just then, as Daphne let the happy mask fall to reveal her tiredness, her constrained sadness, that made Cynthia think she could ask the question.

"Yes," Daphne said. "Yes, very much." Her eyes were cast down now, her face slanted away from Cynthia.

Cynthia chewed on the skin of her little finger for a moment, thinking. At last she said quietly, "I can't be David for you. I can't stay here for you."

Daphne did not change her expression or tone of voice. Gently she said, "I never said you should, Cynthia."

There was some loose skin around Cynthia's thumb, which she began to peel. Although she could not articulate it to herself, this strange act felt like something she could *do* while she tried to come up with the right thing to do or say. Daphne looked over at Cynthia, and her face was so full of love that Cynthia felt both thrilled and threatened.

"Do you think," Daphne said, "that you could remember how to play the Moonlight Sonata? I'd love to look at the fire and hear you play that."

"Well, I haven't played for ages, and Dad doesn't have a piano. I'll make a million mistakes. But sure," Cynthia said.

She moved to the piano at the far end of the room. Daphne got up onto the sofa, stretched out, and stared into the fire. Cynthia played.

The music was slow and soothing, although Cynthia's rendition of it was not particularly soothing, with all the clunkers she hit. But the music built and repeated and built some more, and when she had finished, Cynthia looked over to see that her mother had fallen asleep. She crossed the room, took up a quilt from her mother's bedroom, and brought it into the living room. She bent over her mother's sleeping figure and tucked the quilt around her so that it would not fall off. Daphne's breath was deep and regular. Cynthia looked into her relaxed face. Then she turned to put the screen in front of the fireplace, and went up the stairs to her little bedroom in the attic.

When Daphne heard the upstairs door open and close, she opened her eyes. She didn't move. She lay there looking into the fire but seeing instead an encounter that had taken place between her and Hudson that afternoon.

They had been at the college, in the outer office, on either side of Daphne's desk, which held, in addition to the usual pile of files and papers, a little artificial evergreen tree that Daphne had decorated with candy canes and red-and-white-striped peppermints. It was almost five o'clock and everyone else had left earlier for the Christmas-carol celebration at the college chapel.

Daphne and Hudson were exchanging Christmas gifts. They did this every year. At first the presents had been small, even silly, but with each passing year they became more serious.

Daphne's present was rather chiding and mischievous; she gave Hudson a book entitled *Parallel Lives,* a nonfiction book about five Victorian and rather sexless marriages.

Hudson handed Daphne a small velvet box. Inside was a pair of small brilliant earrings: two rubies surrounded by diamonds.

"Hudson!" Daphne said. "I can't accept these!"

"Please," Hudson replied. "They will be beautiful on you. With your coloring."

"But, Hudson, they must have cost the earth. I really can't accept such an expensive gift."

"They were my mother's," Hudson said.

Daphne looked at him. "Oh, Hudson . . ." She would have embraced him, but they were separated by the desk.

They were separated by the knowledge of Claire.

In any case, Fred Van Lieu came along then, needing a ride because his car was in for repairs.

"Merry Christmas," Daphne and Hudson

had said to each other. Hudson had left. Daphne had put the little box in her purse, where it was still. She cherished the present. She liked thinking of the two heart-red gems, gleaming valuably, secretly, in the darkness.

She decided to sleep on the sofa tonight. The fire would keep her warm.

7

That night, after the holiday dinner at the Millers', it was easy for Jack and Carey Ann to get Alexandra to go to bed. They simply surrounded her in her crib with the dolls and stuffed animals Cynthia had given her, until there was scarcely enough room for the little girl herself. Alexandra rolled luxuriously in her nest, sucking her thumb, looking around her at all the new treasures, the look on her face cherubic and blissful, the look that parents sigh to see.

Jack put his arm around Carey Ann as they left their daughter's room. He hugged her against him so that when they entered their bedroom, they naturally sank down on the bed together. They lay on top of the covers, on their sides, fully clothed, looking at each other.

"Carey Ann," Jack said. He was very much in love with his wife.

"Wait a minute," she replied. "Let me take this thing out." She was wearing white wool

273

slacks and a blue sweater, and had spent hours fixing her hair in an upswept style, fastened on one side with a large beaded sparkling comb. She couldn't get her head comfortable on the pillow with the comb in, so she sat up, pulled the comb out, and her long blond hair slid down around her face and shoulders. "Now," she said, and lay back down and smiled at Jack.

"Did you have fun?" Jack asked.

"I suppose," Carey Ann said, pronouncing it "spose." She arched her head back, thinking. "I like Cynthia. I like the way she dresses and walks and carries herself. She's got style. She's so slender and graceful. I just couldn't believe it when she gave Lexi that box of toys."

"I don't think Daphne was very happy about that," Jack said.

"I know. I could tell. The old cow. What a selfish old broad! Why *shouldn't* Lexi have those toys? Cynthia certainly won't be playing with them anymore, and Lexi will have a ball. See what I mean, Jack, about Daphne? She's uptight, or coldhearted, or something. Not to want little Lexi to have those toys."

Jack was silent a moment. "I think those things have sentimental value for her," he said. "You know, looking at those pictures in the album, Daphne didn't look much different from how she does now. But look at the difference in Cynthia. It's absolute. Daphne probably just wanted to keep those things around to remind her of the days when her daughter was little."

"Maybe," Carey Ann said dubiously.

Jack ran his hand lightly from his wife's shoulder up along her neck to her face. "Angel face," he said. He didn't often say things like that because it was hard for him to, but right now he was very much in the grip of strong emotions that he could not define or even realize had infested him but that had been growing more powerful in him, about him, all evening. When he spoke, his voice was thick with love. "Let's have another baby, Carey Ann."

Carey Ann's blue eyes flew wide open. "*What!*" She jerked back from his hand as if it had the power to impregnate her right on the spot.

"I said, let's have another baby." Jack grinned.

"Are you seriously *crazy?*" Carey Ann was so troubled she sat up in bed and stuck some pillows behind her back and leaned against the headboard and crossed her legs tightly, one over the other.

Jack sat up too. "No, I'm not crazy. Carey Ann, I thought you wanted lots of kids. You told me you wanted lots of kids."

"Well, I've changed my mind. I don't want lots anymore. Or at least not now." Carey Ann kept her profile to him.

"But why not? I don't understand. I thought you . . . don't you love Alexandra?"

"Well, of *course* I love Alexandra. I *adore* Alexandra. She's the meaning of my life, Jack, you know that. I just don't want any *more* kids, not yet. Not now."

"Why not?" Jack brought his voice back down to a reasonable tone. He wanted to be a reasonable man even though he was totally baffled.

"Because . . . oh, a million reasons." Because of Jack's pleasant voice, Carey Ann turned to look at him. She counted on her fingers. "First, I want to get a degree in early-childhood education. Now, I just can't do that and have another baby too. I really want that degree, Jack. Second, I don't think it would be fair to Lexi. All these changes, the move, the new house . . . well, it would be just too much to throw a new baby in on top of it all. Until we get all settled. Third, you know what a mess a new baby is, no one gets any sleep for a year, and you've got to think of your career, your papers you have to write, all that stuff you're pressured to do. Why, you can barely keep up with it now. All your life you're dying to write a novel and you're always depressed because you can't write that novel and you know you sure wouldn't be able to do *that* with a new baby around, and you would be so miserable. And fourth . . . well, fourth, you know how I feel about my figure. I'm only now getting it back. I just can't stand the thought of getting all blimpy again. Not for a while."

Jack stared at his wife as if she were something he had just pulled from a Cracker Jack box that he had to learn how to put together. "Maybe," he said slowly, "if we had another baby, we could ask your parents to help us like they did last time. You know, we could have a housekeeper/baby-sitter sort of thing. Then you could still do your degree."

Now Carey Ann looked at him as if *he* had just come from a Cracker Jack box. "*What* are you talking about?" she said, shaking her head in amazement. "You nearly have a hissy fit every time my parents give us *anything*. I can't believe after all the speeches you've given me about *not* taking anything from my parents, about growing up and being independent and having some pride and all that stuff, I can't believe you're saying this! Besides, in Kansas City we had a bigger house, there was room for a live-in housekeeper. We don't have room for one here."

"I could give up my study. We could make that into her bedroom."

"Then where would the new *baby* go? Jack, the house is too small. Where would you write?"

"Then she wouldn't have to be live-in. She could just come every day."

"And the baby would cry all night and you and I wouldn't get any sleep, not to mention Lexi not getting any sleep. She'd be cranky all day, and you wouldn't get your work done and I'd be too foggy-headed to even think of doing any work. Jack, *what* has gotten into you?"

"What's gotten into you?" Jack responded. "You're the one who wanted to have a big family. Now you're acting like I'm Charles Manson or someone crazy because I want another child."

Carey Ann's chin jutted up and her lips clamped tight. She had a bad memory for names and events, Jack knew, and she was probably trying to remember just who in hell Charles Manson was, and she was angry that Jack had mentioned someone she didn't know about. He should have said Jack the Ripper or Richard Nixon.

"Well, I'm sorry, Jack," Carey Ann said. She drew away from him, rose, went toward the bathroom, talking as she walked. "I guess

278

I can understand how you're feeling, a little, but I'm sorry. I'm just not ready for another child." She went into the bathroom and shut the door.

Jack sat on the bed a moment, stunned. Then he got up and went to the door, pressing his nose nearly on the wood. "So that's it?" he asked. "That's *it?* Discussion over, the end, good-bye? Your word is law and you're just going to walk away?"

Carey Ann opened the door so fast it made Jack dizzy. She stood there holding up her slacks with her hands. "Jack, I had to go to the bathroom," she said slowly, like someone teaching an idiot child the alphabet. "What has gotten into you?"

"Well, I just don't think it's fair," Jack said. "You make up your mind about something, and that's it. You won't even discuss it."

Carey Ann edged past him and went to the closet. She began to undress, hanging her clothes up neatly, slipping her nightgown on over her head. "I'll discuss it," she said flatly.

"Oh, great. Thanks a lot," Jack said. "You'll discuss it, but your mind is *totally* made up. Right? You'll 'discuss' it, but I'll just be wasting my breath."

Carey Ann looked at Jack. She was wearing a pink flannel nightgown with a little bow at the neck and she looked about three years old. "That's pretty much how I felt when we were 'discussing' moving back east," she said. "Your mind was set about that and there was no way I could change it."

Jack scratched his head. He was trying to hold on to his temper. "Are you *punishing* me, then?" he asked. "I mean, since I made you come back east, is this your way of getting back at me?"

"Oh, Jack!" Carey Ann said, exasperated. She yanked the covers on the bed and plopped down. "No, I am not trying to punish you."

"Well, I can't exactly have a baby by myself," Jack said. He glared at his wife, then went into the bathroom. While he brushed and flossed his teeth, words galloped through his head like horses in a race, Sarcastic vying with Righteous, edged out by Reasonable, with Romantic finally taking the lead. Carey Ann looked so pretty in her nightgown. He could talk with her about this another time.

And he did. He talked with her about it for the next four days, right through Christmas Eve, Christmas Morning, and Christmas Day. Talked *at* her was more like it. No matter what he said or how he said it, Carey Ann just looked at him, a saint of patience, like a cow eyeing an irritating gnat. It was a strange

Christmas. Jack had had a vision in his head of how it *should* be, and although he knew that vision was a collage of Charles Dickens at his most sentimental, memories of his Christmases as a little boy, and television commercials for a frozen turkey containing a pop-up plastic thermometer, still he had thought it not completely unrealistic. This vision involved a Christmas tree that touched the ceiling, Alexandra ecstatically (but silently) absorbed with her new toys on the floor next to the tree, Carey Ann bustling around in the kitchen cooking pumpkin pie, and himself seated by the fire with a good novel and a brandy, while snowflakes floated dreamily past the window. Reality did not live up to this vision. It was impossible, of course, in the first place, for them to have a tree that touched the ceiling — their living room had a cathedral ceiling and there were no twenty-foot trees available, or if there had been, at four dollars a foot they couldn't have afforded one. Still, Jack had been dismayed to find that this year Carey Ann wanted a tree that *stood on top of a table*. A little short tree. A pathetic little twerp of a tree, the kind that one saw in movies about very old lonely unloved widowers in New York City apartments, the kind that got only three small ornaments, four wrinkled icicles, and no lights.

It had been terrifically cold and windy the night the Hamiltons went out as a family to get the tree. First they had had dinner at Howard Johnson's as a treat, then they had piled in the car and driven out to the country to the farm where the best trees were sold. Jack had wanted to come out earlier in the season to walk the fields where the rows of trees were planted, and choose their own tree and label it — even cut it themselves, that seemed like a romantic thing to do — but Carey Ann had vetoed that idea. She said she didn't see anything *romantic* about watching Jack make a fool of himself with an ax, which he had never used before in his life, while she and Alexandra stood around freezing. Still, he hadn't realized that she had her heart set on a *short* tree. *Families* didn't have short trees!

"It will just make things so much easier," Carey Ann had said. She had Alexandra in her arms and was bouncing her a little. "That way, I can leave the room without worrying about 'someone' pulling the lights off and causing a fire or taking the ornaments down and trying to eat them." Carey Ann was talking through her teeth in a tense monotone, as if that would keep Lexi from knowing whom they were talking about.

"Carey Ann, Alexandra's two and a half," Jack said. "Last year she was younger!"

Carey Ann rolled her eyes. "Last year we were all younger."

"I mean last year she was more of a baby, she got into things more. This year she minds. This year she won't tear the tree apart."

"I really don't want to be bothered with it," Carey Ann replied.

"Bothered!" Jack shouted. He realized that he'd raised his voice enough to cause several other families to look over at him. "Who is *bothered* by a Christmas tree?" he hissed at his wife.

"You're not home all day with *her* and a tree," Carey Ann said. "I am. I have papers to do, things to do. I can't be a watchdog. Besides, we're leaving late on Christmas Day. A great big tree just isn't *necessary.*"

Jack stared at his wife, turned around, and walked away, down the row of cut and bundled trees that leaned against each other like a vast drunken forest. He walked until he was clear out of the Christmas-tree area and standing so far away from the farmers'-market shed that he was outside the circle of light and in the dark. It seemed even colder here. A dark shape huddled against a wire fence; a pile of greens, the crooked tops of trees that had been removed to shape the evergreens, and gnarled hacked-off stumps. This sight filled Jack with a terrible sadness. He stood, hands shoved down deep in his parka pocket, staring at those useless greens.

"Jack." Carey Ann spoke softly, right at his shoulder. "Honey, remember, we've talked this all out. I asked you if you wanted to go to Kansas City with me and you said you didn't. You said you have so much work to do. You said you want to try to write a paper over the break. You said you didn't *want* a big Christmas. You said you didn't want a lot of fuss. You said it would be just fine if I took Lexi with me for a while and left you alone in the house, with all that peace and quiet, and you could work. You said you wanted some *serenity*, remember? You don't want a big tree cluttering up the house."

Slightly mollified, Jack said, "I don't think a big tree would exactly clutter up the house."

"You'd be surprised. Right after Christmas, all the needles start falling off. You can sit right there and hear them, they sort of sift down with a little whispering noise, a little 'ping,' it's just like a dripping faucet, it could drive a person crazy. And when you take a big tree out of the house, it sheds all its needles in a great big *trail* and they poke holes in the vacuum-cleaner bag so dust and stuff starts fooming out all over and you *never* get all the needles up — if you go barefoot, you get one stuck in your toe. Not to mention Lexi."

Jack stared at Carey Ann. This is really wonderful, he was thinking, this is really just *charming*. Christmas isn't even here yet and already Carey Ann is complaining about cleaning up after it.

Carey Ann stared back at Jack. As if she could read his mind, she said, "I don't have the time this year to do a mammoth Christmas and clean-up. I'll be starting courses for *credit* in January. There are some books I need to read before then. I'm beginning from so far behind everyone else. It can take *days* cleaning up after Christmas. And I won't be here to do it this year. And I don't think you have time either."

"Alexandra — " Jack began.

"Alexandra will have enough excitement with two Christmases, one at our house and one in Kansas City. Not to mention the airplane trip and the fuss my parents and friends will make over her. Jack, you can't have it both ways at once. You *said* you wanted a quiet Christmas so you could work."

So he had sighed and shrugged and put his arm on Carey Ann's shoulder and gone to the front of the farm to find a short tree.

Then there had been all the parties. Daphne's had been pleasant enough, low-key, relaxed, intimate — well, he always enjoyed being around Daphne, and Alexandra and

Carey Ann had had a good time too. The day before Christmas Eve the English department had held, late in the afternoon, an informal Christmas party to which spouses and children were invited, and Jack had wanted Carey Ann and Alexandra to come — he had *really* wanted them to come. First, because he wanted Carey Ann to get to know the people he worked with so when he told her about them she understood what was going on, and because he thought she'd like them and like being part of his life, *included.* Then, too, he had to admit to less charitable feelings — he wanted Hudson Jennings and any of the rest of the department who had seen Carey Ann come steaming in with the baby in her arms, or heard her crying, to see Jack and his family as a happy and united whole, not squabbling and tense as they had been that day. But Carey Ann had chosen to take Alexandra to the kiddie party that her play group was giving with a bunch of other mothers and children. They had even arranged for a Santa Claus to visit. Jack understood how that party would be more fun for his two girls; still, he missed them. He drank too much spiked eggnog and got home with a terrible alcohol-and-sugar headache.

That night they had had to go to the Jenningses' for another Christmas party — a formal one, without children. That had been pretty dreadful. They had sat in stiff subservience with some other junior faculty members, nodding politely and laughing deferentially as Claire expounded on the history of certain seasonal traditions, and Hudson, their chairman and hero, sat in almost dutiful silence. Jack was sure he was going to get it from Carey Ann when they got home, and what could he say — it *was* a boring party, Mrs. Jennings was a drip and a humorless snob. But to his amazement, Carey Ann had taken the entire thing lightheartedly. "Poor dried-up old guys!" she had said. "I'll bet you they never fuck. Oh, honey, let's never let ourselves get like that!" And they had made love with abandon, reveling in their youth and health and energy. That night in bed had been the best part of the entire holiday for Jack; it was the only time that Carey Ann really paid any attention to him.

Christmas Eve the three Hamiltons had gone to the Curriers' for an early dinner. They had been invited because Shelby Currier and Carey Ann had become such good friends, and Alexandra enjoyed playing with little Aaron. Watson Currier's brilliance in chemistry was legendary and he looked pleasant enough, but Jack had never met another man with such capacity for silence. Perhaps he had

287

visions of chemical formulae dancing in his head; whatever, he hardly spoke all evening. While the women and children laughed and chattered, Jack and Watson sat with glasses of Scotch, brooding at the fire. If Jack asked Watson a question, the man would, with obvious effort, drag himself up out of whatever deep pit of thought he was mired in, and reply, but his replies were monosyllabic, sometimes little more than grunts. Jack gave up. It was enough that Carey Ann and Alexandra were happy, and there were worse things to do than to sit drinking good Scotch by the fire. They ate dinner with their plates on their laps, because of the children, who got silly and played a little game of being dogs and cats and mice, crawling to the adults' knees to mew or squeak for food, which the adults obligingly dropped into their offspring's mouths. It did keep the little ones happy and involved so that at least the mothers could carry on their conversation. Jack, being so uninterrupted by Watson, listened to the women talking and admired them for their ability to sustain a train of thought, an idea, over and through the clamors and intrusions of the children. He had not realized that Carey Ann had such talents — no, it was that he had not realized before now that this actually was a talent deserving of respect.

Then they had gone to a local church to watch a Christmas pageant, which thrilled Alexandra, who went wild over the baby Jesus, calling out, "Baby! There's a baby!" What, Jack wondered, did Lexi think *she* was? Was she glad to see another living human creature smaller than herself, or did she identify with the baby? At any rate, her ecstasy wore her out and she went to bed easily, giving Carey Ann and Jack plenty of time to put out the Santa Claus stuff.

That night in bed, Jack tried once again to convince Carey Ann they should have another child, and once again Carey Ann gently and reasonably refused. Then — what had come over him? gotten into him? he wondered secretly, and Carey Ann asked the exact questions point-blank — he asked Carey Ann to come home from Kansas City sooner than she had planned. Not to be away for two entire weeks.

Carey Ann swooped down all over him, kissing him with silly smooching sounds. "What's come over you? You are so adorable! Oh, you sweet ol' honeypie, I'll miss you too, but, Jack, I've been looking forward to this trip for ages. I have so many friends I want to see, and we'll just have to spend forever talking about stuff, so many things have changed. And then there's Daddy and Mommy, they don't think two weeks is long *enough* for me to be with them. Besides, Jack, it's going to be a real treat for me, I can tell you. I won't have to cook or do dishes for two whole weeks."

Jack watched while a gap the size of the universe opened between him and his wife. This special effect of their marriage seemed to be happening more and more these days. Forget getting Carey Ann to change her mind — he couldn't even seem to get her to see his point of view. Even while they made love, he felt estranged from her. In fact, it was sort of awful, their lovemaking that Christmas Eve. He could tell that Carey Ann was doing it out of charitable intentions, not passion. Well, she was kissing him and cuddling and fondling and moaning and all that stuff, but he knew she was doing it from gratitude and benevolence, a sort of marital noblesse oblige. Still, his body responded.

Which was why he felt so very odd the next day. He woke up, with Carey Ann lying next to him, and felt the most awful ache of loneliness. He was lonely for his wife and she was right there. He was intolerably melancholy all day long, even while taking pictures of his daughter going saucer-eyed over her Christmas loot. Even while he helped Carey Ann pack, while he drove his wife and child to the airport in Boston, where they boarded the giant plane that would fly them across half the continent to Chicago and then on down to Kansas City. Carey Ann, her face flushed pink with excitement and happiness, couldn't stop kissing him. She was nearly jumping up and down with pleasure. She waved and waved and had Alexandra wave and wave as they climbed the ramp and entered the gleaming airplane. Then they were gone.

Jack stood out at the window, watching as the slender silver jaw of ramp clamped up closed and shut. He felt his loneliness hurting him. His loneliness filled him and transformed him and confused him, so that he was like an adolescent, wild with loneliness, which, in spite of the night before, expressed itself all throughout his body as a powerful, demanding, desperate sexual lust.

Seventeen years ago, the Millers had spent Christmas with the Krafts. Daphne, pregnant with Cynthia, was just surfacing from the murky and somnambulant depths of morning sickness. She was exhausted all the time (although soon, within a matter of days, she would begin to feel the superhuman strength and optimism she felt for the rest of her pregnancy) and she was still subject to attacks of nausea, when the world wavered before her sight like a distorting mirror at an amusement park, and she would have to shut her eyes tight and lean against something, or sit down, to keep from throwing up. She constantly ate crackers and even carried plastic sacks of saltines in the pockets of her coats.

"You do not feel like cooking for Christmas," Laura told Daphne. "Don't be foolish. Let me do it. I love to cook. I am healthy. You cook when I am pregnant! Besides, Otto will be home, I will want to cook his special favorites, his delicacies; he will be expecting that."

Otto was on sabbatical that year and was spending it in Germany. Because Hanno was now four and in preschool, and because the Krafts were such zealots about their son's education, Laura had remained in the States rather than disturb their child in his formative years. Otto came home once that fall semester, and for a prolonged stay at Christmastime, but Daphne wished he would never come home, would stay away forever. She and Laura had such a good time without him around. What golden mornings they shared! Joe would go off to teach, and Hanno would go off to preschool, and Daphne would crawl back in bed — in the mornings she was almost paralyzed by her sickness. If she moved at all, she would vomit and nearly faint. Tucked up among the covers, a towel over her eyes — for even light, in those first three months, made her dizzy — Daphne would talk to Laura on the phone. For hours. About everything. It was like reliving her life. It was like reliving Laura's life too. They examined every detail, described each major moment, until Daphne had as clear a vision in her mind of the striped black-and-white dress Laura was wearing when she met Otto, as she did of the clothes she wore the day she heard Joe Miller defend her to George Dobbs. Laura was jealous of the way Joe and Daphne's relationship had begun; nothing nearly so romantic had happened between her and Otto. And as the weeks passed, it grew clear that Laura envied Daphne much else besides. Laura did not love her husband with the passion that Daphne felt for Joe. Or *had* felt for Joe before she entered into the overpowering world of pregnancy.

Daphne, curled among blankets and pillows, unmoving, blotted by her body from participating in the present, grew bored, and began to move more freely in the world of words, in her past, finally into the dark secret depths of her marriage. Laura told her details of her sexual life with Otto. Daphne reciprocated. Or tried to. There wasn't much to tell Laura those days, because Daphne had no interest in sex at all, and in fact was so sick that when she and Joe did make love, all her attention was focused on not throwing up while he toiled in and around her, an ocean of sex rocking the boat of her body into such seasickness that she clutched at the sheets.

When Otto returned home four days before Christmas, his presence became a barrier between Daphne and Laura. The long luxurious morning phone calls ceased. Daphne lay in bed, her strength returning, wondering what Laura and Otto were doing. She could not find out — Otto was there all the time, Laura never had enough privacy to call Daphne for a real talk. For three months it had been as if Laura and Daphne were the primary pair; the *real couple* — and now here Otto was, back again, claiming his wife, breaking the women's alliance, and when Daphne tried to turn to Joe, she realized there was something missing now. He had gone further and further away from her, into his work, into the complicated fields of his intelligence, and Daphne, who had before been like a light, shivering and diffuse all around his life, now was shrunken and concentrated into a single beam that illuminated only one small corner of his life. He did not find her swelling belly attractive. He was not excited about the baby. He was increasingly aloof, and even when Daphne began to emerge from her cocoon of nausea, so that she was *there*, engaged, when they were making love, what she felt more than

294

anything else was a cold loneliness that made her want to cry out urgently for help. But if she tried to speak of this to Joe, he turned away. He said, "Nonsense." He went to sleep.

That year on Christmas Day Joe and Daphne went to the Krafts' in the late morning, after they had exchanged Christmas gifts and opened the gifts sent to them by relatives. Joe and Otto wanted to spend the day cross-country skiing, working up an appetite for the Christmas feast Laura was preparing. The Millers' house that year had been scarcely decorated for the holidays — Daphne had been just too out of it to do much. By contrast, the Krafts' house was a Christmas fantasy. Laura had hung every window, lintel, and picture frame with evergreens tied up with red ribbon. In front of their huge picture window stood a fat Christmas tree, bearing small fat candles in little saucerlike pieces of crinkled tin, as well as apples, tangerines, gingerbread cookies, and exotic glass and metal ornaments in vivid stained-glass colors. The air was fragrant with cinnamon and almond, and the friends began the day with a brunch of stollen, scrambled eggs, champagne, and coffee. Daphne gave thanks aloud that her morning sickness had receded just in time to let her appreciate the holiday food.

Little Hanno wandered around the table

where the four adults sat, playing quietly with the toys he had received on Christmas Eve. From time to time he would climb up on a chair to munch at his food and watch the adults, who laughed more and more as the champagne disappeared from the bottles. He was a good child, angelic on that day, with his blond hair curling in a halo around his head. Laura had knit him a navy-blue sweater patterned with white snowflakes, which he wore tucked into his gray leather lederhosen. He looked like a child from a fairy tale, and acted like one too; he was so good. Finally the men, after making a roaring fire to return to, pulled on their boots and coats, packed the Krafts' gunmetal-blue Mercedes with their skis and poles, and drove away to the countryside. Laura and Daphne were left alone — Daphne felt a delicious thrill of anticipation at the thought of an afternoon alone with her friend. Well, almost alone — they would take Hanno for a long walk, and later, he would nap.

"Hanno," Laura said the moment the men had driven off, "how would you like to listen to your new read-along record while Daphne and I do the dishes? Then we'll take you for a walk." She settled her son by the stereo in the living room, closed the brass curtains so that the fire could not spark out onto the rug, and led Daphne into the kitchen.

That day Laura was wearing cherry-red velour slacks and top with black velvet boots; the slacks accentuated how very long and sleek her legs were. She had pulled her long thick brown hair up into an elaborate twist — in Germany, she said, women of a certain class did not wear their hair down in public. Daphne was wearing an old maternity jumper that Laura had given her, a blue silk thing that flared out from the bosom. Underneath was one of Daphne's own blouses, white silk with lace at the cuffs and neck. She had expanded so much that she couldn't button the blouse at the breast or waist, but the jumper was high-necked and hid this. This was the first time Daphne had put on maternity clothes, the first time she had realized that she really would have to wear maternity clothes.

"Let me see your stomach!" Laura commanded when they entered the kitchen. This room was warm from the heat of the oven and aromatic with Christmas fragrances; it was like entering the cave of a witch.

Obediently Daphne raised her blue jumper. Her white cotton underpants covered her pubic hair but could not stretch any further; her belly swelled out in a full rosy bowl above the strip of cloth. Her silk blouse hung down

297

unbuttoned, parted like curtains, revealing the drama of her body.

"No stretch marks yet," Laura said. "Good. Here. I had Otto bring this for you from Germany. You must do it like this every morning first thing when you get up, every night last thing before bed. Then you never have stretch marks." She opened a large jar of cream and began to massage it into Daphne's skin. "Like this, little circles," she said, demonstrating.

Daphne looked down at her stomach, which had become such an "object," and watched as her friend swept the cream around in little swirls until it had dissolved into her skin. Laura's light and efficient touch was both relaxing and stimulating; Daphne stood smiling, and wished it would go on forever. Joe did not touch her like that anymore, just to caress her, to make her feel good, without sexual motives lurking — had he ever? (Had she ever wanted him to?)

"There!" Laura said triumphantly, and capped the bottle. "You should be grateful I got this for you. It is very expensive and very hard to find. It's only sold in Germany."

"I must pay you for it," Daphne began.

"Oh, don't be silly!" Laura said. "Of course you will not pay me for it! What are friends for?" She leaned forward and hugged Daphne. Their breasts bumped together and their perfumes mingled brightly in the brief embrace.

"Now!" Laura said. "We must clean up the kitchen quickly so we can do something else before we start cooking dinner! You clear the table. I'll rinse and stack the dishwasher."

As Daphne moved from room to room carrying dishes, she seemed to be moving in and out of white flashing light. It had snowed for the past three days, and now the sun was out — an absolutely perfect Christmas Day, a white Christmas, sparkling. The sun on the snow was so brilliant through the modern house's great picture windows that it almost chimed, luring, and Hanno jumped up in the middle of the recorded story and ran to his mother, crying, "I want to go outside and play!"

"Just one moment," Laura said. "Let me start the dishwasher. There. Now, where is your snowsuit?"

Daphne pulled on her boots and coat, then watched as her friend bundled up the little boy. It seemed to Daphne that when Laura bent over to tug on Hanno's snowpants, her face took on a puffiness around the eyes, a white and vulnerable tint. Daphne looked away, looked back. Laura had straightened and was pulling on her own coat — the warm luscious fur Daphne envied. She smiled at

Daphne, but still Daphne thought her friend's face looked slightly bloated, as if the skin was tense with withholding. Had Laura been crying? Laura turned to look at Daphne, and her glance was moist.

"Ready? Here we go!" Laura said gaily. She pulled on black sunglasses against the winter glare. How beautiful she looked, how European! The sleek hair, black fur, long red legs, high black boots.

The two women pulled the little boy on his sled down the street toward the local park. Hanno sat, a little king, holding on with one hand, eating snow with the other. The runners of the sled made shussing noises in the snow. The air glittered.

"Otto is having an affair," Laura said.

Daphne tripped on a crust of ice and snow. She grabbed on to her friend's arm to right herself, and in doing so, stopped them both.

"Laura!" she said, looking her friend in the eye.

"Mama!" Hanno, the little despot, yelled, unhappy to be halted.

Laura began walking again. Her voice was low. Daphne, walking next to her, studied her friend as she talked: she saw the swollen eyes brim and spill their tears.

"It has been the most horrible time of my life," Laura said. "He will not sleep with me.

300

He has promised *her* he will be true to *her!* And I his wife!"

"Snowman! Mama, there's a snowman!" Hanno yelled, pointing.

The women turned back to smile. "Yes, snowman!" Laura said.

"I don't understand," Daphne said. "What do you mean?"

"I mean while Otto was in Berlin, he met a woman. A young woman, of course. A young blonde. How these aging professors love their young blondes. He has been fucking her for the past four months! The entire time of his sabbatical. When he came back home to visit this fall, he slept with me and did not tell me. He thought it was only infatuation, you know, a middle-age obsession. But now he tells me it is *serious.*"

"Oh, Jesus Christ, oh, God," Daphne said. "Oh, Laura, I'm so sorry. What can you do?"

"What can I do? I think there's nothing I can do. Believe me, I have thought of nothing else for days. Daphne, there is nothing I can do!" She spoke the words slowly, like instructions from a manual in a foreign language, as if only now grasping the meaning. "He tells me he loves her. Sonya. He tells me he has tried to stop loving her, he has tried to stay away from her, but he cannot live without her."

301

"Oh, Laura," Daphne said again. She was weighted down with sorrow for her friend.

They had arrived at the playground, and Laura arranged her son safely on the sled, then gave a push that launched him down the hill. No one else was there. The two women watched a moment as the little boy, as gleaming in his snowsuit as a cardinal, slid down the snowy hill that swept away from them in a long and gentle descent. His wild laughter rose back up at them, a reverse avalanche, as bright as the sparkling air. At the bottom of the hill he threw himself from the sled and tumbled and rolled as far as he could go, screaming with delight. Then he stopped and looked back up the hill at his mother.

"I want to go again!" he called.

"You must come back up, then!" she called back. "Grab your sled and pull it up the hill."

Hanno looked at her suspiciously for a second, perhaps remembering winters before, when she or Otto had made the climb up the hill with him seated on the sled.

"Come on!" Laura called, clapping her hands together. Tears were streaking her cheeks, glistening in the bright sun — Hanno was too far away to see. The little boy grabbed the rope and began to pull his sled up the hill.

Laura waited until Hanno was launched downward again before going on. "He met her at the university. She is a doctor. And listen to this. He wants to get the university there to offer him a job. A full-time and lucrative and prestigious job. He could go back to Germany and live with this new woman. Have a new wife, a new life, somewhere with no one who remembers me to frown at him."

"I just can't believe this," Daphne said. She was beginning to cry too.

"I know, I know," Laura said. "I can't believe it myself. But this is what I have been hearing for days. Everything. Every detail. He is angry at me because he is hurting me, and so he punishes me for making him feel guilty. So he tells me what they do together. She likes it like a dog. Like a boy. Even in the ass — "

"Stop it," Daphne said. Her breath had caught in a snarl at the base of her throat. She was gagging on her breath.

"He tells me she is everything to him, his man and his woman. I never was comfortable with such things. She loves it."

"Stop it!" Daphne shouted. She grabbed Laura and turned her to face her. "You must leave him. This is too awful for anyone to bear. Laura, he should not tell you these things. You should not listen. You should not let him tell you such things."

"Oh, do you think I like it? Do you think I

like to hear and envision such things?" Laura was shouting at Daphne, and she put her hands on Daphne's arms, while Daphne's hands were still on Laura's shoulders, so that the two women were almost in an adversarial embrace, and they nearly shook one another in their rage. They were both weeping. Then Laura let out a low harsh howl and collapsed into Daphne's arms. She wept on Daphne's shoulder, and Daphne wrapped her arms around her friend and held her and rocked her, or rather, the two women swayed together as they stood in the cold and burning snow.

"Mama?" Hanno asked. He had reached the top of the hill and stood, sled rope in his hand, puzzled at the sight of his mother and her friend.

Laura pulled away from Daphne. She bent, her face red and wet, picked up her son, and set him down firmly on the sled. She set the sled in the right direction. The obliviousness of childhood was an amazing sight to Daphne, and she told herself she must remember this when she had a child of her own. For Hanno was shrieking with anticipation of the next downhill run and did not notice his mother's face. Daphne reminded herself that to a four-year-old everything adults did must seem bizarre and unexplainable — so why should he question this? What *he* needed was being done. Laura pulled him to the edge of the hill, gave the sled a push, and off he went, laughing.

"When we return home, we must be normal," Laura said. "Otto does not want me to talk to anyone about this. Not even you."

"Well, my God, who *cares* what Otto wants at this point!" Daphne shouted. "What rights does he deserve to have?"

"Look, Daphne, I must try to save my marriage," Laura said. She had pulled a paisley silk scarf from her pocket and was drying her soaked sunglasses with it.

"Why?" Daphne yelled. "Why on earth would you want to?"

Laura looked at Daphne. "Wouldn't you?"

"No! No, I would not! If Joe did to me what Otto is doing to you, I would make him move out of the house, I would see a lawyer, I would divorce him right away!"

"How very American of you," Laura said dryly. "Disposable husbands. Like disposable diapers."

"I would never share my husband," Daphne said.

"No? Not if your pride cost you everything? You wait until that baby in your tummy is a real child and see how you think then. You will want his father in the house.

You will want his father in his life. You will want to stay home and take care of the child. You will not want to be forced to go out to work. When you have a child, everything changes. I'm telling you, Daphne, you become a tigress, and life is all about protecting your child."

"Never," Daphne said. "Never just that."

"You wait." Laura glared at Daphne, and Daphne glared back.

Hanno was there again, then, needing his mittens readjusted and snow removed from the neck of his suit. Laura retied his bright muffler and pushed him off down the hill.

"In Europe, it is common for a man to have a mistress," Laura said. She was catching her breath and calming down. She seemed almost ironic now. "My father-in-law did. My father did. No man who has worked hard all his life wants just a fat old wife to have sex with. In my heart I knew someday Otto would have an affair. I just did not expect it quite so soon. Or that it would be so serious to him — that he would call it love."

"I would never stay with Joe if he had an affair," Daphne said. "Especially not if he spoke to me about it the way Otto is speaking to you."

"How pure the world is for you, Daphne," Laura said. "I predict that it will not always remain so uncomplicated."

"Still — " Daphne began.

"Who knows?" Laura interrupted. She seemed at once angry and somehow amused, as if she knew secrets Daphne did not. "Perhaps in your marriage it will be you who has an affair. Who lusts after someone else. Who sleeps with someone else."

The two women stared at each other. Hanno came whining back up the hill, his face frosty, his nose running. Other families were arriving at the hill, whooping and calling.

"One more time, then we go home for hot chocolate," Laura said to her son.

"So you really *do* know what you're going to do," Daphne said. "You're going to hang on. You're going to wait this . . . Sonya out."

"Yes," Laura said. "That is what I am going to do. That is what I can do."

When they got back to the house, Laura made them all hot chocolate with marshmallows, then put Hanno down for a rest time with his new books. She worked in the kitchen, stuffing the goose and roasting it, preparing the rest of the Christmas feast. Daphne, helpless in her pregnancy, fell asleep in front of the fire. When she awoke, the men were home, and Laura had done something to her face so that there was no sign of her tears, no sign at all of her grief, except for a slight puffiness around her eyes. The Christmas dinner was very gay, with much champagne and delicious food and laughter. Daphne could scarcely look at Otto, she despised him so; but she tried to act normally toward him so he would not guess that Laura had told her of their secret. Daphne did not want to betray her friend in any way.

Jack kept busy the first three days after Christmas. He worked furiously on his essay from morning till late afternoon. Then he forced himself out into the cold silver air and walked along ice-clotted country roads for an hour — it was too icy to jog. In the evenings he read novels while eating heated-up canned stew, and drank so much beer to ward off not only despair that he hadn't written one of those novels but also envy of the men who had, that he felt bloated. He told himself he was getting a lot done.

But the fourth morning, when he awoke, the silence of his house made him lonely. The windows were white with empty winter air, and the wind howled. He was sexy and wanted to make love. He wanted to cuddle his daughter, to hear his wife's voice. At least he could call her on the phone. He needed the caress of her voice to take the ache from this long vacant day. Shoving all the pillows up behind his back, he sat up and dialed Carey Ann's parents' number in Kansas City.

His mother-in-law answered the phone. "Jack? What's the matter?" she asked immediately, alarm in her voice.

"Nothing's the matter." Jack laughed.

"But it's prime time! Why are you calling?" Her voice was stern. Maternal. Protective. Sensible.

Jack felt his mother-in-law's voice reduce his love to the impulses of a horny adolescent.

"I just wanted to talk with Carey Ann," he said. "And with Alexandra. I, um, have appointments all day and just wanted to see how she is."

"Well, she's asleep," his mother-in-law said. "She was up late last night with her old high-school friends. They had such a good time, it was like old times. She didn't get to bed till after two, I'm sure. I'd hate to wake her up now. Are you sure nothing's wrong?"

Frustration welled up in Jack. He was not a violent person, but now he felt a strong urge to punch something. If there had been a button at hand, courtesy of the Twilight Zone, that would have disposed of his mother-in-law forever, he would have pushed it.

"No, no, nothing's wrong," he said. "Don't wake her. Just tell her I called. Hey, what about Lexi? Surely she's up by now."

"Oh, Beulah has her. She's already dressed her and taken her out for a walk. So Carey Ann can have her sleep."

"Well, tell Alexandra hello for me too," Jack said. He wanted to say "give her a kiss for me," but was afraid it would make him sound . . . what? . . . weak? . . . in his mother-in-law's ever-mistrusting judgment.

Determined not to be gloomy, Jack jumped from his bed, did twenty deep knee bends and twenty sit-ups, then took a long invigorating shower. He cooked himself a mammoth breakfast with Prince's *Purple Rain* album playing at full volume on the stereo. The stand-up cutout of Prince and his motorcycle was in his study closet, the only place in the house Jack could find for it. After breakfast he took it out and brought it into the living room. He placed it next to the fireplace, right by a chair, so that he could sit on the sofa and look at the fire and have someone to talk to. Prince, savage, untamable, all purple and black, seemed to glare with disgust at Jack.

"Man," Jack said aloud, Prince speaking to Jack, "you should be ashamed of yourself. What are you, pussy-whipped? You are pathetic, man. You are boring! Get out and *live!*"

"Look," he said to the Prince cutout, "I love my wife. I love my daughter. I don't really want to be wild. I want to be happily married, bourgeois, faithful. I'm the man all those women in *Newsweek* and *Ms.* are looking for. Phil Donahue isn't any better than I am. And where's my wife? Where's my child?"

Prince didn't answer, so Jack went off into his study and sat down at his desk and tried to concentrate on his essay. He had gotten a good start; it should have been easy to get back into. But his mind kept going back to Carey Ann.

Now he knew what men meant with their jokes about women always changing their minds. They weren't talking about the frivolous things that men joked about — women changing their dresses at the last moment, or their hair or the restaurant they wanted to go to. Carey Ann's changes were major. Jack was sure that in the few years he had been with her, before marriage and after, he had remained basically the same person. He had always told her the truth about what he wanted in life, and he had stuck by that. But now here they were beginning just their fourth year of marriage, and Carey Ann had already changed three times. At least. Major changes. First she had wanted — she had passionately affirmed that she really wanted — to be a wife and mother. She had loved Jack

311

before their marriage and in the early months with a passion that made Jack certain that no one else on earth had or ever would have any love better than theirs. Then the baby had come and she had changed. She had gotten all mopey. She had gotten emotional, strung-out, extreme, weak, and weepy. She had been depressed about everything, and then, what was worse, she had been *brave* about their life together. She had been a martyr, leaving her home and family and friends so that he could teach. Now she had changed again, all of a sudden, into this person who wanted seriously to pursue a degree in childhood education, who didn't even want to take time to put up a Christmas tree. What next? What would she change into next?

It wasn't fair. Jack shoved his desk chair back and stalked from the room. Prince was still standing against the fireplace wall, looking cool.

"It really isn't fair, you know?" he said to Prince. "I'm keeping my end of the bargain, I've always kept my end. *I* haven't changed. I'm the same person she married. I haven't decided to . . . oh, go to medical school or drop out and smoke dope."

Prince stared at Jack from his purple motorcycle. His gaze said clearly: I always knew you were a fool.

312

Well, this was certainly the way to go mad. Stand around in the morning talking to a cardboard figure. Jack pulled on his parka and gloves and slammed out of the house. He didn't know what he was going to do, but he would do *something*.

He drove into Westhampton, which was as quiet as a stage set. As beautiful, too, with its sloping snow-covered lawns and quadrangle, the old stone buildings decorated with icicles. There was some action on the main street, cars and people passing now and then, but the students were gone, and that was what made everything seem so bare. Jack took the stairs to the third floor English/History offices three at a time. The heat was on, and a few lights here and there, but most of the offices were dark and no one else was around. It was spooky and depressing. He sat in his office with the door open in case someone passed by, and did some paper shuffling. He looked out his window at the campus spread in all its winter glory beneath him. Everything was as lonely and cold as the moon.

He locked his office and walked over to the student union, which was open for the faculty and staff today, and ate a cheeseburger and french fries while pretending to read a book that had come in the mail, a new study of the works of Jonathan Swift. It was so boring he read the same paragraph three times. What an awful mood he was in! Usually he would relish this peace, usually he begged for it; he needed this kind of solitude in order to get his work done. But something had turned against him now. Or gone sour.

Crumpling his paper napkin, Jack finished his gloomy cheeseburger and dutifully rose to dump his garbage in the bin and put his tray on the used stack. From behind his back came the sound of familiar laughter, and he turned to see Daphne walking into the cafeteria with Pauline White. Jack thought: *Snow White* — for Daphne's short thick hair was as black as a raven's wing, her skin was as white as snow, and her lips and cheeks were as red as blood. And there was about Daphne a resonance, a glow, a vitality, that was almost mythological. She always seemed to mean more than she was, at least to Jack, or she brought a dimension to his life that expanded the way he saw and felt about the world. He felt drawn toward her. It was amazing to him that she was always laughing, always with other people, her friends. He felt shy.

But he approached the table where Pauline and Daphne were seating themselves, busy now taking off their winter paraphernalia and piling coats, mittens, mufflers, purses, on the chairs beside them.

"Oh, hi!" Daphne said, looking up and seeing Jack. "How nice to see you! How are you?"

"Oh, fine," he said. "Carey Ann and Alexandra are gone, you know. For two weeks." He turned to address Pauline, a tenured member of his department, and also a very nice woman. "Visiting her parents," he explained. "In Kansas City."

"So," Pauline replied, "are you relishing your solitude or hating it?"

"Both," Jack said, and everyone laughed.

"Well, join us for lunch," Daphne told him, gesturing at a chair next to her, and for one flash of a moment Jack almost did. He almost pretended that he hadn't eaten yet (but what if the old broad in the cafeteria line made some crack about his having two lunches within thirty minutes?); but then he shrugged.

"I've already eaten," he said. "Just finished. And I should get back to work."

"Well, sit down a minute and have a cup of coffee with us. I want to know how your Christmas was. Lexi must have been in heaven."

"Yeah, well, all right, I will have a cup of coffee," Jack said.

As they went through the line and settled down at the table and talked about the Christmas just past, Jack became uncomfortably aware of powerful and bizarre sensations tumbling around inside him. He kept looking at Pauline, addressing his remarks to her, because he was terrified that the two women might notice how he felt when he looked at Daphne. There could no longer be any doubt about it: he had a crush on her, a violent, irrational, fierce adolescent crush. She was wearing a pair of gray flannel slacks, a white shirt, and a long red cardigan, hardly an outfit to drive a man wild with desire, but he was wild with desire. The red of her sweater and earrings was as bright as apples or cherries; he was hungry, he wanted to bite into her; and everything about her was so bright, so intense. Her eyes really sparkled. Daphne's breasts were so large they swelled outward like a shelf, and when she moved, the neckline of her button-down shirt shifted, revealing pale freckled skin.

He had to keep looking away. He knew his throat and cheeks were red from blushing. He had to leave, he had to get back to work, but he was as entranced as a man in a magic spell.

"Listen," Pauline was saying, "what are you doing tonight?"

"Well . . . " Jack hesitated.

"A whole gang of us are going into Greenfield to the new Chinese restaurant and then we're going to see the late show of *Lady-*

Killer," Pauline told him.

"Good God," Jack said, "why are you going to see that? It's supposed to be grisly."

"That's just the point," Daphne said. "We've all decided we need something to off-set all this good cheer and goodwill."

"It's supposed to be a first-class horror film," Pauline went on. "The reviews have been raves. It's an excellent body-slasher movie."

"Sounds like a contradiction in terms." Jack grinned.

"Come on," Daphne urged. "It will be good for you. Get you away from your books for a while."

"Douglas is coming, and Marcia Johannsen and her husband, and I think Hank and Ellie Petrie. It'll be fun!" Pauline said. "Then you can drive Daphne and we won't worry about her driving alone on country roads at night."

Jack looked at Pauline. Are you blind?, he thought. Have you no eyes? Do you know what you're doing?

He looked at Daphne. He was dazzled.

"All right," he said as casually as he could. "That'll be great. I'll go. What time shall I pick you up, Daphne?" He felt a hot flush of blood rise up his neck and face, the source of which was surging powerfully at the base of his torso, so that he felt like a volcano rumbling and welling, ready to burst, and his skin was tense and sensitive with the pressure of holding him back.

8

After Christmas seventeen years ago, Laura had taken Hanno with her to Germany, where Otto was finishing his sabbatical year and having his affair with Sonya. That year while working at the University of Hamburg, he had lived in his parents' home, the sensible thing to do because he was on half-pay from the college in Massachusetts and had to support his wife and child, to keep up the mortgage payments on their American house. Someday he would, perhaps, make money from the German-American textbook he was working on, but he had not received a large advance on it. Someday he would, absolutely, receive a lot of money from his mother's estate — at least a million dollars, although the German death taxes would take their own lion's share. Still, he could afford to be a poor college professor for a while, and it was in keeping with that role that he lived in his parents' home while on sabbatical.

If his father, that unloving tyrant, were

319

alive, Otto probably would have stayed else-where. But his father had died three years ago, and now his mother was weakening with her age and her loss: with her domineering husband gone, she was like an outline of a woman, the substance and color drained away. She did not know what to do with herself. Her life had been in every way ruled by her husband's needs and wishes and demands. She did not say: "All I can do now is die," but that was what she was trying to do. She slept, or sat, listless, through the days.

The Kraft family house in Hamburg was large, brick, with a splendid walled garden. There were many entrances, and Otto was a man now, so he came and went as he pleased. Once there had been live-in help, but now old Mrs. Kraft and Otto managed to get along with only one dough-armed middle-aged apple-cheeked woman coming in every day to clean and to cook a large hearty meal for the evening. Sometimes Otto came home to share a dinner with his mother, sometimes not. Mrs. Kraft livened up with her son around, and listened with respect if not with comprehension to his dutiful dinnertime conversation about his work, his text, current events, what was good on television, politics. She sat, old, curved, white-haired, trying to die, nodding with pleasure just to hear her son speak, not ever once thinking of agreeing or disagreeing with any one thing he had to say.

Of course she did not know about Otto's lover, Sonya. If she had, she would not have been surprised. She would not have been even upset, for this happened, this was how men were. It had happened to her, it had happened to all her friends, it was life. And she wanted her son to be happy. Perhaps she suspected: many nights, especially in late November and early December, Otto did not come home to sleep in his old room in the corner of the second floor. Perhaps she suspected, perhaps not. What she thought didn't matter, not even to Mrs. Kraft.

Laura did not tell Otto that she was going to come with their son to Germany. She was too smart for that. She was not a cipher like her mother-in-law. She drove Otto to the airport after their dreadful Christmas holiday and said a cool good-bye. Otto was addled by then, desperate only to get back to bed with his mistress and incapable of talking any more with Laura about divorce. He had another semester of his sabbatical — another five months in Germany in Sonya's bed — and he could not see beyond that. So he got on the plane, blind with love, unsuspecting, and Laura went home to pack. Three days after Otto arrived in Germany, Laura arrived, with

Hanno in her arms and trunks and suitcases spilling out of the taxi. Mrs. Kraft, opening her front door, was so surprised she almost didn't recognize her daughter-in-law, and when she saw her grandson, so blond and chubby and beautiful, she began to cry.

"We miss Otto too much," Laura said. "We do not want to spend another semester without our husband and dada."

She embraced her mother-in-law, who let her into the house, naturally, and by the time Otto came home from the university, there was the entire second floor of the house given over to a bedroom and playroom for his son, and his wife's clothes unpacked in the closet of the corner bedroom, her silk dress hanging against his tweed jacket.

Daphne knew all this because this much, in detail, Laura had written to her. She had known, too, in advance, that Laura was going to do this. She had helped Laura pack. She had driven Laura and Hanno to the airport. Still, she could not believe it when Laura was really gone. The world became as blank as a white sheet of paper. Her best friend in all the world was gone. How would she get through her pregnancy without her? At this stage in her life, when she was bulging and lazily obsessed with her maternity, she would rather have had her husband gone than her friend. It was terrible.

After that first long, triumphant letter, Laura continued to write, but differently. Her letters were without the vivid warmth of their friendship. Perhaps she was afraid that Otto would get hold of her letters and read them. More likely she was hoping that this was only a horrid phase in her life and she didn't want any written record to remember it by when it was all over. She did write lengthily, bossily, about Daphne's pregnancy.

"Are you using that European salve on your belly twice every day? You'd better, or you'll be sorry. Do you need me to send you some more?

"Are you eating liver for lunch every day like I told you? And don't forget brewer's yeast and wheat germ. Remember, you are *making* that child. Whether that child is healthy or not, superior or not, depends on each and every thing you put in your mouth.

"I hope you are remembering to take a long walk every day. It is good for your muscles and your stamina, you must build up stamina for the birth process."

And finally, "It is time you are practicing your Lamaze breathing every day now. Seriously, and regularly, each day, so when the baby is coming you will be doing your breathing naturally and with experience. This is very important."

Daphne was achingly lonely in January and February. She even cried, she missed her friend so much. It was strange how it was Laura instead of Joe she needed so much to talk to — about clothes, being pregnant, the nursery decor, TV shows, books, food, her mother-in-law. She had shared with Laura secrets of great or little importance that she could never have told her husband. Joe would rise and eat a sparse breakfast, go off to teach, and Daphne would sit at the breakfast table with her healthy cereal and decaffeinated coffee, looking down at her global stomach. Who was the most important person in her life now? Joe or Laura? Who was the most necessary? She felt like a traitor to Joe, and she tried to get closer to him, to get back their old animal intimacy, but he was very busy with his course work, his committees, his scramble to the top. She read in women's magazines that this was how it was with "young marrieds." The woman was concerned with the new babies, the man with his career. So she relaxed and did not chide herself for missing her friend.

But she was so desperately lonely for Laura. Sometimes, when she was dusting or cooking, sentimental songs would come on the radio, and they would make Daphne think of Laura, and Daphne would cry. Especially she missed laughing with Laura. It seemed that with Laura, as it had been with her best friends in school and college, there was an element of lunacy, of hysterical, almost dangerous wildness. She had never laughed like that with Joe. Perhaps it was a female thing, that crazy laughter; perhaps it would frighten or repulse men to see women so loony, so witchlike in their cackling, helpless crowing mirth. And after all, in honesty, it was quite often something about a man or men that caused those shrieks. Or something foolish they had done long ago with a man or boy.

It was Laura who caused Daphne to get out and make new friends — although Laura had no idea of this. In one of her letters to Daphne she mentioned an afternoon she had spent with an old university friend, a woman who was recently divorced, and Laura wrote Daphne how intelligent this friend was, how beautiful, how fascinating, how sad and amazing that her stupid husband had left her, and so on. Daphne felt a real cramp in her stomach when she read that part of the letter, and then she felt a hot rush of anger. Why, she was jealous! She was as physically jealous that Laura had spent an afternoon with an old *fascinating* friend as she would have been if

Joe had come home praising another woman's looks.

Then Daphne passed herself in the hall and caught sight of her face in the mirror — what a harridan! She was wearing one of Joe's old sweatshirts, which was stretched to the seam-breaking point over her enormous belly. Her hair stuck out all over — when had she had it shaped last? And her face! She was scowling like an old battleax, frowning and pouting and glooming away like a spoiled child.

"Very nice," Daphne said to herself in the mirror. "Very attractive, I'm sure."

After that low point, she got herself in control. She made an appointment to have her hair cut and styled that very afternoon, and she went on from there to search out other women friends. There were the other faculty wives she met at all the university functions. She especially liked Pauline White, although she was also a little shy around Pauline then, because Pauline, unlike Daphne, had followed through and gotten her Ph.D. and was not just a faculty wife but a faculty member. And Pauline was four years older than Daphne and had a son in kindergarten. Still, their friendship began then, in its own jerky, clumsy, cumbersome way, and that friendship lasted.

For a while she was very close to some of

the other pregnant women she met at the Lamaze courses. Several of them were solicitous of Daphne, because Joe came with her to the first Lamaze meeting at the gym at the Y and would never come again. He thought the pregnant women were vulgar, showing off, all those bodies on the floor, stomachs swelling up in the air, all those fat legs spread out all over while the men knelt next to the women counting or rubbing backs. Daphne remembered how Joe had leapt to her defense long ago, and now she wondered if his courtliness, his protection of her right not to know that the word "cock" might have an earthy connotation, was perhaps at base symptomatic of some deep prudishness in Joe.

Or perhaps he just truly found a gymnasium full of puffing, blowing, waddling, graceless women, women blown up and crassed out by biology, unattractive. It was true that as her pregnancy advanced, Joe was less interested in making love with Daphne. Some men found pregnant women sexy; Joe did not. He loved Daphne, but now in a rather abstract way. And that was all right, because he used up all his energy teaching, writing articles, grading essays. He was not out having affairs — he was in their dining room, working late at night at the table, drinking pots of black coffee, working in a world of words and ideas, far away from Daphne's carnal realm.

Joe fainted before she had the baby. He fainted before they even got into the delivery room. Daphne had just been admitted to the hospital and had come from the bathroom, where she had put on a particularly skimpy cotton gown. She walked into the labor room, where Joe sat uncomfortably on a chair looking at the chart on the wall that depicted how his wife's cervix would dilate wide enough to let a grapefruit pass through. She smiled at Joe, and her water broke. Daphne grunted — a woman in labor and delivery makes sounds of bestial intensity, sounds she never makes any other time — and grabbed the wall to brace herself against an enormous contraction, and her bare legs sticking out from the graceless gown went bowed as she bent, and a flood of bloody water gushed out between her legs and onto the floor.

Alarmed, helpless, Joe watched, turned white, and fell sideways off his chair onto the floor. When the contraction was over, Daphne called for a nurse to come help her husband. After he recovered, the doctor sent him off to the cafeteria for coffee, with orders to remain in the waiting room until it was all over. They were grateful that they had found out so early in the birth that Joe was not a delivery-room type. Fainting fathers often caused havoc for doctors.

Joe did rush down to buy a huge bouquet of flowers for Daphne when Cynthia was finally born. It was early June, and the college was out for the summer. He was working on papers for a journal, but this was as relaxing a time of the year as possible, and for a while — a day — he was caught up in Daphne's euphoria.

"Look what we did!" she kept saying. "Look what we made!"

"She's very nice," Joe said, holding his new child gingerly.

"Nice! She's beautiful!" Daphne insisted.

Cynthia was a beautiful baby, and not all babies are beautiful. But Cynthia was. Daphne called Laura long distance to give her the news, and Laura whooped with joy.

"A daughter!" she cried. "This is *wonderful*, Daphne! She can grow up and marry Hanno! We can be mothers-in-law together!"

The truth was that Laura really seemed more excited about Cynthia's birth than Joe did. Why was that? Daphne would never, ever, know. In any case, it almost didn't matter, because Daphne was totally wrapped up in her baby. Her eyes opened and closed on Cynthia; Cynthia was the first and last thought of her waking day and Cynthia was the substance of her dreams at night — when she slept. There were all those middle-of-the-night feedings. Two weeks after Cynthia's birth, a large package arrived in the mail from Germany. It would be a blanket, Daphne guessed, cutting the thick cord, tearing off the brown wrapping paper. Or a soft embroidered baby dress.

It was a present for Daphne, a sumptuous red velvet lounging robe. Real velvet. It was very clever: it had a row of tiny glittering ruby-red buttons from the hem to the plunging neckline, but these were only decorative; the robe had a zipper hidden in a front panel, so that Daphne could easily unzip the bodice to nurse the baby.

"This is for you, my dear!" Laura had written on the enclosed card. "You deserve it for all your work — don't you! I am so proud of you and I can't wait to see Cynthia. Now, when you get depressed and feel dumpy — and you will, we all do — put on this robe, which will be splendid with your black hair."

Daphne put on the robe. It *was* splendid with her black hair. And it made her seem slender again, it flowed and swirled around her body, hiding her widened waist. The workmanship and material of the robe were the most excellent Daphne had ever seen on any garment in her life — and seventeen years later, when Cynthia came home from her father's to spend Christmas with her mother, it was that robe that Daphne wore to entertain. It was a timeless and superior garment.

Daphne was glad to have it that summer, even though it was too hot to wear most days. Laura was right: she put it on when she was feeling depressed and dumpy, and it helped her see into a future when she would look and feel attractive again. Daphne spoke on the phone almost every day with several of the friends she had made in the Lamaze class; as the women had their babies, the conversation naturally changed in focus from their own bodies to their babies' bodies. Daphne had never been happier in her life, for Cynthia was beautiful and adorable and good and gave Daphne immense pleasure. With her baby at her breast, Daphne felt a deep and complete sense of connection with the spiritual and physical source of the universe.

At the same time, that deep and complete connection was causing a chasm in her marriage.

The tenth day she was home from the hospital, she had to make an emergency phone call to Joe. Now that the baby was in the house, he had moved all his papers and his typewriter out to his office at the university, for as cramped and tiny as it was, at least it was quiet — no baby squalling there.

"Joe," Daphne said, "I need you to bring me some medicine from the druggist right away."

At the time Daphne called, Joe was sitting in his office talking with Hudson Jennings about Henry James.

"What's wrong, Daphne?" Joe asked, alarmed. "Is the baby okay?"

"Oh, she's fine. It's me, Joe. I need to have a bowel movement and I can't unless you get me some medicine."

This information stunned Joe into silence.

"My system got all screwed up when I delivered Cynthia," Daphne elaborated. "They told me I couldn't leave the hospital until I had had a bowel movement, so I lied because I wanted to go home. I've only had three bowel movements in ten days and I'm in agony. But delivering Cynthia gave me hemorrhoids — "

"Daphne. Just tell me what you need," Joe interrupted.

" — and it hurts so much to go to the bathroom, I don't want to but I have to."

"Daphne," Joe said. He was clenching the phone against his head so that none of Daphne's words would escape into the room, into Hudson's hearing.

"Could you get me some Preparation H and some laxative suppositories? And bring them

332

home right away?"

"Yes, good, fine, good-bye," Joe said.

When he arrived home with Daphne's medicine, Joe was furious, and he let Daphne know it. He had never been the sort of man comfortable with buying his wife sanitary napkins, and these items made him almost writhe.

"You might like to know that you interrupted a conversation with Hudson Jennings!" Joe said through clenched teeth, each word sounding like a curse.

"Well, Joe, I'm sorry, but I'm in pain," Daphne said. She grabbed the brown paper sack and hurried into the bathroom.

Joe left, slamming the door, to go back to the university.

That night Daphne tried to talk with him about it all. In spite of the heat, she had put on the red velvet robe because it made her look lovely, and she drank a vodka tonic even though she knew some of the alcohol would get into her baby's system when she nursed her, and she made an effort to be loving and attentive to Joe. Earlier in the day she had talked to several other new mothers from the Lamaze class about Joe's strange new coldness, and they said that this often happened with men. The men were jealous of the new babies and of the affection their wives lavished on the babies, and the men grew surly in reaction.

"Right when you don't have the energy to do it is the time you have to vamp your husband, or your marriage goes down the drain," one of the new mothers said.

So Daphne tried that night, but Joe was oddly unvampable. He was irritable from the heat, and his writing was not going well, and he found it frustrating, he said, to have Daphne cuddling and kissing him when they couldn't have intercourse for five more weeks.

"We could do other things," Daphne said.

Joe looked at her, uncomprehending.

Daphne was so tired, so tired from giving birth and staying up most of the night the past ten days with the new baby and from carrying the child, the weight, the lovely weight, causing her arms and shoulders to ache. She was so tired that the last thing in the world she wanted was to make love to her husband with her mouth, but she slid down to the floor, leaned against his legs, and began to unzip his pants.

"Daphne, for God's sake, stop it!" Joe yelled, and jumped up off the sofa.

"Joe," Daphne said. "What's wrong?"

"You're just being . . . repulsive," Joe said.

"I am? How? It's not like we've never done this before."

"That was different. We were being lovers. Now it's like . . . like you're doing me a favor. Taking care of me."

"Well, what's wrong with that?" Daphne asked. "We all need to be taken care of sometimes, in all sorts of ways."

"Daphne, just don't push it," Joe said, sighing. He sank down into an armchair and leaned forward, hiding his face in his hands. His voice came out muffled. "I'm sorry. I know I'm not doing this fatherhood business very well. I don't know. I just don't feel comfortable with it. My nerves are all shot to hell . . . I don't know when Cynthia's going to start screaming. It's like living in a tornado zone."

Daphne went over to kneel next to Joe. She put her head on his knee and wrapped her arms around his legs. He leaned back stiffly in the chair, not touching her. "We'll go away," she said. "We'll get a baby-sitter and go to a motel for a night. Just the two of us." It was not what she wanted to do at all.

"Daphne," Joe said, "give it a rest. I love you. You know I love you. We're just in . . . a kind of phase right now. I mean, God, how can I say this without hurting you? I know it's going to change, Daphne, but right now you just don't . . . excite me sexually."

Daphne sat very still for a moment, frozen

into that moment. The irony: their physical closeness now, as she knelt with her arms around her husband's legs and her head on his knees, and yet they were so very far apart. (If only he would put his hand on her head or shoulder as a sign of affection, but he didn't, as if afraid she would misinterpret.) Earlier in their marriage she would have jerked herself away from him, flung herself away from him, offended, would have shouted something clever and cutting at him, and gone into her bedroom, or the kitchen, and he would have followed, and wrapped his arms around her and pulled her to him and appeased her. Earlier in their marriage they had been more passionate in their fights and more eager to make up quickly.

Now she could not fling herself away in one great dramatic scene. He would think she was being shrewish. He would not come hold, appease her, he was not even now putting his hand on her arm. She was so tired with the baby, and he was so tired with his work; they did not have the energy for the scenes and reconciliations that they used to.

And she knew that Joe was right: this was only a phase in their marriage. If love was like an exotic country — a tropical-island paradise, Fiji, Tahiti — then marriage was like the whole wide world, with its oceans of tur-

336

bulent passion and its lakes of calm and its busy cities and, too, its wasteland stretches of arid, vast, monotonous desert. In the middle of a desert it was difficult to believe that one could ever come to the margin, see mountains or freshwater streams again. One kept on moving on faith, one had to, in order to get through and out.

So. Here they were, suddenly, when she least expected it, in the desert of their marriage. But the belief that they loved each other — the institution of marriage itself — was like a vehicle they were riding in together (trapped in together, if one wanted to be grim about it) that would carry them along until they reached the end of the desert and a change in the climate of their lives.

How sensible she was, not a hysterical female at all, pretty good for a woman battling with postpartum depression, Daphne thought. Very gently she extricated herself from her embrace around her husband's legs. Very calmly she said, "I think I'll take a bath now. Cynthia shouldn't wake." Very rationally she walked across the living room and down the hall to the bath.

The hot steamy water relaxed and refreshed her. Just lying down for a few minutes relaxed her. She almost fell asleep in the tub. When she rose and was toweling off, she looked at

337

herself in the mirror. She hadn't done this — looked at herself, full length, naked — since the birth of her baby.

But now she stood naked, studying herself critically, ready to drip. There she was. All of her. So much of her. Dripping. What she noticed first of all, as who could not, was her stomach. Laura's famous European salve had not worked, and now silver minnowy stretch marks swam across the gleaming bowl of her stomach, while, below, her pubic hair curled like seaweed. Actually, her stomach looked more like a giant plastic baggie full of fish than a bowl — the skin was loose and her intestines sagged untidily inside. If she moved a little, took a few dance steps — wow, what a dazzling array of directions her body went into, breasts jouncing this way, stomach jiggling that. Even her thighs were still swollen — even there, at the top of her thighs, between her legs, the fishy stretch marks swam.

And her breasts. Well, men were supposed to like big breasts, weren't they? Her breasts were huge, and in their fullness both beautiful and alarming, as if they had become articles of their own, great bulging attachments with the veins as bright as if they had been drawn on the outside of her skin with a blue felt pen and nipples straight out of *National Geographic*.

There were brown circles under her eyes.

Well, of course there were. She hadn't slept for more than three hours straight through in ten days. Above her mouth was a little brown mustache of pigment, which the doctor said often came with pregnancy and birth and would eventually go away. A similar brown blotch had appeared just between her two eyebrows, giving her a frowning, idiotic look.

What a treat she was to look at. She didn't hate her body — she was proud of it, look what it had just done! If only Laura were here to share the scrutiny, how they would laugh and shriek with pleasure, alarm, and glee at what Daphne had become. Perhaps if she joked about it with Joe? Perhaps he would join with her in a good laugh? Marriage was not only about sex.

Daphne put on her nightgown and brushed her hair. Disguised in flowing cotton, she looked pretty. She would go be friends with Joe.

When she got to the living room, she found that Cynthia had awakened during her bath, and Joe was holding her now, rocking her. She had to take the baby from him and nurse her. This was the way it was to be, then — why had she not known it, everyone had told her in advance, but she had not really understood: having a baby in the house, in one's life, really altered the marriage, and everything within it.

Cynthia was beautiful, but she was sickly. In the early months she had colic, that mysterious ailment that made her cry for three hours every night while Daphne rocked and walked the floor with the baby in her arms, sometimes crying herself from frustration at her inability to make her infant happy. There was then a period of peace for about three months, and then in the winter Cynthia began to get earaches and ear infections along with colds that caused her little pink nose to run constantly with the most unattractive green mucus.

It was in late August, when Cynthia was not quite three months old and still crying every evening with colic, then waking in the middle of the night for a feeding, that Daphne had a phone call from Laura at five o'clock in the morning. Daphne had put Cynthia back to bed only an hour before. Drugged with sleep, she grabbed up the receiver to stop the ringing, but for a moment was too exhausted to do more. Next to her, also tired, Joe muttered, "Jesus Christ. Who is calling at this hour?"

"Daphne," Laura said. The air around her words crackled and hummed with distance. "Daphne, are you there?"

"Laura? Are you all right?"

"We are coming home today. You must meet me at the airport with a car. Can you do that?"

Through her weariness, joy surged. "Oh, Laura, of course we'll meet you," Daphne said. "How are things?"

"I'll tell you when I see you," Laura said.

Logan Airport in Boston was two and a half hours away. Daphne insisted that Joe drive. "Laura is your friend too," she said.

"And so is Otto," Joe countered.

"But Otto may be with Laura, for all we know. She said 'we.'"

"'We' may mean just Laura and Hanno. And I have work to do."

"You always have work to do. Now, look, I can't drive through Boston with Cynthia in my arms. You don't want to stay home and baby-sit Cynthia. And I want Laura to see Cynthia right away, I can't wait to show her to her. Besides, Laura will be hurt if you don't come. And if Otto's there, and everything's fine between them, all the better."

But at the airport it was not Otto who climbed down the ramp from the airplane with Laura and Hanno, but old Mrs. Kraft. Laura looked stunningly beautiful. She had gotten very thin and had had her hair cut like a boy's, short and shaggy, with long bangs

341

that fell down into her eyes. She wore a gray jumpsuit and high gray boots and lots of silver jewelry, and Daphne, in her navy-blue corduroy jumper and white blouse, both of which had been chosen because they unbuttoned at the bodice so she could nurse, felt dumpy and unsophisticated in comparison. Hanno, blond and rosy-cheeked, was wearing a sailor boy's outfit with a wide white collar and a white hat with a blue ribbon. When he saw Daphne, he grinned shyly, looking up under the brim of the hat with great cornflower-blue eyes.

Daphne put Cynthia in Joe's arms and grabbed Laura and both women hugged and hugged each other, laughing and crying at once. Laura felt as tiny and fragile as a bird in Daphne's arms, and when Daphne pulled back, she saw the dark circles under her friend's eyes, the deep sadness there.

"Daphne, Joe," Laura said. "I want you to meet my mother-in-law, Mrs. Kraft. She is coming to stay with us for a while." Laura shot Daphne a look that said quite clearly: Don't say a thing. Don't ask.

So it wasn't until much later, when both Hanno and old Mrs. Kraft were tucked away in bed, that Daphne learned what was going on in her friend's life. She and Joe had brought champagne to celebrate Laura's return, and

Daphne had spent the morning airing out Laura's house and stocking the refrigerator with milk and other necessities, so finally the three friends sat in the living room with champagne and cheese and crackers and baby Cynthia snoozing on a blanket on the carpeted floor near them.

"Welcome home," Daphne said, toasting her friend.

"Yes. Welcome back," Joe said.

They all drank, then Laura said, "Well, here it is. Otto is wanting a divorce. He is coming back to teach, he will be here in a few days, but he is bringing Sonya with him. He has it all planned. By mail he has already rented an apartment for the two of them. By mail and phone he has already contacted a lawyer."

"Oh, Laura, no," Daphne said.

Laura reached into her purse and pulled out a pack of cigarettes — a new habit for her. She crossed her long sleek legs, tossed her head, lit up. "Mrs. Kraft is unhappy about this. An affair she would not mind, but divorce for her son is out of the question. She is on my side. She knows I have done nothing wrong. There is a chance, she thinks, that together she and I and little Hanno and perhaps the college community can exert enough influence to change Otto's mind."

"What do you think?" Joe asked.

"I think she is too optimistic!" Laura said, her eyes filling with tears.

"Oh, well!" Daphne said, standing up and pacing the room in her agitation. "Well, you shouldn't take him back anyway, even if he would come. Laura, where's your pride? He's going to bring that Sonya person back here to live with him? How does he think poor little Hanno will feel? Look, Laura, Otto's being an incredible shit about all this."

"You never did like him," Laura said.

Daphne stopped. "No. I didn't. I admit that." She paced again, restless with energy, anger, plans. "I've always thought he wasn't good enough for you. I'm very sorry you are being hurt and that it's all happening this way, but maybe it's all for the best. Now you can start a new life. Why, you can do anything, Laura! You could go back to school, you could get a degree, you could get a job, you — "

"Oh, Daphne, don't you know me any better than that?" Laura said, waving her cigarette around. "Don't you know I'm irretrievably domestic? I am just a hausfrau." Raising a hand to forestall Daphne's objection, she went on. "This is not an insult! This is what I want to be! I like being a housewife, I like being in a home, that is what I want my life to be about, making a home cozy. Don't look so scornful. There's nothing wrong with that, is there, Joe?"

Joe, caught between the two passionate women, shook his head morosely, looking as if he'd rather be anywhere else in the world. "No, no, of course not," he said.

"Well, then, you will find someone else," Daphne said. "Laura, you're a beautiful woman, you're bound to have lots of men fall in love with you."

"Oh, Daphne, you are so kind in your thoughts of me," Laura said. "If the father of my child does not love me, how am I to believe another man will?" She leaned forward to stub out her cigarette, and when she sat up again, her face was silver with tears.

"Oh, Laura, Laura," Daphne said, going to her. She could not bear this, to see her friend in pain. She sank onto the sofa and wrapped her arms around Laura and hugged her. "It will be all right. I promise you." This made Laura sob harder.

"I have only wanted in my life a husband, house, and children," Laura said, pulling away, lighting another cigarette. "I have not wanted jewels or fame or excitement. I have only wanted what is usual. And I have been very good — you see this house, you have eaten my food! You see my child, he is a beautiful, healthy, happy child! I am a very nice woman! How can Otto leave me?"

"He's a fool, Laura, he's just a *fool*," Daphne said, crying.

"You're a man!" Laura said, crying, leaning toward Joe. "You tell me. What do men want? What have I not given Otto? What do you see are my failings?"

Joe looked miserable enough to cry himself. He was not used to talking about such intimate things. He paused, reflecting, and Daphne would have bet money that at that moment he was frantically searching his mind for some appropriate quote from Shakespeare, Donne, Byron. Something about love and loss. "Love is for man a thing apart, 'tis woman's whole existence"? No, that wouldn't do.

"Otto and I are colleagues, but we have never confided in each other," Joe said at last. "I couldn't speak for him."

Daphne glared at Joe. What a namby-pamby answer, what a coldhearted answer!

"You think it's sex, don't you?" Laura said to Joe. "Oh, I know you think that, that's how men think. Well, I wish you could know how I am in bed. I am wonderful in bed. I am passionate and innovative and — "

"Laura," Daphne interrupted. Joe was turning beet-red at this talk and she didn't

346

want her husband to think her best friend was crude. "Laura, stop. It's not you. You are wonderful in every way. We know that. It's Otto. There is some sickness in him that is making him act this way. Now, you can't change him. You just can't change things. You have to move forward. Make plans. Look into the future."

In Daphne's mind it was all so clear. She could have made a chart, a list, for Laura to follow, step by step, day by day, that would take her out of this slough of misery and into the bright clear light of a free life. But Laura kept wallowing in her despair. She kept not wanting to believe that Otto would really leave her. She kept trying to think of things that would make him stay. Daphne talked about the future; Laura responded by describing an episode from the past, when Otto loved her. Joe sat watching, saying little, turning gray.

Later, in the car, on the way home, Daphne said, "You were so unresponsive, Joe, so unkind."

"I didn't mean to be unkind," he said wearily. "I just didn't know what to say. I can't change things. It seems to me that Laura's going to have to realize that sooner or later."

"But you could have given her a little more

sympathy," Daphne said. When Joe didn't reply, she went on, "She *is* a wonderful person, don't you think, Joe? She's beautiful and a fabulous mother and homemaker. Do you think she has any flaws that would drive a man away?"

"No. Of course not. But marriages all have secrets. I honestly don't think it's my place to judge Otto."

"You, you are so dispassionate!" Daphne said.

"Yes, exactly. That's what I'm trying to be. I am not on Otto's side, nor on Laura's."

"But Otto doesn't need help, and Laura does!"

"Then you help her. There is nothing I can do."

"You are retreating more and more into your mind, do you know that?" Daphne said, turning on Joe in a sudden fury. Cynthia, asleep in her arms, stirred at Daphne's raised voice, and automatically Daphne jiggled the baby back to sleep. She lowered her voice but kept the anger in it as she spoke. "It is all books for you, and college committee meetings and exams and student essays and articles and lessons, words on paper, words on paper, all words on paper! You don't feel anymore. You don't *feel* for me or for Cynthia or for poor Laura! You are pretending to be a flesh-

and-blood man with a family, but you are becoming J. Alfred Prufrock. You are measuring out your life with coffee spoons. You are so *contained!* How can anyone reach you?"

They had pulled into the driveway of their house and Joe had let the motor run so the car heater would warm them against the strangely chilly late-August night. He sat very quietly staring straight ahead of him while Daphne raged. When she was finally quiet, he turned to look at her. "That's not true, Daphne," he said. He reached out and pulled her to him, and kissed her on the mouth for a long time, the two of them leaning into each other over the baby, who for once, miraculously, slept. And who continued to sleep after they went into the house and she was laid gently in her cot while Joe and Daphne tiptoed to their own room, where Joe made passionate love to Daphne in their wide married bed. It was the first time since Cynthia's birth that Joe had been so amorous with Daphne, and her body responded to his, it was like a homecoming. As Joe lay on top of her, his naked skin sliding against her naked skin, she cried in sexual ecstasy and then in happiness — her body had come back to her.

Later, when Joe had rolled over and she lay against his chest sheltered by his arm, Daphne cried again. "Oh, poor Laura," she said. "She doesn't have this and we do. We are so lucky. Poor Laura." She looked up at Joe and saw irritation settle across his face. It was not wise of her, she thought, to speak of Laura when she was lying with her husband. It was like bringing an irrelevant and annoying element into the warm intimacy of their bed, a piece of sand, a ringing phone, a bad dream.

The weather turned warm again and September and October were golden months, but then it began to rain, then snow, and it seemed that year that a great cloud, as bleak and cold as cinders, settled over New England. In April, when everyone was longing desperately for spring, it rained and rained and rained, battering down the daffodils.

Cynthia had almost continuous colds, earaches, ear infections, and had to go through a series of visits to the medical clinic. The doctors spoke of surgery to put drains in Cynthia's ears. The furnace faltered and failed and the repairman told Daphne it would be a waste of their money to keep fixing it; it had to be replaced. That was an unexpected and unwelcome expense — they had been hoping to take some kind of vacation over the Christmas holidays or spring break, to go somewhere warm and sunny, but now of course they couldn't. The new furnace and Cynthia's medical bills took all their money.

Things got worse and worse for Laura too. Otto went through with the divorce. More horribly, he showed up everywhere with his Sonya, who was not at all what Daphne had expected. She saw Sonya at a large faculty party — although she did not speak to her and would not speak to Otto. Sonya was young, younger than Laura, but much larger, a great strapping blond milkmaid type with a wide stupid face. Yet she was a doctor and was setting up practice in town. And faculty wives started going to her — Sonya was a gynecologist — and singing her praises. How gentle she was, how sympathetic, how intelligent.

Predictably, people began to invite Otto and Sonya to their dinners and parties and to avoid Laura. Otto, after all, had the tenure, not Laura. Laura saw her lawyer, the therapist she had begun consulting at Daphne's suggestion, the mothers of little Hanno's friends, Mrs. Kraft, and Daphne. It drove Daphne crazy that now, when she, Daphne, thought Laura should be out getting a job, or working on a degree, or going to art openings or concerts at the college, or, hell, even sitting in bars flirting with strangers, anything to expand her life past its little core of misery, Laura spent almost all her time at home, keeping house for Mrs. Kraft and Hanno.

Finally, in May, the sun blossomed in the sky, and flowers and flowering trees and bushes of every imaginable color bobbed and dipped against fences and houses, above the streets. Trees leafed out, dappling the lawns beneath them with shadows, staining the roads with shade. Cynthia, eleven months old, crawled off the blanket Daphne had spread in the backyard, and, intent on catching a bird pecking away in the tall grass by the hedge, pushed herself up with her fat pink hands and ran. Her first steps. She didn't get very far, not on those fat untested legs, but she did run. A wobbling, bobbling run, but still a run. Daphne called everyone she knew to report: Cynthia had not walked when she took her first steps, but had *run*.

With the warmth, Cynthia's colds and ear infections disappeared, and although she went through life at a hellish pace in the day, she began to sleep through the night, and also to take long afternoon naps. Daphne's energy returned. She planted petunias, geraniums, nuzzling her nose into the spicy green leaves; she planted impatiens and hung baskets of fuchsias, dug in the earth to plant hollyhocks and morning-glory seeds. She joined an exercise club at the Y, left Cynthia in the playroom with the baby-sitter and other children, and did aerobics three times a week. It was as if her life had been given back to her.

One late-May evening Joe came home from the college to find his two girls, as he had come to call them, reclining in the backyard. Cynthia had fallen asleep, wearing only her diaper, in the playpen Daphne had set out in the shade. Daphne was wearing a swimsuit, trying to tan her very white and slightly sleeker body, and she was reading a delicious romantic novel. A pork roast was on the charcoal grill, filling the air with its rich meaty scent, and she had set out an ice bucket and tonic and vodka and crackers and cheese on the patio table.

"How are you?" Joe asked, fixing himself a drink.

"I'm fine. I'm in heaven, actually," Daphne said, stretching. "This is heaven."

"Yes, I can believe it, looking at you," Joe said. He sat down on the chaise next to her.

"Look. I'm getting tanned," Daphne said, and pulled her suit down at her hipbone to expose the tanning line.

"Yes. You are." To Daphne's surprise, Joe bent and kissed her on the belly, light but intense kisses, from her belly button down past the tan line, down to her pubic hair.

It was so sudden a thing for Joe to do, and so erotic. Daphne placed her hand in Joe's thick hair and leaned back on the chaise, closing her eyes. She felt her thighs go lax. She could smell the sun on her hot skin. *The neighbors*, she thought, but unless they were peering out of their second-story windows, they couldn't see. *Cynthia*, she thought, but the baby slept on.

"Joe," she whispered huskily.

"You smell like the sun," he murmured, burrowing his face into her.

"Joe," she said. "We should go inside."

He didn't answer. Or rather, not in words; he responded by reaching up to put one hand over her mouth, gently, while with the other he peeled her suit away from her crotch and thrust her legs apart with his head. Daphne took Joe's fingers in her mouth for a moment, then felt all control slipping away. She dissolved onto the chaise, turning her head toward the shade, raising one hand to cover her face, and then, after a while, biting the inside of her arm to keep from crying out and alarming the baby.

Later, when Joe and Daphne were eating their pork roast and baked potatoes and fresh tomatoes at the patio table, with Cynthia scooting around in the garden in her little round green walker, Daphne said, "You've never done anything like that before."

Joe looked sheepish. He grinned. "You know, I'll be absolutely honest with you. I

354

think it was a real instinctive male-domination thing. When I came out and saw you so fat and happy, so completely *smug*, as if you were enjoying every pleasure the universe had to offer, I couldn't stand it. I wanted you to remember you need *me* for pleasure too."

"Joe," Daphne said, amazed. "How could you ever think I didn't always remember that?"

"I'm just telling you how I felt," he said. "You're always asking me to tell you how I feel, so I'm telling you."

And even later, when they had put Cynthia to bed and were sitting together on lawn chairs in the backyard, watching the blue fade out of the brilliant sky into a deep gray, Daphne rose and knelt before her husband. She ran her hands over his shoulders and down his chest and abdomen. She unbuttoned his pants, and began to unzip them.

"No," Joe said. "Not out here."

"But I — "

Joe pushed Daphne away, almost roughly. "Not here, Daphne. I just can't."

She rose and pulled at his hands. "Then come inside," she said. And they went inside and made a ferocious, very animal love, but Daphne would always think about that night and wonder what it meant: what sort of woman was she, who could be ravished under

the sun while the baby lay nearby and who-
knew-who was looking out of the windows, or
what kind of man was Joe, always to need the
dark?

9

For the nine months of the school year, the year that Daphne in her mind called "The Year of the Divorce," Otto went every Sunday to the house where his son and mother and almost-ex-wife lived. Daphne of course was never witness to these occasions, but according to Laura, she and Mrs. Kraft served Otto slices of his favorite tortes, and coffee, and brandy. Otto asked his mother how her health was, and what she was doing with herself, and what the news was from home, and what she thought of the New England weather. Then he took Hanno by the hand and led him off to an afternoon of museums, or movies, or ice skating, or swimming in the college pool, and then a snack of pizza. When he brought Hanno home, he knocked on the door and waited for Laura to reclaim their son. He did not go in, but left immediately.

Those Sunday meetings were the focus points for Laura's conversations with Daphne.

She would come to Daphne's on Monday for coffee and spend the morning repeating every word the fugitive Otto had said, trying to discover in his words some sign of dissatisfaction with Sonya, some hidden need to return to her.

"His collars are frayed!" Laura would say to Daphne, leaning across the kitchen table, terribly earnest. "Before, Otto would *never* go out with the slightest thing wrong with his clothes. No spots on his tie, no buttons missing, no threads hanging, and here he is with his shirt collars frayed. She is not taking care of him!"

Daphne sometimes thought these conversations would drive her mad. She loved Laura and wanted to help her through this terrible time in her life, but Laura seemed so stuck. She shied away from any talk about the future, about her life after the divorce. If Otto said by chance, "You're looking very nice today, Mother. It must be spring. You too, Laura," Laura spent the next week like a mad alchemist trying to extract the magical out of the banal. "He complimented me! He has not complimented me for weeks. What do you think this means? Perhaps he is coming around!"

By Friday, when Otto's past visit had been squeezed dry of any real hope and Laura had heard about some dinner party where he cuddled with Sonya or a trip the two took over Christmas or spring vacation to Cozumel or Montreal, Laura would plunge into a dreadful depression. Fridays were miserable days. Laura would weep and weep.

No matter what Daphne said, no matter how brilliant a plan she put forth for Laura's future, the Friday sessions always ended the same way.

"Well!" Laura would say finally, lifting her head and tossing her hair and lighting a cigarette. *"This* Sunday will be different! This Sunday I will — " And she would list what she would do: wear a dress with a slit in the side to show off her great legs, or short shorts; make Schwarzwalder Kirschtorte, Otto's favorite cake; let Mrs. Kraft answer the door and stay out of the room for a while — then make a dramatic entrance.

When Daphne tried to talk to Joe about Laura, he grew impatient. He rolled his eyes. "What's the matter with the woman?" he said. After a few months, it got to be a private joke with Daphne and Joe:

"Laura still suicidal?" Joe would ask over dinner.

"Yes."

"What a surprise."

"Well, do you think she should move

back to Germany?"

"Not if she prefers living in the States."

"Do you think she could get a job?"

"Of course she can get a job. Any idiot can get a job."

"Maybe a job would take her mind off Otto."

"What will take *your* mind off Laura?"

Daphne learned not to talk much about Laura. It made them both seem so dull, she knew, like a scratched record, the same things repeated ad nauseam.

But in May, when the world was luxuriant and luscious with flowers and fragrance and warmth, Daphne had an idea. The Millers were eating on the patio again; she had grilled hamburgers and they had turned out perfectly, thick and juicy on their onion-seed buns. She had crumbled some of the hamburger meat into little bits and put them, along with crumbs of cheese and slices of banana, on Cynthia's high-chair tray. Cynthia loved catching the food between her fingers, feeding herself, then sucking her fingers. Birds sang around them, and flowers bloomed: it was bliss. Daphne and Joe had found each other again sexually, too — that was part of the idyll.

"I've had an idea!" Daphne said. "I'm so unimaginably *stupid*. How could I have gone through this terrible winter without thinking of it? Joe, we have to have a cocktail party. Or a dinner party. Just a few married couples, so it isn't too obvious, and Laura, and every single man at the college."

Joe groaned.

"Really, now!" Daphne said. "Really, Joe, come on. This is exactly what Laura needs. She's just going to curl up in a ball mourning that gross Otto the rest of her life unless we help her. She'll come to our party, and when those bachelors get a good look at her. . . ! Think of it! She'll never be lonely again."

Joe groaned again. Then he reached across the table and stroked Daphne's cheek. "You are an incurable romantic. You are Mitzi Gaynor singing 'A Cockeyed Optimist.' But we should have a party. We owe a lot of people. And it's a good time of year. All right. Let's do it."

"Oh, God, Joe, I'm so excited!" Daphne said.

The next few weeks Daphne's head was filled with visions. It was the same fantasy with variations. Laura meeting a young professor: their eyes would connect across the crowded room, they would walk toward each other, talk, smile, and leave the party early to go make mad passionate love. Or: Laura meeting an older professor, one with some

361

elegance and savoir faire, who would appreciate her European charm. He would woo her with compliments and make a date to take her to the best restaurant in the area. Or . . . The possibilities, the fantasies, were endless.

The night of the party could not have been more conducive to romance. It was a cocktail party so that more people could be invited, but Daphne had put a pink paper tablecloth on the redwood picnic table and laden the table with food: a huge ham, sliced thin, with interesting mustards and breads and pickles; cheeses; meatballs simmering in chafing dishes; deviled eggs stuffed with caviar; vegetables and dips for the dieters; stuffed mushrooms; a silver platter piled high with seedless green grapes, strawberries, apple slices, and plums. The round glass-and-metal table they used for outdoor dining was large enough to hold the ice bucket and glasses and bottles of liquor and soft drinks. Daphne hung brightly colored Japanese paper lanterns from the trees and the sides of the house and put short fat candles inside colorful paper bags on the lawn. The backyard glimmered like a fairyland. It looked magical — something wonderful could happen here!

Daphne wore a low-cut summer dress and tied her hair up with a scarf. Finally she had lost the weight of pregnancy and birth. The classes at the Y had gotten her back into shape, an even better shape, very hourglass. Joe was attentive; whenever he was near her, he put his hand on her arm or waist affectionately; proprietorially.

Laura looked wonderful. These were the days when hippies influenced fashion, and she wore a paisley minidress with a matching paisley headband and dangling earrings. Daphne heard one of the faculty wives say to Laura, "Darling, your legs are a sin." "They are?" Laura exclaimed, alarmed. "No, no, you're taking me wrong," the woman said. "I mean they inspire lust in all our husbands. And envy in all the wives."

Daphne watched Cynthia at one moment (was the baby-sitter really keeping the baby away from the burning candles?) and her friend at the next. Laura was approached by many men. Of course, they had not invited Otto and his Sonya, so Laura was, Daphne thought, as free to flirt as a teenager at her first dance. But where were Laura's expansiveness, vibrancy, wonderful low laugh? Every time Daphne watched Laura, Laura looked stiff and somber.

So when the party was finally over and all the guests had gone, Laura, instead of going off to dinner with one of the men, or going off for another drink, or taking someone back to her house, or any variation on the themes Daphne had envisioned, remained behind, alone. She helped Daphne and Joe clean up, then sat at the kitchen table with them while they had a makeshift dinner of party leftovers. It was late. The party had gone on forever. The baby-sitter had put Cynthia to bed and gone home.

Joe said, "Ladies, if you'll excuse me, I'm going to pass out," and with a mocking smile at himself, weaved off to bed.

As soon as he was out of the room, Daphne leaned forward over the kitchen table. *"Well?"*

"Well?"

"Well, Laura! Did you . . . meet someone nice?"

"I met many nice people."

"Oh, for heaven's sake. You know what I mean."

Laura was stirring a huge pile of sugar and quite a lot of milk into her coffee. This seemed to claim her entire attention. Finally she looked up at Daphne.

"I am grateful for what you tried to do. I know you were hoping I would meet someone special. And there were some nice men. But, Daphne, they all seem so young, or frivolous, after Otto."

"But why not enjoy someone young and frivolous for a while? I mean, Laura, you don't have to look at every prospective man as a future father for Hanno. This is the time in your life when you should just have some fun."

"Meaning sleep around."

"Well, yes, why not? Yes!"

Laura sipped her coffee. "I don't think I want to sleep around. I don't think I would be comfortable with it."

Daphne eyed her friend appraisingly. "You surprise me. No, really, I'm serious. You are so . . . sensual, Laura. You love the things of the senses so much — everything around you, you make appealing. Your food, your clothes, your house — "

"And that makes you think I would like to sleep around?"

"That makes me think you would like sex. Oh, come on, Laura, think about that Hal Dodson, what a gorgeous man he is. Don't tell me he doesn't make your juices flow."

Laura looked amused and superior. "What a way of putting it. Listen, for this conversation I need some brandy in my coffee."

Daphne accommodated her friend, poured some in her own coffee, then settled back in her chair. "So?"

"We've been needing this talk when booze makes us honest," Laura said. "You've been driving me crazy all year now. Telling me just to go out and get laid."

"Really, I haven't put it quite so crudely."

"But that is what you mean. If I had gone off tonight with that Hal Dodson, you would have been happy? If I had gone to his house and slept with him?"

"Yes. Happy and envious. I'll admit it."

"Daphne, he's much younger than I. We couldn't possibly ever get serious about each other."

"So what? Why not have one night of pleasure?"

Laura smiled at Daphne, a slow, almost seductive smile, looking up through her lashes as she sat with her head tilted down. "Because," she said softly, "it would not be pleasure for me."

Daphne just stared at Laura, waiting.

"I know I've said how good I am in bed with Otto, innovative and so on, and that is true, Daphne. I am good in bed for a man. But I'm not so good in bed for myself. Oh, here it is in graphic vulgarity for you. Maybe this will take that puzzled look off your face. Daphne, I almost never have orgasms. It is very hard work for me even to try. To tell you the truth, I really don't like sex. When I hear you raving on about how you feel about Joe or how you lust after Hal, I know my body just operates differently from yours."

"I don't believe this," Daphne said. "I don't believe this."

"My *dear*, you know so much about me. But you do not know the deepest things. I'm telling you now. You know how poor I was as a child in Germany. I've told you the story of my mother holding my hand and crying because I was hungry. I vowed that would never happen to me. I would never let my child go hungry. So I did what was necessary. I found a wealthy man and married him and made him happy. Well, for a while, ha. *That* is what all that 'sensuality,' as you call it, was about. That's what all women's charms are about, when you come down to it, you know. Making the home alluring so the man will stay in it and bring us some money. Give me more brandy."

"You'll be sick if you drink any more, Laura," Daphne warned, but Laura reached across the table and poured brandy into her empty coffee cup. "At least let me give you a glass."

"This is good for you, you know," Laura said, after taking a large swallow. "You are such an idealist, such a dreamer. You need to know some things. You need to admit some things. Face facts. All women are whores, in a way, aren't we? We need to keep our men happy so they will support us."

"Laura, you're drunk. You're saying awful things."

"Oh, come on, Daphne, sometimes you irritate me so much! You like to hide from the truth in your romantic literature. Your poetry. Men are basically animals. They are different from women, they'll sleep with any woman who offers, while a woman has to work very hard to keep a man in her home."

"Laura, you're just cynical because of Otto. Not all men are that way."

"*Every* man is that way. Every man, Daphne."

The two women stared at each other. Then Laura said it.

"I could make your Joe sleep with me, you know. I could. I could get any man to sleep with me."

Daphne felt chilled and shivery and sick.

"That doesn't mean marry. That doesn't mean love. That just means have sex. Men are promiscuous. We are all only pretending otherwise for the sake of civilization. Oh, look at your face, you look like a child and I've just stepped on your dolly. Sometimes you are just a baby."

"Well, you make me very sad. I'm very sad for you. If that's how you feel."

"Don't be so superior."

"I'm not! I don't mean to be. Laura, truly I

am sorry for you. That you don't think men can be faithful. That you can't just enjoy sex — "

"And you can. Enjoy sex. You are the great sex queen."

"I didn't say that! What's gotten into you?" Daphne felt the night and the conversation and her friendship with Laura slipping away past her control or imagination.

She rose from the table. "I think I see a light in the backyard in one of the paper sacks. I'm going to go out and check it. I want to be sure I've extinguished all the candles. I'll be right back."

It was after midnight, but the early-summer night was bright with stars and moonlight. The air was fragrant and warm and slightly humming with insect noises and small animal rustlings. She had kicked off her high heels and walked through the grass, which was dewy now against her feet. No candle was burning; she knew that. She had only needed to get away for a moment, to think. But in case Laura was watching, she walked to the end of the yard and bent over a paper bag and looked in. She took a deep breath of the clean night air, then turned to go back to the house.

Halfway to the house, she saw Laura coming down the lawn toward her. Laura had not kicked her heels off and she seemed very tall and as thin as a taper. Behind her, the kitchen glowed with light, so that Laura's face was shadowed and unreadable. To Daphne's surprise, she came right up to Daphne and drew her against her, folding her in an embrace.

Holding Daphne against her, she said, "I have made you angry, and I never want to do that. You are my best friend. I need you." Laura was crying now. She leaned against Daphne, her arms wrapped around her, and her words came like puffs of breath against Daphne's temple. "I'm sorry if I offended you. You must not hate me. Don't hate me. I love you so much, Daphne."

"I don't hate you, Laura," Daphne said. "I love you too."

"Oh, Daphne," Laura said, and kissed Daphne firmly on the mouth.

Shocked, Daphne drew back, pushing herself away from Laura.

"Oh, God, I'm so drunk," Laura said. "I must go home. I am so drunk." She began to walk up the lawn toward the side of the house, headed toward the front, where her car was parked.

"You shouldn't drive, Laura," Daphne said. "Not drunk."

"You're right," Laura said, and, veering off, made it to the long lawn chaise. She collapsed onto the striped crisscross of fabric.

"I'll spend the night here."

"You can't! You can't sleep out here!"

"Why not? It's a warm night. This is comfortable. My mother-in-law will take care of Hanno. Daphne, I have a headache. I want just to go to sleep. Go away."

Laura turned on her side and raised her arm to cover her face. Daphne stared at her. Somehow it seemed so . . . disreputable for Laura to sleep the night outside on a lawn chair. But she went into the house and found a light summer blanket. By the time she got back, Laura was asleep, or seemed to be, so Daphne wrapped the blanket around Laura, being sure to tuck the bottom under the cushions so it wouldn't fall off in the night. Alcohol seemed to be steaming from Laura's breath and every pore, mingling with the night's fragrances.

Daphne went inside to her bedroom, to the bed made warm by Joe.

When Daphne awoke at eight the next morning, she looked out the windows and found that Laura and her car were gone. She fixed two huge mugs of coffee and brought them back to bed.

Daphne told Joe about the conversation with Laura — omitting a few things: not telling him that Laura said she could get Joe to sleep with her; not telling him how Laura had kissed her. She must have been so very drunk.

"Isn't it sad, isn't it surprising, Laura not liking sex, not being able to have orgasms," Daphne said. "I mean, to look at her, you would think — "

Joe shifted uncomfortably next to her. "Really, do you think you should be telling me all this? Surely she meant this to be confidential."

"Joe, she must know I tell you everything! Wives do that, they tell their husbands everything."

"Still . . . " Joe said.

"But *really*," Daphne pressed on. "Don't you think it's just amazing that Laura is that way about sex? I mean, Joe, looking at her, at the way she moves and talks and touches people, you'd think she just loved sex, wouldn't you?" She waited for Joe to answer. He grunted noncommittally. "I don't know," Daphne went on, musing aloud, "you just never know about people, do you? You never know what's really hiding under the surface. I mean, Laura is my closest friend and we've talked about everything, I thought I knew everything about her — and now look." She turned toward Joe. "I don't know what to do to help her."

"I don't think there is anything you can do."

"Oh, there must be. Think how lonely she is. And I can't help but think that it was marriage to that horrible Otto that made her think she doesn't like sex. Anyone married to Otto would hate sex and men. Poor Laura."

"What are you going to worry about when Laura's happy?" Joe asked, laughing, pulling Daphne close to him. "Listen, if I could get you to forget her and remember me for a while, perhaps we could take advantage of Cynthia sleeping late . . . "

"Oh, Joe," Daphne said, and put down her mug and wrapped herself around him. He was so very much *there* — all masculine and muscular and physical — and she quickly forgot anything else.

Summer brought several changes. Otto and Sonya went back to Germany for the three months of school vacation, and Mrs. Kraft, resigning herself to the divorce, went with them. Laura, suddenly so alone, and realizing that at the end of the summer she would be legally divorced and Otto and Sonya would be married, went into a deeper depression. She seemed unable to take control of her life, to make even minor decisions. She spent more and more time at Daphne's house. Sometimes she even sat there with Hanno, watching TV. Often she stayed for dinner, helping Daphne cook it or clean up after. Those evenings, Joe would retire to his study as soon as possible.

But the more unexpected change came from a phone call for Daphne: the head of the English department at a nearby community college said that they were looking for a temporary part-time freshman-English instructor for the fall, and Pauline White had recommended Daphne: would she be interested? She was ecstatic. She accepted the job. Joe was happy for her, for he knew it was what Daphne wanted, and they could use the extra money.

But "How can you leave your little baby?" Laura demanded. She was strangely angry with Daphne. "What kind of mother are you?"

"Laura, Cynthia is a year old now. I've been with her constantly for a year. I'll teach only two mornings a week. It's not going to harm her for life to be with a baby-sitter. Don't be crazy. Oh, I can't wait, I love teaching so."

After the phone call, Laura began to take care of Cynthia for an hour or two in the mornings or afternoons while Daphne dug out old textbooks and lesson plans. The women didn't plan it that way; it just fell naturally into place, since Laura and Hanno came over almost every day to lounge around with Daphne and Cynthia. Daphne bought a large blue plastic wading pool to put in the backyard, and while she worked inside at the dining-room table, Laura would sit in a bikini, drinking iced tea, watching her son play in the water, or helping little Cynthia toddle and crawl in the pool. Daphne would lift her head from a passage in an essay, and hear the shrieks of children's laughter, and Laura's low laugh, and think how happy she was.

At the end of the summer, Laura said to Daphne one afternoon: "I think you should hire *me* to baby-sit Cynthia when you teach."

Daphne was sipping some iced tea, and she kept her head lowered so that Laura wouldn't see her face. What was she to do? She wanted to put Cynthia with a sitter who had other babies Cynthia's age. But she didn't want to hurt Laura's feelings.

"But Hanno will be in kindergarten," she said. "You don't want to waste your time baby-sitting."

"I never think of baby-sitting as wasting my time!" Laura said. "That's the most important work in the world, caring for little ones."

"But, Laura, I mean, you should get a real job. One where you could make a decent amount of money."

"I am getting quite a decent amount of money in the divorce settlement," Laura said. "Otto is being very generous with child support too. And I will own the house clear and free. What do I want with more money?"

Daphne gave in. That evening, when she talked it over with Joe, he seemed uninterested — whatever Daphne wanted to do was fine. So the fall began, and Laura came to the Millers' house two mornings a week and Daphne went off to the community college to teach. Daphne would return home to find Cynthia in clean clothes and giggles, the house immaculate, and a freshly baked cake or bread sitting on the kitchen counter.

"Don't complain," Joe said one evening as they finished one of Laura's cakes late at night, when Laura had gone home. "This is the best thing I've ever eaten. If it makes her happy — "

"I feel like I'm exploiting her somehow."

"You're only letting her do what she wants. She volunteers all this. You didn't ask her to cook. You didn't even ask her to baby-sit."

"But, Joe, somehow it just seems wrong. It seems as if . . . oh, I don't know, as if she's demeaning herself. My best friend, cleaning our toilet. Don't you see?"

"Your feminism is running away with you,"

Joe said. "Stop a minute and remember all Laura has said. She really likes housework and cooking. Not every woman finds housekeeping demeaning."

"Well, *you* wouldn't want to spend every day of your life at it," Daphne said.

Joe just looked at Daphne and sighed, letting his expression carry the message that she was now going past the rational in her thinking.

So the semester unrolled. Joe taught, Daphne took care of Cynthia and taught, Cynthia grew and blossomed into a strong-willed and active little girl. Laura and Hanno spent Christmas with the Millers. Then Daphne took Cynthia down to Florida, where her widowed mother had retired. She returned after two weeks to find that the college wanted her to teach again, two courses, and Laura said she wanted to continue baby-sitting Cynthia. Much of Daphne's energy went into the teaching, but underneath the steady pattern of her days ran an electric current of tension. She could not feel comfortable with all that Laura was doing. It just seemed wrong. She wanted more for her friend's life than baby-sitting and housecleaning.

In May Pauline and Douglas gave an enormous cocktail party. Daphne spent hours cajoling Laura into going and then planning with her what to wear. She had more fun getting ready for the party with Laura than with Joe, because Joe had been grouchy recently, one of the results of a large and painful hemorrhoid. After the doctor assured him it was not dangerous, he would not die of it, Daphne stopped worrying and found it secretly amusing. All the fuss he'd made over getting her hemorrhoid medicine after Cynthia was born! He deserved to suffer the same ailment, really he did. She tried to tease him about it, but he got angry.

"It's painful, dammit!" he said. "It's nothing to laugh about!"

"Joe, sometimes you are such a *priss!*" Daphne said in return.

Joe had to drink a thick and slightly sickening fiber drink at night, and the doctor gave him a special cream to apply to the hemorrhoid twice daily. Joe was afraid the medicine would stain or smell. The hemorrhoid was so large that the doctor wanted to ligate it in the office, but Joe became ill at the thought. The entire episode embarrassed him horribly.

"You should be a woman for just one day," Daphne said. "God, how I would love it. I'd love it if you were a woman for just one day — after having a baby, or when you're having the first few days of your period. Talk about mess! And staining! And smells!"

378

"For Christ's sake, Daphne, must you carry on like this?" Joe asked, stomping off into the bathroom for privacy.

He didn't want to go to the Whites' party because he felt so awful. "Oh, no," Daphne pleaded. "Please, Joe, I can't go without you and I really want to go!" He finally agreed, as long as she would agree to leave when he got too uncomfortable. But it was a smashing party with lots of guests and food and booze, and before long Joe, like the others, was laughing and talking.

Daphne had been having a good chat with Pauline but she kept her eye on Laura as she talked, to see if Laura was hitting it off with any of the men. Otto and Sonya fortunately had not been invited, but several attractive single men had.

When Pauline went off to check on the caterers, Daphne went searching for Laura. Laura seemed to be on her way outside toward Joe, no doubt looking for Daphne.

This is ridiculous — Laura shouldn't spend all her time with Joe and me just because she feels safe, Daphne thought. I must get her to mingle. She relies on us too much.

The backyard and patio were not lighted, because the evening was so chilly that Pauline thought everyone would want to stay inside. But several couples and groups were standing around in the dark, talking in low voices or smoking. Joe was leaning against the side of the house, looking out at the dark garden, drink in hand.

Laura, her wineglass in her left hand, approached Joe and slowly slid her right hand around Joe's waist, up under his shirt.

"Hello, Asshole," Laura said, laughing her low luxurious laugh.

"Christ, Laura, not here!" Joe said. He put his arm around her shoulder and steered her around the corner of the house, out of Daphne's sight.

It was as if she had been struck by lightning. Daphne stood unmoving, both hands pressing against her belly, where the bolt of knowledge had speared in with its electric shock. She had dropped her drink, but the glass had landed on the grass at her feet and did not break.

There had been moments like this before, moments when she knew that from this point on her life would be completely changed. Horrible moments: when her father told his family he was dying of cancer. Miraculous moments: Cynthia's birth. It was as if the physical absorbed the knowledge before the understanding could take it all in, and one was left with a numbed mind and a rubbery body, poor flash-struck thing, containing the jagged terror.

Was it possible that she had told Laura about Joe's hemorrhoid? But, no. Never. Joe was such a privacy maniac that he would have been furious if Daphne had told anyone. Well, then, could Joe have told Laura, casually? He had scarcely been able to talk to the doctor about it; he couldn't have told Laura unless they were intimate.

"Beautiful evening, isn't it?" Hudson Jennings was standing next to her.

Daphne looked up at the tall, slender, elegant man with his beautiful brown long-lashed eyes. She must be giving off vibrations, fumes, sparks, she was so radically hit. Didn't he notice anything?

"Yes," she managed to say. "Beautiful evening."

"But still a little chilly to be outside. How do you like teaching at the community college?"

Hudson was always so kind. "I like it very much." What would *Hudson* think if she told him she was standing here in agony because she had just discovered her husband was having an affair with Laura because Laura had called Joe "Asshole"? She would have to explain it all, Joe's hemorrhoid, his mania for privacy. A great bubble of hysteria welled up

381

inside her. "Excuse me, Hudson, I think I'm going to be sick."

She escaped from him and rushed into the house and to the downstairs guest bathroom in time to vomit out her drinks and food, but not, she realized, as she lay gasping against the door, not the terror and the grief that now spread through her body.

"Daphne?" Joe was knocking on the door. "Are you all right? Hudson said you were sick."

Daphne crawled to her feet and opened the door. There he stood, her husband, looking so innocent, slightly worried, slightly annoyed.

"Yes," she said. "I'm sick. Please take me home."

Joe reached out his hand to support her, but she shook it off and hurried on ahead of him. They went out the back door and around the side of the house, so that they would not have to explain their departure to everyone. As soon as they were in the car, Daphne said, "You are having an affair with Laura."

Joe looked over at her, then back at the road. "Where did you get that idea?"

"Asshole," Daphne said.

"What?" Now he was startled.

"She called you Asshole. In such an endearing tone of voice."

"Christ, Daphne, and because of that you think we're having an affair?" Joe exhaled angrily. "Look. I was home once, when you were teaching. I had to come home to get some papers, and I was feeling terrible, and she was baby-sitting Cynthia and she asked how I was and I told her. That's all. That's hardly having an affair."

"Joe, don't lie to me," Daphne said. "I'm not a fool." When he said nothing, she went on. "I heard her tone of voice, Joe. I saw the way you touched her. And I know you. I know you wouldn't tell her about your hemorrhoid unless it was because you couldn't make love. Just as it kept you from making love to me." Saying those things made them more vivid, and she cried out, "Oh, God!" and began to weep. "How could you, Joe, how could you?"

"Daphne, get hold of yourself. You're imagining things. You're imagining all of this," Joe said. "Now, look, we're home. Dry your face. You don't want the baby-sitter to see."

For a few moments Daphne was able to pretend normalcy in front of the sitter, but the moment Joe went out the door to drive the girl home, she flew, frenzied, into Joe's study and began tearing through his drawers. She was looking for love letters, for signs of Joe's affair with Laura. She pawed through files and letters and term papers, sobbing again, and did not know Joe was back until she saw him standing in the door.

"Jesus Christ, Daphne, have you gone mad?" His face was livid.

"Tell me the truth!" Daphne screamed. "For God's sake, just tell me the truth! I can go on after I know, but I have to know the truth."

"I've told you the truth, Daphne. You're being ridiculous," Joe said, and turned and walked away.

If he had crossed the room and embraced her, saying softly, lovingly, "Daphne, how could you even think this? You know how I love you," perhaps she would have calmed down and believed him. Instead, she stood, shaking, listening to her husband go up the stairs. Joe had seen that she was in pain and had walked away. No longer her chivalrous knight.

Was she crazy? Was she imagining all this? She felt like a top spinning out of control, ready to topple and smash onto its side.

She raced up the stairs. Cynthia was sleeping calmly, and Daphne did not linger there. She was afraid her horror and anger would poison the air of the baby's room. She went into the bedroom and stood looking down at

Joe. He had undressed and was now on his side of the bed, turned away from her side. He was either asleep or feigning sleep, his breath low and steady. How could he fall asleep now? If he had wrapped his arms around her, if he had cajoled and comforted her, telling her he loved her alone in all the world, what would have happened then? And why hadn't he done that, why had he responded with such cool anger? God, she hated him! — and yet she loved him, he was her husband, her lover, her life, and she knew she would not be able to come into this bed of theirs, this marriage bed, again, until she knew the truth.

Grabbing up her car keys, she raced downstairs and out into the night. It was only a few minutes' drive to Laura's. Daphne drove, not seeing the headlights on the dark road but Laura's hand on Joe's waist. At Laura's house, she pounded wildly on the front door, hoping Laura was home from the party.

Laura peeked through the curtains to see who it was, then opened the door. She was wrapped in a light blue robe, and had creamed all the makeup off her face so that she looked bleached and shadowed under the overhead hall light.

"Daphne? What's wrong?"

Daphne pushed her way into the house.

"You are having an affair with Joe," she said.

Laura pushed her hair away from her eyes. "So," she said. "He told you."

Now what had been suspicion was certainty, and Daphne thought she would die of the pain on the spot. Of course she didn't die; she stood there for a moment, looking idiotic, not capable of speech.

"He told me he didn't want you to know. I wonder why he told you. Look, come in, let's sit down and have some brandy."

"How long?" Daphne said, standing in the hallway, her hand clenching spasmodically around her car keys.

"What?"

"How long have you been lovers?"

"Since Christmas. When you went to your mother's with Cynthia. I invited him to dinner. You knew he came to dinner . . . "

Daphne remembered. Joe had called to tell her he missed her and Cynthia, and had said he was going to dinner at Laura's that night, and Daphne had said, "Oh, poor darling." She knew he didn't care for Laura. "At least you'll get a good meal," she had said.

" . . . and things just happened. Please. Don't look like that. Come have some — "

Laura reached her hand out to take Daphne by the arm, but Daphne backed away from the other woman with a violent repulsed move.

"You incredible horrible pathetic repugnant *bitch*," Daphne said.

She went out of the house then, not bothering to shut the door, got in her car, and drove back home.

Joe seemed to be still asleep. She turned on the lights, bent over him, and shook him awake.

"Wake up," she said. "We have to talk. Now."

"Jesus, Daphne, it's one in the morning."

"I've been to Laura's. She told me the truth. You and she have been lovers since Christmas."

"Goddammit," Joe said. He pushed himself up to sit on the side of the bed and buried his head in his hands, his elbows on his knees. "I'm sorry," he said, his voice muffled. "You weren't supposed to know yet. I'm sorry."

"Joe, how could you? Oh, Joe," Daphne said, and the tears began to come. "I thought you loved me."

"I do love you, Daphne. But I love Laura too. And . . . she needs me."

"Why? Why does she need *you?* She was my best friend. Why couldn't she have an affair with someone else?"

Joe looked up at Daphne, then down again. His voice was very low. "Because she's in love with me, Daphne. She's been in love with me for a long time. She's not a frivolous woman, she's not promiscuous, she couldn't help how she felt. She didn't want to do this. But you can't help whom you fall in love with."

Daphne backed off a few steps, as if she had just encountered something diseased or hideous. How smugly — oh, yes, smugly! — Daphne had passed Laura's confidences along to Joe, as Laura all along intended her to do.

"Oh, God, I see it all now," Daphne said. "Laura has orgasms with you, doesn't she?"

"Daphne, don't be so crude."

"Answer me! Doesn't she! She has with you what she's never had with any man before, what no other man has ever been able to give her. Right? Am I right?"

Joe lifted his head. He was fighting a smile. "As it happens," he said, "since you insist on knowing, you're right."

"Oh, Joe, you *fool*. You pitiful fool with your masculine vanity. Don't you see what a sucker you are? What a sucker I've been? Jesus, God, Joe, Laura has been playing us as if we were marionettes!"

"Daphne —"

"Joe, Laura's lying. She's desperate, she's cunning."

"I know when a woman has an orgasm," Joe said. "I think you would credit me with that much by now. I know when a woman loves me."

The pain was so wrenching that it made Daphne bend double. For a few moments she could only stand, arms pressed against her stomach, huddled over herself, and she could not prevent the moans that came, in all their bestiality, from her throat.

"Daphne — " Joe said, his voice harsh.

She moved away. She knew she was not a pretty sight. The injured one is never a pretty sight. Still, she could not stop herself from crying out, because he was her husband.

"You'd better calm down or you'll wake the baby," Joe said.

His coolness made her angry, and that helped. Daphne crossed the room and sat in a chair, blowing her nose in a tissue while Joe, who slept naked, rose and put on a T-shirt and a pair of jeans.

"Do you love her?" Daphne hated the way her chin was quivering. Couldn't she at least keep some dignity through all this?

"Yes." Joe sighed. He ran his hand through his hair. He looked away, and then he looked right at Daphne. "Yes. I'm sorry, Daphne. I don't know what happened. I love you too, still, but in such a different way. Laura needs me, while you . . . Christ, Daphne, you didn't even suspect until tonight! I've even thought maybe it has helped you out in a way. You're always so busy with the baby and your teaching. But Laura has time to listen to me. And she really listens. You always . . . because you work in the same field, you always seem to think you have to give an opinion or even argue with me. Besides, Laura loves cooking and keeping a house, and you hate all that stuff — "

"You're going to marry her!" Daphne cried.

"Christ, Daphne. Let's not get into that now," Joe said miserably.

"No, Joe, let's do get into it. I need to know. You've got to tell me. Are you going to marry her? Are you really going to leave me and Cynthia and marry Laura?"

Joe looked at Daphne. He said, "I'm sorry."

Daphne's last mainstays of dignity were swept away by a flood of grief. She bent her head into her hands. While she cried, Joe quietly, in his deliberate, unhurried way, packed a suitcase.

"I'll come back for the rest tomorrow," he said finally.

All Daphne had left now was fury. "Don't," she said. She stood up, letting her anger blaze. "By tomorrow the rest of your things will be dumped on the front lawn."

"Daphne — " Joe began.

But she interrupted him. "I hate you," she said. "I hate you, and I hate Laura. Laura is a slut. She is a shark, and you are a sucker. God, Joe, you've really been taken! I'm so embarrassed for you!"

"Don't be," Joe said. He turned his back on her, left the bedroom, and went down the stairs.

Daphne stood at the head of the stairs looking down. "I will never forgive you!" she called. "I wish you nothing but evil! I hope your hemorrhoid is really cancer. I hope Laura gets breast cancer and dies. I hope — "

But the front door was shut on her words, which were only air, and Daphne was left to face the rest of her life.

10

Daphne left work to go home early. After all, it was Christmas holiday for the college, and although she and the other secretaries dutifully showed up as they were supposed to, not much needed doing. The wild scramble had been in the weeks just before Christmas, when several professors were desperate to get their papers ready for the conference on American history being held in San Francisco the last week in December. The new wild scramble wouldn't start for another week, when the college opened for its month-long winter term and then again when second semester started at the beginning of February.

It was too bad she had had to come in today. She had hated leaving Cynthia alone. Cynthia would be leaving the third of January to go back to high school — and her father. Daphne would not see her again until . . . When? No one could say. Cynthia would leave for Europe at the beginning of the summer with Joe and Laura, and they would tour the Continent, and finally settle in London, where Joe had a visiting professorship and Cynthia would try to get into an acting school.

To make it as an actress, one had to start as young as possible; of course, London was the place for her, not this idle backwoods burg. Daphne understood all that. Besides, what a wonderful adventure for a young girl, a summer in Europe! And of course Laura, who spoke fluent French as well as German, and had friends and relatives everywhere, would provide deeper and more meaningful experiences than any ordinary tour.

Who would not want such things for her child?

At the base of the Vermont hill, where the paved road became dirt, Daphne pulled to the side and let the old Jeep idle. She leaned her forehead down onto the steering wheel. Would she ever in her life be free of pain? She was the Seven Sins Incarnate. Pride, Envy, Covetousness, Gluttony, Wrath — Wrath, Wrath. . . . Her mother's words echoed in her mind: "Anger hurts you more than the person you're angry at; it eats away at you and makes you bitter and mean, while the person you're angry at lives most of his life unaware of that passion." Yes, Daphne thought as the snake of bitterness flicked away inside. Her mother had been right. Joe, Laura, they could not be touched by her anger now, not in any way at all. They never could be. They had the power to hurt Daphne, through Cynthia, but although they were guilty, they were also free, unpunished, untouched. Right now they were in Idaho, spending their Christmas vacation skiing — oh, where was the justice in that? Where was the justice in anything? How could it be that Joe, who had given nothing to Cynthia for the first sixteen years of her life but the basic child support the courts ruled necessary, who had not remembered his daughter at Christmas or on her birthday, who had not written letters to her or telephoned her or visited her on his trips back east — how was it that he, with a snap of his fingers, a flick of his whim, could summon his daughter into his life? How could Cynthia have gone? Daphne understood it from an intellectual point of view — Cynthia's need to know that her father loved her; her hope of being "discovered" if she lived on the West Coast; her desire to get out of the overly proper, stifling atmosphere of the small New England college town — yet Daphne would never understand in all her life how Cynthia could have left her, left *her*. She hated her daughter for her easy desertion. She loved Cynthia, and wanted her happiness, but still,

394

there was that hate, born of betrayal.

Daphne lifted her head. All around her the countryside was deep in snow. The trees that lined the road dipped beneath the weight of snow that glossed their branches. It was not five yet, but the sun was almost gone and shadows laced the ground into a latticework of gray on white. No birds sang, but tiny rabbit tracks crisscrossed everywhere, and suddenly Daphne envisioned an entire colony of rabbits, white rabbits with pink noses and ears lined as if in pink silk, dancing in the snow, weaving in and out of the shadows, "Keeping time, Keeping the rhythm in their dancing, As in their living in the living seasons . . . "

She was going mad. But there was something about rabbits that suggested family, and home and hearth and familial love. Peter Rabbit, and then the book by Margaret Wise Brown, *The Runaway Bunny,* in which the baby bunny says he'll run away and the mother bunny tells the baby she will always find him and bring him back. The mother hopes to keep her child safe no matter how far he ventures into the world. This seemed to Daphne the truest book ever written. Cynthia had loved the book as a child. But of course Cynthia was not a child anymore. As Pauline had said, sooner or later all children left their parents. It was just that for Daphne it had happened sooner. And mother love might feel bigger than the world, but in truth it was never as strong.

Daphne put the Jeep in gear and started home. Always before she had thought of herself as a survivor, as a triumphant person, no matter what life threw her way. Even buying her tiny ramshackle cottage had been an act of courage and of spunk, she thought, but lately she had lost her energy. There were times, Daphne thought, when Life ought to *give* you something. When there ought to be *something given,* unexpected, free of charge, a gift not even thought of or wished for, a surprise. Now she couldn't think what it would be for her, but still she wished it would happen. It was what she needed. She was working as hard as she could to make her life come out all right, but now it was time for Life to make a contribution. For it couldn't be possible that, now that she was so old, forty-six, Life would do nothing but just take and take away?

The Jeep rattled and crashed down the lane, destroying the rural peace. Daphne parked and went into her house. Cynthia was lying on her stomach on the living-room floor, surrounded by photo albums.

"Hi, Mom, how are you, God, you should look at these!" Cynthia said, smiling up at Daphne.

Daphne hung her coat on the rack near the door, and pulling her red cardigan around her for warmth, sat down next to her daughter. "Listen," she said, "a bunch of us are going into Greenfield to see that new slasher movie. And we're going to a Chinese restaurant first. Want to come with us?"

"Oh, Mom, I can't. I told you. I want to spend the night at Donna's. She's expecting me anytime. Can you drive me down?"

Daphne ran her hand through her thick hair. "Oh, Jack is going to take me to Greenfield so I don't have to take the old clunker. But we can drop you on the way." She looked at her watch. "He should be here any minute."

She started to get up, but Cynthia said, "Wait a minute. I really want you to look at these. I've made a collage. I'm going to take it back with me."

First Daphne saw only that the photo albums had been ransacked and rifled. Here and there pages had been stripped bare. She started to protest, then saw what Cynthia had done. On a large piece of construction paper she had attached pictures of almost every birthday cake she'd ever had. There was the famous Doll Cake: a Barbie doll in the center, the cake the doll's tiered dress, covered with pink ruffles of icing. The famous Train Cake, when Cynthia had insisted on having ten friends to her party, and Daphne in a fit of creativity had taken small bread-loaf pans and made eleven little chocolate cakes, iced them, laid them on a track of red licorice, and given each boxcar its own special load of candy: root-beer logs, M&Ms, jujubes, jelly beans, chocolate balls. The wheels were Oreo cookies and the steam from the engine was made of marshmallows stuck together with colored toothpicks. All the children had gone crazy on seeing it. What a work of art it had been. And there were the horse cake, the flower cake, the balloon cake.

"These are all just so fabulous, Mom! You were so clever!"

"I know," Daphne agreed. "They were wonderful. I always thought that if you ever went to a psychiatrist and said I had never loved you, I could take him the photographs of all these cakes to prove otherwise."

"Oh, Mom," Cynthia said impatiently, "I'd never think you didn't love me. God." With one quick fluid motion she pushed herself up off the floor. "I've got to get my overnight stuff packed." She went out of the room.

Daphne sat looking at the mess on the floor, photo albums and magazines and nail polish and tissue boxes opened and piled every which way, a Diet Pepsi bottle under the coffee table, an apple core on the rug. She started to call Cynthia back, then thought: No. It wouldn't take long to clean it up tonight, and why risk a confrontation when Cynthia was going to be here only a few more days?

She went into her bedroom and lay on the bed a moment, just resting. She was tired so often these days. She supposed she should change, but her gray flannels, white shirt, and red cardigan were so warm and cozy, and what would she change into anyway? It was a casual night, she didn't have a date, they were all just going to a Chinese restaurant, which wasn't formal at all, and a slasher movie. Oh, this is the way to become an old lady with ringworm curls and dried food on your bodice, she told herself, and heaved herself up. She put on a long, oversize, stylish black sweatshirt-dress and her high gray suede boots. No jewelry except for dangling gold earrings.

"Oh, wow, dude, sexy!" Cynthia said from the doorway. She came into the room, walked around Daphne, scrutinizing her. "You know, you don't look thirty-two. All my friends say they can't believe you're thirty-two. Are you really that old?"

Cynthia's affectionate teasing pleased Daphne. She put out her arms and drew her daughter next to her. Side by side, they stood looking at themselves in the full-length mirror on Daphne's closet door, the black-haired mother, the honey-haired child.

"What can I say?" Daphne said. "We two Miller broads are lookin' pretty good these days."

Cynthia snaked her arm around her mother's waist and pulled her closer. "It's true," she said. "We're a pair of jewels."

This time Jack got Carey Ann on the phone.

"Hi, sweetie pie," she said, her voice little-girlish and light. "How are you?"

"All right, I guess. How are you?"

"Oh, Jack, I'm just having the time of my life! So's Lexi! Everyone just adores her. All my friends say she's just the prettiest baby they've ever seen, and everyone wants to run out *right now* and get pregnant! Everyone says if there are a lot of little baby bastards in Kansas City in nine months it's going to be all my fault! And, Jack, Daddy and Mommy gave me so many fab presents for Christmas! Jack, Daddy gave me a white fox coat! Jack, wait till you see me in it, I look so beautiful you'll just drool! 'Course they have loads of presents for me to bring back to you too, honey."

"Well," Jack said, trying to get some enthusiasm into his voice, "that's very nice of them. What are you doing tonight?"

"Oh, just the greatest thing! A whole bunch of us are going out to the club for dinner. Beulah and Mommy and Daddy will take care of Alexandra, of course. She's having so much fun she won't even know I'm gone. I'm afraid she's getting dreadfully spoiled here."

"Who all's going to the club?"

"Oh, you know, Sharon and Trish and Christie and Pattie, even though I don't really like Pattie, I never did, you know, but she's still part of the group, and some of their boyfriends, and, Jack, some of my old beaux will be there too, but promise me you won't be jealous — I mean, you know I won't flirt with them or anything. They're all fellows I've known forever, and I just want to hear about what they've been doing with their lives and what's going on. There will just be a pile of us out at the club."

Jack was silent. "The club" sprang up before his eyes — he had been there many times, and he knew the private banquet room the group would probably be given. There would be one long table, or two, if there were enough people, and the room was done in a glittering art-deco style that made you feel slightly time-warped and disoriented, free of responsibility, as if anything you did in that room had no connection with real life, as if once you walked out of that room, everything you had done there vanished from all memory. He bet the waiters there had seen some sights. Instead of candles on the table there were small lamps, the bases metal statues of naked ladies or naked men, their arms raised to hold up the light, with the shades in stained-glass patterns of grapes and leaves and flowers that threw crazy-quilt shadows on the tablecloth. Similar lamps hung against the walls, with fringed shades hanging down. The chairs were a decadent tarty red velvet on gilded wood, and the room was thick with Oriental carpets. The waiters, their long hair slicked straight back and greased down, wearing tuxes, all handsome and probably gay, stood at the doors with their hands crossed at crotch level, white towels hanging from their arms, always alert for an empty wineglass. It was at this club, in this room, that Jack had been served, for dessert, a concoction of chocolate and booze named "Satan's Breakfast." The club was about as midwestern-native as Al Capone.

"You'll probably be there all night," Jack said.

"Probably," Carey Ann agreed. "I just can't wait. It's going to be so much fun to see everybody together again. 'Course, I'll miss you, Jack, I wish you could be here too. But don't worry, I'll talk about you all the time. If you feel your ears burning tonight, you'll know why. Listen, sweetie, I really want to talk to you forever, but I've got to go get ready. I haven't showered or anything."

"All right," Jack said, not very graciously.

Carey Ann heard the tension in his voice. "What are you doing tonight, sweetie?" she asked.

At least she did that much, Jack thought. At least she had the sense to spend a little time paying attention to him, at least she had cared. He felt soothed. She did love him.

"A bunch of us are going down into Greenfield. To a Chinese restaurant and then to a slasher movie. *Lady-Killer*."

"Oooh," Carey Ann squealed. "I'm glad I'm not there! I hate that kind of movie. Imagine a bunch of college professors wanting to see a thing like that! Who all's going?"

"The Whites. The Johannsens. The Petries." Jack paused. "I'll probably drive Daphne down and back."

"Now I'm really glad I won't be there. That old Queen Hen," Carey Ann said. "Listen, Jack, I've really got to go."

A tornado of fury boiled and spun inside Jack: he was jealous of her with her old friends, why wasn't she jealous of him driving

403

around at night with Daphne?

"Can I speak to Alexandra?" he asked.

"Well . . . she's eating now." There was silence while Carey Ann put down the phone and wandered off. "Here she is," she said.

"Hi, Lexi!" Jack said.

Silence from the other end.

"Lexi, this is Daddy!" Jack said.

"It's Daddy!" Carey Ann whispered at the other end of the phone. "Say hi to Daddy, Lexi!" Then laughter, and Carey Ann's voice came on. "Jack, she's the cutest thing. When I said, 'It's Daddy,' Lexi took the receiver and looked into the little holes!" She went back to her daughter. "Lexi, say hi to Daddy."

"Hi, Daddy," Lexi said. Her voice sounded far away, and dubious.

"Hi, Lexi. I love you, honey." Jack felt as if he were calling out over the miles, trying to reach his small daughter with the drift of his voice. Over the phone the miles of air between them intersected and carried who he was away, he knew, before he could get to Lexi.

"Sorry, Jack, she ran off back to Beulah. Beulah was giving her cinnamon toast. You know it's hard for her to understand how the phone works. Don't worry, she won't forget you. We'll be back before you know it. I've got to go."

"Wait!" Jack said. He was angry, lonely,

404

desperate, he was spurned again by the two females he loved. He was so overwhelmed with emotions, but not one of them could he speak aloud now. If he said any of this to Carey Ann, she would laugh, or get mad and think he was trying to spoil her fun, or, worst of all, she would try to appease him in a voice that made it clear she thought he was being a real baby about all of this.

"Well, what?" Carey Ann was saying impatiently.

He couldn't think of anything to say: Do you miss me? Do you love me? Do you think of me when you go to bed at night? Are you glad you married me? Do you wish you were back in Kansas City for good with all those dumb hunks your father approves of?

"What are you wearing tonight?" he asked. Carey Ann always liked to talk about her clothes. This would keep her on the phone a little longer.

Carey Ann broke into peals of laughter. "Imagine you asking me that!" she said. "You never know what I'm wearing! You never know what I'm wearing when you're looking at me!"

"That's not true!" Jack protested.

"Oh, honey, yes it is. You just don't care about clothes, but that's all right. Anyway, I'm wearing a new dress tonight. You haven't seen it. An off-the-shoulder sequined, slinky sort of thing. A real drop-dead kind of dress, the kind I could certainly never wear at your old college 'functions.' Functions — don't you just love it? That's what I tell people here. Back east they don't have parties, they have functions. Honey, I just have to go now!"

"All right. Call me tomorrow, why don't you? I love you, Carey Ann."

"I love you too. You know I do! 'Bye, now!"

The receiver was buzzing in his ear before he had a chance to hang up. The buzzing seemed to be the sound of all those miles of space mushrooming like a black cloud, expanding the distance between him and his wife.

Jack and Daphne were at ease with each other at the beginning of the evening. At first, leaving Plover for the drive down into West-hampton, Cynthia had been in the car with them, so full of high spirits that she leaned over from the back seat, looking from one to the other so fast her flying beaded earrings nearly hit Daphne in the face, snapping her gum with exuberance, saying, it seemed to Daphne, "like," or "you know," or "excellent," with every breath. They dropped her at Donna's, and as Jack pulled away, the car filled with silence. Jack and Daphne looked at each other and burst out laughing.

"You wait!" Daphne said. "You just wait!"

And talking about children — Cynthia, Alexandra, and then their own childhoods — kept them occupied until they reached the Chinese restaurant, where the Whites and the others were waiting. Then they were engulfed in the general noise and gossip of academics on holiday.

The Chinese food was wonderful. In the way of good parties, everyone seemed terribly clever. But *Lady-Killer* was so trashy that after a whispered vote, which caused some of the others in the audience to yell, "Shut *up!*," the group of eight filed out of the theater to the cries of the third doomed woman in thirty minutes.

The group stood around in the lobby, a regular committee, incapable of decision, until Hank and Ellie Petrie announced that they were all going to a local bar where there was dancing on weekend nights. It was a good place, dark but clean, and slow old rock-'n'-roll favorites pulsed through the room hypnotically. Daphne and Jack danced, but only once, and the rest of the time they sat at opposite ends of the table, separated by all the others.

It was only at the end of the evening, in the

car on the way home, that a sense of awkward-
ness fell between them. Perhaps it was the
silence in the car after the noise of the bar; and
the air was so cold it seemed hostile after the
bar's smoky warmth. The moment she sat
down on the icy car seat, Daphne had the
strangest urge to slide across and snuggle
against Jack for warmth. It was just a quick
welling-up of animal need.

But of course she wouldn't do that. Daphne
could tell Jack was nervous now — she was
older than he was, and had been a divorced
woman long enough to notice the signs of a
nervous man. Jack kept fiddling with things,
the heat gauge, the radio, the back-window
defrost, and the bright lights: every now and
then he switched the wrong thing and the
windshield wipers, which were unnecessary,
came flashing across their vision. "Sorry!" he
said each time, almost yelling.

Oh, dear, Daphne thought, how am I going
to make him comfortable? The drive back to
Plover would take the better part of forty-five
minutes, and most of it along dark country
roads. The bright streetlights of Greenfield
were a help; it made them feel as if other people were still around, but once they hit the
long black stretch of Route 2, they were as
stranded with each other as two astronauts on
the moon. Or two teenagers on their first date.

Daphne had not forgotten his kiss during the fall. Well, how could she? It was the only real kiss she'd had in about two years. She said to herself: Jack is thirty-one. You are forty-six. You could truly be his mother. She said to herself: Jack is married. You know what you think of women who mess with married men.

Still. The mind by nature is made to fade when faced with the powers of the body, like the moon fading in the sky when the great sun rolls over the horizon. What has seemed rational and clear by silver light in a black sky suddenly is impossible even to find when the sun takes over so completely, blazing through the senses. This was what Daphne was feeling within her body now, a sunrise. Gently a heat came rolling up inside her body, spreading its rays to every part, so that her limbs and fingers and skin, which for a while had seemed numb to her, now tingled with life. Desire, quick and dense and pervasive, streaked through her abdomen and legs.

Men's bodies. Women could talk all they wanted about liberation, but they would never be free of the love of men's bodies, and no liberation could ever be as sweet as union with a man one loved. David had been older than Jack when he and Daphne became lovers, and although he played tennis and golf, he had developed an alcoholic softness around his chest and belly. Still, the hair on his chest and abdomen had pulled her gaze down his torso like a summons every time, another one of nature's tricks, pointing the way to that magical package between the legs. The vulnerable balls. The cunning penis, shaped like the arrow that pierces the heart. When David had been drinking a lot, he was impotent, and they came to accept this and not attempt anything. Then his penis would hang, a tough useless weed in his crotch. But when he hadn't been drinking, it swelled up like steel, and this was why Daphne loved David, why women loved men, because they were soft and hard at once, silk skin over brick muscles, rampant penis over fragile balls, rigid prick thick with cream.

Jack was so young. His body, she had noticed — she had thought of it often — was firm, from youth and from his running. His thighs were long and hard and hairy, bestial. His black hair, still thick, and his skin, still firm and taut, made Daphne remember young Joe, potent with youth. Even at his best, David had not come more than once a night, but when he had been in his twenties and early thirties, Joe had been able to rest and rise over and over again. Jack would be able to too. Daphne wondered about things:

was Jack's pubic hair wiry or straight and lank? His hair was dark, would his penis be purple or pink in tone? Men's penises were different in spite of what magazines said, or so Daphne had found in her brief experience. Jack was fairly short. Would his penis be?

"Would you like some music?" Jack asked, breaking into her thoughts.

"That would be nice," Daphne said, feeling her face go hot with guilt. How long had she been sitting there in silence, thinking of penises? Frantically she searched her mind for some topic of conversation that wouldn't seem artificial at this moment, but she could think of nothing. She felt like a teenager on a date, as paralyzed by sex as a cobra by a flute, waiting, waiting, hanging in the air.

The car lights flashed on the road signs welcoming them to the state of Vermont.

"I find I like living in Plover," Jack said. "I like leaving the college behind so completely, going into a different state in more meanings than one. Then, going up into a mountain, too, the wilderness, after all that civility, provides a great relief."

"I know," Daphne said, grateful for his easy tone. "You really feel that you're getting away from it all, going into another world."

And as they drove, the wilderness did enfold them, the wooden bridge thumping responsively under the car's wheels, the road becoming dirt, the trees and bushes closing in above and next to them, narrowing the road, stretching out to scrape the sides of the car, nature closing in.

Daphne had left a light burning in her cottage. Jack stopped the car next to her old Jeep, turned off the engine, and looked at her expectantly. She knew he wanted her to invite him in for a drink. She wanted to invite him in for a drink, and more.

"Thank you," she said politely. "For driving."

"Daphne," Jack said. His voice was hoarse. He reached his hand out and pulled her to him and kissed her on the lips. One hand he kept on the back of her head, holding her to him, the other hand he put on her neck, running his thumb under her chin.

Daphne shivered under his touch. He smelled new and clean, as fresh as washed cotton drying in the sun, and his kiss filled her body with light. She pushed him away.

"No."

"Let me come in. Let me spend the night with you."

"No. It would be wrong. You know it would be wrong."

"Please."

It was growing cold in the car. They could

scarcely see each other. But they could smell and hear each other, and it was like being drugged by the gods. Daphne's body turned toward Jack's as if he were the sun.

"Just come in for coffee, then."

"All right."

But once they were inside the house, enclosed in its warmth, Jack took Daphne in his arms and pulled her to him. He put his hands on her buttocks and pressed her hips against his. They were the same height and matched nicely all up and down. Jack was kissing Daphne, her mouth and eyes and neck, and nudging into her, and never in the world had she wanted anything more.

No. Several things in the world she had wanted more. Long ago, for example, she had wanted her husband not to be sleeping with her best friend.

"Jack," she said suddenly, shoving him away, backing off, closing her coat over her breasts and holding it there. "Stop a minute. Listen to me. We can't do this. We mustn't do this. You love Carey Ann. You can't do this to her. You can't do this to your marriage."

"I want you. I've wanted you for months."

"I want you too. But human beings can't go around just taking what they want. Listen, Jack, I've seen this movie before. I've been in this spot before — but on the other side, looking in. I've been where Carey Ann is, I've been a new wife with a little child, and my husband had an affair, and it ended our marriage, and it was awful, Jack. Jack, it was *evil*. And I can't be a person who does the same thing."

"Carey Ann wouldn't know. She probably wouldn't even care. She's so preoccupied with everything else. Everything else matters but me."

"Oh, I know that's what you think!" Daphne began to move across the room, further away from the pull of Jack's power. "But I know it's not true. You do matter to her. She would die if you had an affair. She's just so young, Jack, she's got to get herself organized, she's working on that. You have to stand by her. You can't go off screwing around whenever you feel ignored."

"I don't go off screwing around. I've never screwed around on her. Why are we talking about Carey Ann? I want you. I want to go to bed with *you*."

Oh, he does know how to say the right things, Daphne thought. How nice it was to hear that: Jack wanted to go to bed with *her*. She had imagined this, lying in her lonely bed on winter nights. She had imagined how it would be to have Jack, small, dark, intense, young, firm Jack lying on top of her, skin against skin, the feel of his muscles, and how he would sound, needing, and then being satisfied. She had imagined it all, and now she could have him, and she wanted him. Who, after all, would know? Who would care? No one at the college would suspect this — Daphne was so old, and a secretary. Gorgeous young Carey Ann would never think to wonder about her husband with Daphne — Daphne knew this, knew it every time she saw Carey Ann look her way. So it would be only she herself who would know, and couldn't she finally devise her own consequences?

Jack was walking closer to her now. He had unzipped his parka and she could see the hollow of his neck, she could almost feel the sexual burn of his late-night whiskers against her throat.

She moved back, away from his pull. She shook her head. She was afraid she was going to cry. Oh, God, she thought, don't let me be maudlin. If I'm not going to have any pleasure, let me at least have some dignity about this.

"Jack," she said again, holding both hands out as if warding off a monster. "Please don't come any closer. I want you to leave now. You know I'm attracted to you, but I just can't go to bed with you. You're married, and I can't go to bed with you. I can't do that to you."

"But what do you care about my marriage?" Jack said. He looked so puzzled. "You're not even Carey Ann's friend!"

"No. I'm not. But I'm your friend, Jack. I'm your good friend."

"I don't need you as a friend," Jack said angrily.

"Please. Go."

He stared at her. Then, looking bitter, he turned and stalked across the living room and went out the door, shutting it so hard it shook the little cottage. Daphne stood paralyzed, her back nearly against the wall, listening to the sounds of his car starting up and murmuring away through the snow-covered bushes.

Victory, said her mind, but her body said, *Defeat.* And her body would make her pay. She would not sleep tonight. Her house was as quiet and now seemed as cold as a block of ice. Nothing moved, no sounds, only her body desiring, and all that heated sunrise in her loins and limbs had vanished with Jack, leaving in its stead the touch of the grave, moonshadows, cemetery streaks slipping against her skin. Sex was life and heat; loneliness was this: invisible sleet sliding just under her clothes, chilling her to the bone.

Daphne sank down onto the floor and cried, doubled over, cramps in her abdomen, pain like thirst in her mouth and breasts. It had been two years since she had been with a man. Why was she doing this to herself? Where was the sense of it all?

Dickens, who had been watching quietly from in front of the cold fireplace, waddled over now and stood next to her, staring intently at her, slowly wagging his tail. He seemed to think that Daphne, bent over on the floor as she was, was playing some kind of game.

"Oh, Dickens!" Daphne wailed, and looked up at him with tears streaking down her face.

Dickens pushed his head forward to smell her breath, then sneezed, and went back to lie down in front of the fireplace. He was getting old, after all, and besides, he had seen this before. Not exactly this, but this much agony.

All the times Hudson had driven Daphne home, or stopped by for a drink, or come to help with something heavy, and stood talking in his gentle blink-eyed giraffe way, his need for Daphne steaming from him like a scent, filling her with equal need . . . and then Hudson would leave, and Daphne would sit on the sofa, clutching herself, like a diver who has started down into great depths, then been forced to surface too fast.

Yes. She had been here before. At least one gained this much with age and experience, one gained the memory of coping and thus knew the first steps to take in going on.

She would not sleep tonight, or not easily. She would be restless and unable to read, and — Daphne looked at her watch; it was only a little before midnight! — it was too late to call Pauline for a helpful talk. Not too late to call Jack, though, who, Daphne imagined, was at this moment fixing himself a strong drink. She would have to wrestle with herself as with a devil to keep from calling him or going there; he was so close, and no one would see.

A drink. A strong drink to numb. Music? No. Too sensual. TV? No, it would not be powerful enough tonight. Action: build a fire, find some mending, get out some knitting — now Daphne knew why women all over the world knit away like psychotics. If she had knit every time she yearned for a particular or general man's body, she could have knit a house by now. "Idle hands are the devil's playthings." Did she have that right? It sounded vaguely obscene.

Daphne went through the kitchen and shed and out the back door to the cold night to get some wood she had piled against the wall. She left the door open as she carried in three loads. The hell with her oil bill, she was such a wild and reckless thing. Finally slamming the door against the bitter night, she knelt at her fireplace and built an extravaganza of a blaze. Dickens jumped up at the "whoosh!" the fire made as it caught, then turned around several times and lay back down to sleep. Daphne made herself a big Scotch with ice and dug out her knitting — she was working on an afghan for the sofa. She'd be through with it in no time at all.

What if the phone rang? What if Jack came back and knocked on the door? As she settled down with her feet up on the sofa and the fire blazing, her imagination tugged at her senses. But she would resist even that, in case she weakened. Oh, how would she fight this desire?

Well, there was always memory.

Joe had thought Daphne was unreasonable to be so furious because he was leaving her for Laura. He *had* to do it — why wouldn't she understand?

Laura had been hurt that Daphne was so upset.

She had come over to Daphne's that first day, her eyes swollen with tears. Daphne didn't want to let her in the house, but Laura had Hanno by the hand, and Daphne had Cynthia on her shoulder and was afraid of frightening the children.

So the two mothers of small children, the two women Joe Miller was sleeping with, put

Hanno in front of the TV and Cynthia in her playpen. Then they went into the dining room and shut the door. This final deed they did with accord.

"What are you doing?" Laura had sobbed. "Joe came to my house last night. He says you are violently angry. I don't understand. How can you do this to me?"

"What am *I* doing?" Daphne had asked. She had had no love left in her for Laura. She wanted to kick her friend.

"You're ruining everything!" Laura had said. "How can you be so selfish? You of all people should understand. I am so lonely! You are my friend, you *love* me: Don't you want me to be happy? Why can't you let go of Joe nicely? You have Cynthia. You have your teaching. You love your teaching! You don't need Joe, and I do."

"You're crazy," Daphne had said. "You're a crazy, selfish bitch!"

"No, I'm not!" Laura had said. "I'm your friend —"

"Laura! You betrayed me. You manipulated me. You are taking my husband, my daughter's father. Don't you know I hate you? I hate you. I'll never forgive you!"

"I can't believe you're saying this things!" Laura had said, her English giving way under her emotion. "Why won't you listen to me?

Why won't you understand?"

"Laura, just get out. Get out or . . . I'll hit you. I swear to God I will."

"You'll calm down," Laura had said. "You will get over your anger. I know you will."

What still made Daphne angry, and always would, was how Laura saw herself as the injured party, because Daphne had not loved her enough to want her to have happiness with Joe. Even after all these years it was painful for Daphne to remember that spring, when she and Joe had met only for legal purposes, to sign divorce papers, to sign at the closing of the sale of their house. Joe married Laura as soon as the divorce was final, and they moved to California, where Joe took a job with a university. Daphne told the community college she wanted to teach full-time there, but their enrollment dropped that year and they said regretfully that they didn't know if they could offer her even a part-time job. When Fred Van Lieu offered her the job as secretary in the history department, she had taken it, glad for some way to make money, for some way to order her jagged life.

Her life was still jagged. She was still jagged, and torn.

What could make her whole? Could anything make her whole?

Not an affair with a young married man,

that much was certain.

In the middle of the night, in the midst of sipping Scotch and knitting, Daphne fell asleep. She awoke in the morning, her entire body aching from its cramped bed, and from cold, for the fire had gone out in the night and the first thing she saw when she opened her eyes was the ashy-gray hearth. The afghan she had been working on had slipped to the floor. Besides, it was far too small to cover her yet. She would need many more nights to knit. And she knew she would have them, these long nights alone.

Jack had been awakened this morning by a call from Carey Ann. The weather in Kansas City had taken an unseasonably mild turn, as it sometimes did in the Midwest, and today and tomorrow would be warm and sunny. She was going to leave Alexandra with her parents and Beulah and spend a few days at Christie's farm just outside Kansas City, riding her old horse, Jelly Roll, which she had sold to Christie when she married Jack. In order not to upset her parents, she had promised to extend her stay in Missouri by several days. Jack understood, didn't he? Oh, Carey Ann said, she was so happy to be back home.

"Home," Jack had said. Just that one word.

"What?" Carey Ann asked. She waited, letting the space between them flutter. Then, "Oh, Jack, come on, you're not sulking again, are you? Jack, look. Why do you get so upset when I say I love it here, around my friends and family and the places I'm familiar with? I love you too. I love you *best*. I'm coming back to you soon."

The same old argument. The same old thing. Jack was so angry at Daphne for not sleeping with him and so angry at himself for trying to get Daphne to sleep with him that he couldn't be very civil to Carey Ann. Which did make a kind of sense: if she hadn't left him, he wouldn't be wanting to sleep with Daphne. Here he was, teaching a specialty he didn't like in a department with a chairman he didn't like, and where was his loving supportive wife? Halfway across the continent.

Still, he didn't really want to be unfaithful to Carey Ann. He didn't want to hurt her. He just wanted . . . What? Some affection he wasn't getting. That was all. Something warm and embracing in this hard world.

"Have a good time, Carey Ann," he said, defeated, and hung up.

It was too cold to run outside today, and the dirt road was rutted and slick with ice. He'd run in the gym track, and then work like a fiend on his lesson plans for next semester's courses. Jack pulled on his jeans and a wool sweater, stuffed his running gear into a canvas bag and his papers into his briefcase and headed his car away from Plover. He felt both regret and relief as he drove down the mountain, farther and farther away from Daphne's home, as if he were leaving the scene of an almost-committed crime.

On his way to the college he stopped in the local bookstore to check on his textbook orders. He decided to buy himself a thick new novel to read that night, a treat for himself, whatever he wanted, but as he looked through the fiction section, he found himself growing crankier and sadder, as if the books exuded a poisonous gas. All these damned writers writing! Where did they get the time to write, the money to survive and support their families while they wrote? Half of them no doubt were gorgeous young women who slept with their writing instructors or editors or both, who had fathers or boyfriends to support them. But the other half, the men, how did they do it? There weren't enough hours in the day for Jack to do his courses well and spend some time with his family and still have the mental stamina to write a novel. Would there ever be a time when he could write? Standing in the sunny bookstore, Jack felt Time touch its icy skeletal finger to the back of his neck, a kind of gleeful poke. And he knew that years would go by, years and years and years, and he would be gray and withered and his thoughts would be gray and withered, before he would have time to write his novel.

He left the bookstore without buying anything. Cold air whacked him in the face and lungs; it was a hostile day, and he leaned forward against the wind, holding his muffler over his mouth, thinking of Carey Ann wearing a sweatshirt, riding her horse over the rolling Missouri hills.

Peabody Hall was warm and well-lit, and as he climbed the stairs to his cell, laughter and voices and the hum of machines drifted out to him. Once settled at his desk, he leafed through his books, comparing approaches for next semester. He stopped a while to take an ironic and sly pleasure from Lord Chesterfield's famous letter to his illegitimate son, Philip:

Women, then, are only children of a larger growth; they have an entertaining tattle, and sometimes wit; but for solid reasoning, good sense, I never knew in my life one that had it, or who reasoned or acted consequentially for four-and-twenty hours together. . . . A man of sense only trifles with them, plays with them, humors and flatters them, as he does with a sprightly, forward child; but he

425

neither consults them about, nor trusts them with, serious matters; though he often makes them believe that he does both. . . .

Right on, Chesty, Jack thought. *Women.* Then he went back to his saner self. This essay would provoke discussion; and then they could go back to Defoe's essay on the education of women, which was advanced and liberated for that day and age, and would make his class more tolerant of and disposed toward reading *Robinson Crusoe.*

Jack kept hard at work all day. Perhaps his anger and his frustration were fueling him, but ideas for his classes came fast and easily now, so that he scribbled and typed and forgot to eat lunch. When he finally leaned back in his chair and rubbed his neck, he saw that already the sun was setting in the sky — but they had just passed the winter solstice; it was only about four o'clock. He grabbed up his papers and went down the hall to see if any secretary was around. Someday everyone in the department would have word processors to work on; this much had been promised, but until then, it would be a secretary who would have to transmit his scribbles into crisp Xerox-copied order.

Now, as he walked through the warren of offices, he heard very little. These days, with no students here, everyone went home early, eager to snuggle up with a spouse or at least a hot video and forget the dreary life-denying day. Jack's stomach rumbled inside him and his shoulders cramped. He'd have a good workout in the gym, buy a feast at the local deli, then hide out in his house like a teenager, drinking beer, eating, watching anything and everything on the tube.

He passed the history-department offices, Daphne's realm, which already were dark and empty. He crossed the hall and entered the main office of the English department. Through the windows the sky stretched out forever, gravestone gray. The golden points of lights that glimmered in the distance seemed worlds away. Daphne was at the main desk, working at a computer, wearing a dress in cherry-red wool. She turned and looked up at him and smiled, no embarrassment, a purely friendly smile.

"Hi, Jack. If you're looking for Hudson, I'm afraid you've missed him. He's just left. Everyone's left but me, I think. It's that kind of day. Half the office has flu and the other half is coming down with it. I have to finish a paper for Fred Van Lieu, and my computer's down, wouldn't you know it. Hudson said I could use this one. His secretary's not in today."

Jack looked at Daphne. "I need a draft of this syllabus typed up," he said. "Just one copy. But it can wait. No hurry."

"Sure? I could type it up for you after I finish Fred's."

"No, no. I can wait." Was it his imagination or did Daphne feel as awkward as he did?

"Is that it?" Daphne asked, leaning over the desk to look at the sheaf of scribbled papers in his hand. "Listen, I'll leave a note for someone to type it up tomorrow. Otherwise it will get lost in the shuffle. Let me get a folder for it."

Daphne rose from her desk and crossed the room to take a file folder from the supplies shelf. She moved through Jack's field of vision like a cardinal flashing its colors, its signal of intense bird-bright heat in a cold world. Daphne stretched her arms, reaching for the file folder, and the red wool dress rose too, holding to her form. Cherries, roses, apples, wine: health and heat against the grave. Jack went to her and put his arms around her. In response, she dropped her arms to her sides and lowered her head slightly, as if in surrender, and he kissed the back of her neck many times, nuzzling kisses, breathing in her scent as he kissed her. Daphne stood there, seeming passive, but he could feel her response against his body, he could feel how she was melting against him, and he pressed his torso against her back, and she leaned back into him, still holding her arms quietly at her sides.

Jack moved one hand down to press against her crotch. With his other hand he slowly stroked the front of her neck and then her shoulders and then finally, slowly, he moved his hand and arm down to the shelf of her breasts. Through the layers of wool and brassiere he felt her nipples harden. He hardened in response. Her breasts were as soft as pillows, but heavy, bulky. He held them in his hands and was surprised at their warm mass. He thought of her white flesh beneath the red dress. He moved his hands from her breasts to raise her skirt.

Such good luck. Daphne was wearing high boots with knee-high cotton socks, and a long slip and underpants, but no panty hose. So when Jack had slid the dress up in a bunch around her hips, he could feel the warm bare skin of her thighs, and her cushiony buttocks, intersected by the triangle of silky underwear. Her skin was as smooth and as white as milk. He slid his hand around to her belly and Daphne shuddered against him and caught her breath. She was leaning against him, still passive, letting him do what he wanted, sighing. Jack slid his hand down so that his finger slipped into her pubic hairs, which were wiry and coarse to feel in contrast to her smooth skin. He raised one hand to fondle a breast, with the other deftly crept between her legs and discovered that what he guessed was true: white luxuriant Daphne was made of cream. She cried out, a low-caught cry, and tried to turn in his arms.

There was a noise from somewhere behind them. Someone was strangling? Jack turned slightly and saw Hudson Jennings standing there, clearing his throat wildly. The suddenness of it — his superior there, the embodiment of propriety — sent alarm zinging through Jack's body, which was still, even now, pressing for sexual satisfaction. A strange clanging of feelings set off within Jack's body, and he wanted to laugh and at the same time slug someone. God damn Hudson Jennings!

Daphne was struggling to get her dress down. Her face was as red as her dress. Jack backed away from her, taking deep breaths. He leaned against the office wall, not looking directly at Hudson.

"This would be a fine scene for our students to come upon," Hudson said coldly.

"It's vacation," Jack said, his voice embarrassingly husky.

"And that excuses this display?" Hudson said, not really asking a question.

"Oh, for heaven's sake, Hudson," Daphne said. "You could at least have had the dignity and kindness simply to shut the door and go away and leave us alone."

Jack felt his eyes bulge from his head like a cartoon character's. How did Daphne dare talk to Hudson that way? He looked sideways at Hudson to see how he was taking it. Hudson was nearly vibrating with anger.

"Mr. Hamilton, I'll see you in my office at nine o'clock tomorrow morning," Hudson said, looking at Jack. Hudson turned to Daphne. "And you, Mrs. Miller, may consider yourself dismissed. I'll have Paula deal with the paperwork; I believe you have some sick leave and vacation time coming to you."

"Hudson," Daphne said, moving toward him. "What are you saying?" She was still smiling, as if this were a joke.

"Mrs. Miller," Hudson said. "I'll put it to you quite clearly. You are fired." He drew himself up haughtily. "And don't think that our past friendship will be of aid in making me change my mind. The college's policies on moral turpitude are and always have been firm. I'm sure Fred Van Lieu will concur."

"Hudson!" Daphne said, her smile leaving her face. "You're kidding."

Jack looked from Hudson to Daphne and back again. What was the matter with Hudson? The man looked as if he were about to die of pain. Was he going to have a heart attack? Jack almost wished he would.

"I think the two of you should leave now," Hudson said. "Mrs. Miller, you may come back tomorrow when there are other secretaries here, to get whatever personal things you have in the office."

"Hudson," Daphne said, angry now, "don't you see what you're doing? You're punishing us for doing what *you* want to do and *won't!*"

Hudson turned red, then did an about-face and walked off down the hall. For a moment Daphne and Jack stood in silence, letting it all settle about them.

"Do you think he meant what he said?" Jack asked.

Daphne was white-faced. "Yes," she said. "I think he meant what he said." She moved around the room quickly, gathering up her coat and purse.

"Let me . . . " Jack began, but didn't know how to finish. Let him help? How? "Are you going home? At least we can have dinner together, a drink — discuss what to do?"

Daphne looked at Jack. Her eyes glittered; her face was flushed. She was shaking. "There's nothing to discuss," she said. "I'm fired. You'll have to deal with Hudson, but at least you can be sure he won't spread this around. He's many things but not a gossip. So you won't have to worry that Carey Ann will find out. You'll be okay, Jack."

Jack moved toward Daphne, reached out his hand to touch her shoulder. "But you — " he began.

"I've got to keep away from you, that's the first thing," Daphne said, smiling. Then her facade crumbled and she burst into tears, her face a terrifying sight of raw emotions: fear and anger and grief.

She hurried from the room, down the hall, down all the flights of stairs.

11

By nine-thirty that night, Jack thought he would lose his mind. He so badly needed to talk to someone, anyone, about what had happened, that if Carey Ann had been there, he would have told her, even though one of his main instincts now, clanging through his system like a fire alarm, was that Carey Ann never know, never find out what had happened. He wanted to protect Carey Ann. He didn't want to lose her, he wanted their marriage.

God, what a hell of a mess! And it was all his fault. There was no way around it, it was all his fault. He felt sick with guilt. Somehow he had to help Daphne. Because of him, she had lost her job — which she had had for . . . what, fourteen years? He knew how rocky her life had been lately, how hard times were for her, how little money she had, how little family, how the college in many ways was her home, and now because of his stupidity she had lost her means of making a living and access to the world that was her home. He had to do something.

But what? He couldn't reach her. He had driven home in a rage at Hudson (and in a physical rage at being sexually frustrated in the middle of what had been nearly a dream of pleasure), talking to himself in the car, cursing, hitting the steering wheel, wondering out loud what to do next. The minute he was in the door he had dialed Daphne's home number, but she hadn't answered. He had paced around the house like a maniac, dialing her number every ten minutes, but no answer, no answer. He fixed himself several Scotches, and at eight o'clock stuffed some crackers in his mouth to soak up the booze. His throat had revolted against the dry food. He almost could not swallow. He wasn't hungry. He was so full of guilt and anger and worry, his body seemed stuffed to the bursting point.

Why wasn't Daphne home? Where had she gone? She wouldn't do anything stupid, would she — she wouldn't commit suicide, would she? But why wouldn't she? She had just lost everything. Her job, her reputation, her means of support. Still, Daphne was not the suicidal type.

But where was she? At nine-thirty Jack made a decision. He would call Pauline White and go talk to her about all this. If he didn't, if he tried to make it through the night, he'd go mad, he wouldn't be able to sleep, he'd end up pounding on someone's door and yelling out his problems to anyone. Pauline White was Daphne's closest friend. At least Jack thought she was, and she was a kind and sensible woman. Jack dialed her number and asked if he could come over now to talk to her about an urgent problem. Pauline told him to come.

Pauline and Douglas met him together at their front door. Both of them were wearing robes — matching tartan plaid wool robes, and the same kind of deerskin fleece-lined slippers. What a salt-and-pepper set they were, Jack thought, almost laughing at the sight of them, and then thought: Am I getting hysterical? *Men* don't get hysterical.

"Look," Jack said, "I'm sorry to bother you. A terrible thing has happened. With Daphne. To Daphne. It's my fault. And I can't reach Daphne."

They let him into their warm gracious living room and gave him yet another Scotch and drank Scotch themselves while they listened. To Jack's relief, Pauline seemed almost amused, until Jack told them Hudson had fired Daphne.

"What worries me most is that I can't reach Daphne," Jack said. "On the way here I drove to her house and pounded on the door. No lights are on. I know she's not there."

"Well, you know, her daughter's in town," Pauline said. "Daphne wouldn't do anything rash with Cynthia in town. So don't envision scenes of Daphne slitting her wrists in the tub." She thought a moment. "I'll call Cyn's friend Donna. She might know where Daphne is."

Very quickly Jack's worries were abated and replaced by bafflement when Pauline hung up the phone. "Donna said that Cyn called to tell her that her mother was taking her to Boston for a whirlwind trip. Donna's mother talked to Daphne. Daphne said she had some vacation days with pay and she was going to live it up with Cynthia. They're going to stay at the Ritz, do the museums, go shopping, be wild."

"Oh," Jack said. He felt oddly deflated, somehow shunned.

"This is how Daphne does things," Pauline said, putting her hand on Jack's shoulder as if consoling him. "She is the soul of serenity until there's a crisis in her life, and then she jumps on a broomstick and flies off in a fury against the wind. She bought her Vermont cottage a week after she knew Cynthia was going to live with her father. It's her way of coping."

"But this . . . this is different," Jack said.

"Yes," Pauline agreed. Again she sat quietly thinking.

"Hudson's a damned fool," Douglas said gruffly. "Fool to let her go. The history department will be chaos. Fred will be furious."

"I think I know what will happen," Pauline said. "Daphne will be back from Boston with all the local newspapers in her hands and all the want ads and apartments for rent circled. Yes, I'll bet that's just what she'll do."

"But that's terrible!" Jack said. "That she should have to move. Leave her friends, her home, her life! All because of a stupid mistake *I* made."

"Look, Jack," Pauline said, and the tone of her voice made it seem as though she had really said, "Look, buster." "Daphne could have stopped you. She could have said, 'Don't.' She could have slugged you. You didn't have her bound and gagged. She's responsible too."

"And Hudson is right," Douglas said in his gruff voice. "That was a damn-fool thing to do in an office. In Hudson's office. With the door wide open. You'd think she wanted to get caught."

"Well, it was the end of the day. We both thought everyone had gone home. The halls were empty, the offices were empty. The

438

thing is" — Jack turned toward Douglas, this man he hardly knew, as if supplicating — "I don't know why I did it at all. I mean, Daphne's an attractive woman, but I love my wife. I really do love Carey Ann. I guess I've been lonely and depressed with her gone, but that doesn't explain my lack of . . . judgment."

Douglas grinned, a grimace more than a smile. "If you have to have an explanation, blame it on the academic ego," he said. He was looking across the room at his wife, and Jack remembered that Daphne had told him that Pauline had once had an affair with another professor. Douglas went on. "In our pathetic ingrown toenail of a profession, we are always longing for admiration and attention of any kind from anyone. Every professor you meet is the same. Because we know we don't really matter in the world. We don't make anything useful, not cars or food or houses. If we're really good at what we do, only thirty-two people on the planet can appreciate it, and thirty of those thirty-two hate us for doing it better or first. It's lonely, being a professor. That's all." Douglas leaned forward toward Jack. "This won't be the last time you'll be tempted to be embraced by another woman, but if you're smart it will be the last time you'll succumb. If you're smart, you won't let Carey Ann know about this, and you'll find another way to deal with your needs." Douglas laughed, a short honk of a laugh. "Get a dog. Take up jogging."

"I do jog," Jack said.

"Did you jog today?" Douglas asked. "Should have."

"Well, I'm going to go talk to Hudson tomorrow," Pauline said. "I'd call him tonight, but it's after ten, and he and Claire go to bed early, the old farts."

"You are?" Jack looked at Pauline and was filled with hope. "Do you think you can reason with him?"

"I honestly don't know what I can do with him, but I can make him know how blasted angry everyone will be if he gets rid of Daphne."

"I can count on not getting tenure here," Jack said woefully, the reality of his own situation now dawning on him. He looked at Douglas and Pauline to see if they agreed. "That much is for sure." He waited.

Pauline scrutinized Jack. "Would that break your heart? Not getting tenure?"

"It's been my dream, all my life, to teach here," Jack said.

"But I haven't thought you were particularly happy here."

Jack shifted in his chair and drank more

Scotch. "You're right, I haven't been," he admitted. "Though I guess I haven't understood that till right now. Part of it is they've got me teaching a period I hate — the neoclassic; it's so deadly dull — when I want to teach twentieth-century."

"You're a junior professor," Pauline said. "You're just paying your dues. You know you won't be teaching that forever."

"It's Hudson, too," Jack said. "He's so rigid. He's so proper and so . . . *constipated* with all his damned old rules."

"Lots of parents pay lots of money to send their kids to a school that abides by those damned old rules," Pauline said. "There are reasons for his rules. If you're in a fine old prestigious Ivy League institution, you don't go changing things easily. Hudson has a reputation to uphold. And he's not out of bounds in firing Daphne, you know. Secretaries oughtn't to screw around with married junior professors in the middle of the day right out in open view."

"You're right," Jack said, lowering his head into his hands. The weight of all that had happened, that he had caused to happen, and what was going to come to him because of his actions now seemed to sink onto his back, pressing him into the ground. "Married junior professors shouldn't screw around in

441

public either. I was an ass. I'll have to deal with the consequences."

"You won't be dismissed," Pauline said. "You're a popular teacher, and it would be difficult replacing you right away. You've got a three-year contract, right? I'm not sure what Hudson will do, but he's not the ogre you think he is. He'll probably put you on some kind of private probation. He's not the type to hold a grudge. I know he's cold, but he's capable of generosity of imagination."

Douglas laughed again, his brief bark of a laugh. "It won't take Hudson much 'generosity of imagination' to understand what Jack was up to with Daphne. Poor old Hudson has been mooning around Daphne all his life."

"He *has?*" Jack was shocked. "Then why hasn't he — ?"

"He's married," Pauline said. "He's tried to be a good man." She looked into the depths of her Scotch glass. "Now look where his goodness has got him," she said. "I'll bet he's more miserable than anyone else. Poor Hudson."

"Poor Hudson," Jack echoed, his voice bitter. He was so depressed he thought he might actually cry. "I should go home. Thank you for your help."

Pauline scrutinized Jack. "You're not too soused? I don't want you leaving here too drunk to drive."

Jack stood up. "I'm fine."

Douglas stood up too, and surprised Jack by putting an arm around him in a fatherly way. Looking at his wife, he said, "I find that in times like this, shock and dejection keep one unpleasantly sober, no matter how much one drinks." He patted Jack on the shoulder. "You'll be all right. This isn't as bad as it seems. This is the first time I've heard of Hudson making such a major decision with such haste, and I'll be very surprised if we can't persuade him to change his mind. So this is not the end of the world for anyone."

"You're right, darling!" Pauline said. "He's right, Jack. It isn't like Hudson to make such a snap decision. I'll bet that's why Daphne's gone off to Boston, to give Hudson time to cool down and change his mind. It will be all right. Don't worry."

The Whites' optimism and kindness buoyed Jack up during his drive back to his house in the hills. But once back inside that house, with the cold black night surrounding him, he felt boxed in by loneliness.

The little Christmas tree, the short tree, stood on a table near the glass wall. There were no presents under it, and he had not turned on its lights, so it looked dreary, its limbs drooping. Carey Ann had been right.

Every now and then it would lose a few needles, which would fall with a sifting whispering noise, a ghostly sly secretive noise, causing him to look up suddenly from what he was reading, thinking: What was *that?* Oh, yeah, the tree.

The ghosts of Christmas. A good literary tradition. No ghosts haunted this house — it was too modern for that, although perhaps after this Christmas there would be some. What was dying now, or could die? His marriage? Certainly, if she found out, Carey Ann's trust. Jack leaned against the high wall of glass separating him from the plunge down the mountain and felt the glass cooling his Scotch-fevered face. The cold was almost painful. In spite of the realtor's suave assurances, their heating bill was going to have to be astronomical; this glass might be triple-glazed and thermopaned and ten other technological wonders, but he could feel the cold coming in, and he knew it was coming in all up and down and across the height and width of this wall of window.

Below, far below, a few lights sparkled from cars passing along Route 2 up to Plover and from the few houses unscreened by evergreens. It probably was lonely up here for Carey Ann and Alexandra. It would be even lonelier as Alexandra grew older. When he was a child, one of his greatest happinesses had been to run screaming out the door and across grassy lawns to the homes of friends. Neighborhoods. Children needed neighborhoods. Families needed communities.

One thing was for sure: he wouldn't have gone to Daphne's in a lust-crazed fit if their homes had been in a neighborhood where people they knew might see him going in the door and coming out again.

Did that mean that man by nature would be immoral if he were certain of the security of privacy? Did that mean that Jack by nature was immoral as long as he wasn't worried about getting caught? No. He wasn't so clever. Look how he had behaved in Peabody Hall, of all places.

Things were not going well. Things were not working out right. Things were botched.

Jack poured himself another Scotch, pulled a chair up to the window so that he could rest, leaning forward, cooling his forehead on the cold window. Looking at the black night. Now. He would be logical. Organized. Sensible.

What did he want?

He wanted Alexandra to live healthily and happily.

He wanted Carey Ann to be happy and to love him as she had loved him the first year of their marriage.

He wanted to be a novelist.

And right there his mind screeched to a halt, slammed into the cold hard facts of life: he couldn't support his family, he couldn't keep his daughter happy and healthy if he tried to write instead of teaching. He wasn't independently wealthy. He had to work.

Jack tossed back the rest of his Scotch. At this rate he'd be sloppy drunk and singing to himself before long. He could also count on a wicked hangover. Was this the way to live a life? If he was so fucking intelligent, why was he in this mess? Why couldn't he figure anything out?

"Oh, Carey Ann," he said aloud. "If you love me, why aren't you with me now? If you were here, everything would be all right."

His words, his loneliness, his desperation, his self-hatred, his need, his Scotch, and, not the least, never the least, the most, his love, his love, streaked a crystal path of clarity through his foggy brain, culminating in a thought that blazed in the darkness of his mind like the Christmas star in the night sky:

Why wasn't he with Carey Ann?

The phone was ringing and ringing. *Riiingg!* That was the *sixteenth* time. But Daphne wouldn't answer it. Maybe she would never answer the phone again. Why should she? Who in the world would she want to talk to? It gave her a feeling of power, not answering the phone; she sat at the kitchen table and watched the phone ring, sending malevolent glares toward the device of plastic and wires from her swollen red-rimmed angry burning eyes.

She had held up very well until now, and now surely she had the right to dissolve in a fit of self-pity, righteous anger, despair — grief. *Yes, come on, you snake of bitterness, and uncoil, unwind, stretch out to your full length and slither, flick, flare, through my limbs and veins and nerves and vessels, fill me full. Of bile.* She felt the monster she had always carried within her unleashed now, turning, growing, expanding, pricking, biting, spitting, piercing, ejecting poison into her every cell. If she sat here at her kitchen table, in the dark, if she sat here long enough, she would undergo a metamorphosis and turn into a viper herself, snakewoman, viperwoman: serpent. Yes, and then she would crawl on her belly beneath this house and die.

Cynthia was back in California. At least there was that: she was safely back, and Daphne had spent four dazzling days with her in Boston. Probably it was the best time they had ever had together in all their lives, at least

447

since Cynthia was a mother-loving child. It helped a lot that Daphne had treated herself and Cynthia to all kinds of pleasures. Tea at the Ritz; twenty-five dollars spent right there. Imagine. They saw all the newest movies, and spent an afternoon at the dark, ornate, beautiful, slightly vampirish Isabella Stewart Gardner Museum. Taxis instead of subways, and shopping at Bonwit Teller. Well, they had been frugal then, shopping at the Finale Shop on the top floor, where everything was discounted.

She hadn't let Cynthia have a hint of what was going on. Was that because she wanted Cynthia to remember her, for once, as gay and vivid and witty and splendid, since it would be the last time she would see her mother?

Well, had she thought that? Was that what she thought now?

Daphne sat at her kitchen table in the dark, without the tiniest amount of energy or desire to fix herself so much as a cup of coffee. This morning she had put Cynthia on the plane to California, and now she had called California and heard that Cynthia was safely there. There was nothing else in the world that Daphne wanted. Her stomach disagreed; it growled; she had not eaten since yesterday. But she did not care. Given time, the snake of bitterness swelling inside her would devour her stomach and she wouldn't feel hunger pains anymore.

Daphne sat at the kitchen table in the same pair of black wool trousers, black boots, and black-red-and-white bulky mohair sweater that she had donned that morning, pretending to her usual vanity so that Cynthia would think all was well. After driving Cyn to the airport and returning home, Daphne had been so tired, so enervated, that she had collapsed on this kitchen chair. She had taken her dangling red-and-gold earrings off and placed them on the table side by side and played with them for a while, lining them up parallel or crisscrossing them. That was what she had done today: waited to call Cynthia to be certain she was safely home — she had told Cyn not to call her (she didn't want to answer the phone) — and toyed with her earrings. The slender red-and-gold strips looked like fringe; but she could not braid them, they were too stiff. Finally she had just stared at them, unmoving.

Daphne thought she would just sit there forever. Or, when sleep came, she would wrap her coat around her and put her head down on the table and simply close her eyes.

Could one die so easily? Could one just give up, just surrender, and lie down, wrapped in warmth, and die? Or would the greedy body drag itself, fighting against its soul, over to the breadbox for nourishment? These were interesting questions, Daphne thought. How easy would it be to die? All the years and months and days and hours and vivid terrifying seconds when she had worried about the easiness of death: for herself, when Cyn was a baby and a little child; for Cyn always — car accidents, cancer, drowning in the summer, pneumonia in the winter; and Daphne had prayed every night that her daughter would remain alive. And she had. But all those nights it had seemed to Daphne that death was the easy thing, life fragile and vulnerable and frail. Maybe she had been wrong. Wouldn't it be interesting to see? To see, if at some point in the future days, in spite of herself, in spite of what she truly, *truly* desired, her body betrayed her and ate.

Well, she could take something. She had sleeping pills, she had booze. Why not do that? How serious was she about this death business? Really. She had refused herself a good stiff drink, or rest with the help of pills, because she didn't want the consolation, the reprieve from grief, the fog and numbing, the comfort. She had blanked everything from her mind during the four days she spent with Cynthia in Boston, but now there was no more reason for blankness, and she wanted to let it all in, accept the truth, see her life for what it was, for what it had become.

Dickens was still in the kennel. She had not picked him up yet. Good thing. He would get hungry whether she did or not. She remembered a story she'd heard about an old woman who had lived with her dog for twelve years, a loving couple, until the old woman died one day, and no one knew about it for a week, and when people finally broke into the house to check, they found that the dog, starving, had started to eat the old woman. Daphne could understand that. It didn't appall her. The thought of old Dickens gnawing on her upper arm or thigh didn't bother her. She envisioned him trotting around the house with her femur between his jaws; Dickens would be both proud and nervous, worried even in an empty house that someone would deprive him of his bone. He'd probably try to hide it somewhere, under the sofa, under the bed. Daphne found an odd consolation and a consoling grim humor in this vision. She wished she had gotten Dickens, after all, from the kennel.

But she hadn't. She was alone. It was night, and very cold out, and all beings human or not were tucked away somewhere for warmth. Even she was warm. There was a thought. Wasn't dying of hypothermia supposed to be relatively pleasant? Didn't one just drift off into a dream? Daphne thought for a while about going outside, but couldn't find the momentum to move.

After a while, she pulled the upper part of the coat around her, and, adjusting the hood so that it cushioned her head against the hardness of the wood, lay on the table, her hands in her lap. She closed her eyes. She had cried so much all day, starting as soon as Cynthia walked down the ramp into the plane to California, that her eyes burned painfully. It was a relief to close them. But more tears were building up, misery was bubbling away like a jam in the caldron of her body. God, it *hurt* to be so sad!

Oh, maybe she would take something, everything.

But still she could not move.

There was a knocking on the front door. Not the wind. Who could it be at eleven at night? Who cared? Daphne didn't have the energy to answer, and after a while the knocking went away.

"Daphne!"

The shout, so close by, made Daphne jump and nearly scream. Lifting her head off the table, she looked around; was this it, had she died so peacefully and easily, and that was

God, calling her home?

No. It was Hudson Jennings, standing outside her kitchen window, hands cupped around his mouth, looking in at her. If the moonlight hadn't been so bright on the snow, she wouldn't have been able to make out his features so clearly. His thick dark hair was disheveled and hung down his forehead, brushing against the top of his glasses. He was wearing a cashmere coat with the collar turned up around his neck against the cold. His hands were in thick dark brown suede gloves. Daphne knew these clothes well; Hudson came to work in them every day. But he wasn't wearing his plaid cap. He always wore his plaid cap in the winter. Claire wouldn't have let him out the door into the cold without that plaid cap. Hudson was going wild. Daphne stared at him, thinking all these things, still too tired to do anything.

And why do anything? Why get up, why let him in? He would bumble and stumble and apologize, she assumed. Probably he would say he had arranged for her not to be fired but to work in another department, in another building. Daphne didn't want to work in another department in another building or in his department in Peabody Hall. Daphne didn't want to do anything.

"Let me in!" Hudson commanded, pounding on the window with both fists.

"Go away, Hudson," Daphne said, but not very loudly. She didn't have the energy to yell.

"Daphne! Let. Me. *In!*"

Daphne pulled the hood of her coat over her head and laid her head, thus insulated, back down on the kitchen table, facing away from the window so she wouldn't have to look at Hudson. His noises were muffled. He would go away soon.

When the sound of splintering glass came, Daphne was surprised enough to sit up again. Hudson had put his hand through a pane in the kitchen door, and was reaching in to turn the door handle. The jagged glass sliced into the thick cashmere sleeve; Claire would not be happy about that at all.

Hudson entered the kitchen, stomping his feet to shake off the snow. He looked slightly insane, his hair flying in all directions, his skin blotching red and white with cold, his glasses sliding down the ridge of his nose, his eyes above them as huge as a madman's.

"I really don't want to see you, Hudson," Daphne said. She thought about putting her head back on the table and covering it with the coat, but decided that would be too child-ish. She might as well keep some dignity about her. It was a pleasure to watch Hudson losing some of his.

Hudson crossed the kitchen without speaking, opened the drawer where she kept her odds and ends, and pulled out a roll of tape and scissors. He reached between the stove and sink and pulled out a brown grocery sack. Back at the kitchen door, he framed the broken pane very neatly with a triple layer of grocery sack and taped it on. Then he put the tape and scissors away, shut the door, threw the rest of the sack in the trash.

Then he sat down in the chair next to Daphne's.

"I'm in love with you," he said.

12

The day after Hudson Jennings caught Jack with Daphne, Jack packed his bags and flew to Kansas City to be with his wife. It wasn't until he was at the airport that he remembered he was supposed to see Hudson Jennings that morning; he called the office and left a message with Hudson's secretary that he had been unexpectedly called out of town on an emergency. Let Hudson get pissed off that he didn't show up for the reprimand, Jack thought. How much more trouble could he be in, after all?

He didn't call Carey Ann to let her know he was coming — he thought a surprise would be more romantic — and he didn't plan his life any further than that. Across the aisle from him on the plane was a family with a little girl much like Alexandra. She was three years old, and talkative and strong-willed. Jack had brought a book with him to read on the flight, but he found himself unable to concentrate on it. He sat staring at it, pretending to read, but

456

really listening to the family across the aisle, and even, occasionally, sneaking glances at them.

The mother had her daughter in her lap and was reading to her from *The Cat in the Hat*. The little girl echoed the words, articulating carefully, and traced the pictures with chubby fingers, then finally nuzzled up against her mother, twisting to get comfortable; she stuck her thumb in her mouth, she sighed, she relaxed against her mother's arm, and immediately fell asleep. Her skin was so very white and her curly hair so fine that the little girl looked terribly fragile, and Jack wondered if the mother shouldn't put her seat belt around the little girl somehow; was the mother's arm protection enough?

Jack realized that the father, nearest to him, in the aisle seat, was looking at his face, watching Jack watch the little girl.

"Sorry," Jack said, embarrassed. "Didn't mean to stare. It's just that your little girl is so pretty. She makes me miss my daughter — Lexi — who's just about your daughter's age."

The other father nodded. "I know," he replied. "I hate business trips. Go away one week, come back, and you've missed so much. Jennifer learned to walk while I was gone. Learned to talk while I was gone.

Finally I changed jobs so I could stay home more. It doesn't last, does it? They grow up so fast. Do you have a picture of your daughter?"

Jack pulled a picture of Lexi out of his wallet, and there was Carey Ann too, wearing a red sweater, cuddling Lexi in her arms. The other father was right: this picture had been taken only six months ago, and yet Lexi was different now, bigger and more grown-up.

"Wow," the father said. "She's beautiful, your wife. Honey, look at this. Isn't she beautiful?"

The woman took the picture and studied it. "Yes. And the little girl is too." She leaned forward around her husband to smile at Jack, keeping her daughter pressed against her breast. "You're a lucky man," she said.

They talked some more, in the manner of polite people who find themselves confined in the same small space, until the father suddenly yawned loudly in Jack's face.

"Sorry," he said. "It's the motion-sickness pills. They make me drowsy."

"Don't believe him," the mother said, leaning forward again. "It's Valium. He's terrified of flying." She grinned.

Jack smiled back, then returned to his book, which he still could not concentrate on. So it wasn't so unusual, fathers loving their children, giving up certain things to be with them; look what that father had done. Maybe Jack was a wimp, or a nerd, or even — what was that word they used to hear? — "pussy-whipped," or, more elegantly put, "uxorious," but he loved being with his wife and daughter, and he wanted to be with them, and he wanted them to be happy. Maybe fate had randomly put this doting father at his side to show him it was all right to be the way he was, that he was not alone.

And something else was nudging at his thoughts. It was . . . What?

Jack nodded, suddenly caught up in a realization: well, no wonder the Skragses didn't want their daughter moving halfway across the continent. She was their only child. They loved her. Of course everyone moved everywhere these days, no grown child would ever think of staying in a place just to be near her parents — in the name of success and accomplishment, it was necessary to move where the job was — but that didn't make it right, or at least the *only* thing that was right, the *only* right way to live. A wash of sympathy and respect swept over Jack, and he understood that Carey Ann's parents were not control-crazed monsters but just parents who loved their only child.

Jack rented a car at the Kansas City airport

and drove out on Route 291 to Liberty, where Carey Ann's friend Christie had her farm. Jack had forgotten how pretty the land around here was, with its rolling hills and sloping pastures and gleaming streams flashing back the sun's light. Christie, whom Jack knew only through Carey Ann, was married to a vet and spent her time raising purebred long-haired German shepherds and Appaloosa horses. Their farmhouse and barns were set at the top of a hill next to a ravine where scrub oak, persimmon, cedar, and soft walnut trees sprouted miraculously from crevices in the rocks to race each other upward to the sunlight. Vines of ivy and poison oak and sumac wound around some of the tree trunks, and on this winter day the ravine flickered with light as the wind blew the trees, exposing snake colors, the rocks of the ravine glittering with quartz and fool's gold, serpentine and shale.

Jack stopped his car in the long gravel driveway and stood for a while just looking down into the ravine, and across the drive, where the pasture sloped away from the outbuildings. From inside the house and behind one of the barns, dogs barked an alarm. He walked toward the house, meaning to knock on the door, and then he saw two riders galloping across the back pasture toward him.

He went around the house and leaned on the white rail fence to watch. Christie was riding a huge Appaloosa Indian-style, without a saddle or bridle, using only a rope to rein, and Carey Ann was on her horse, Jelly Roll. Carey Ann had her hair in braids and was wearing jeans and a sweatshirt, and when she jumped off her horse and came to throw herself in Jack's arms, she smelled of sunshine and fresh air and horse sweat and exuberance.

"Jack! Honey! Baby! Darling! Sweetie! I don't *believe* this! Oh, God, I love you! Oh, God, you feel so good to me!"

This was Jack's Carey Ann; this joyous girl. She was all over him, hugging him, kissing him, laughing, crying, talking a mile a minute, and Christie's Appaloosa danced nervously away, shaking its head and snorting with nervousness at all this action. But Jelly Roll, who had often in her life been greeted exactly the same as Jack was being greeted now, was used to Carey Ann's ways and began to nibble at the winter-stiff grass.

"What are you doing here?" Carey Ann said at last, pulling herself away from Jack enough to give him breath to answer.

"I missed you," he said simply. "And there are some things I want to talk to you about."

"Is anything wrong? At the college?"

"No. Not at all. I just . . . missed you."

"Oh, Jack," Carey Ann said, and tears began to streak down her face. "I missed you too. You are the sweetest thing." She collapsed against him, sobbing, hugging him, kissing his shirt and neck, and he held her, feeling her animal warmth and energy against him, hugging her to him.

"Why don't you two go on into the house and, uh, get reacquainted," Christie said from her perch on her horse. She sidled up along Jelly Roll and grabbed her reins. "I've got, um, a really important appointment in the barn that will take me exactly one hour. Okay?"

"Oh, thank you, Christie!" Carey Ann said, and hurried Jack toward the house. "Do you want some lunch, Jack? No? Good!" she said, pushing him down the hall past the kitchen to the guest room, where her things were. She peeled off her jeans and sweatshirt, revealing underpants of cotton with strawberries on them. Those panties and her slenderness, her braids, her face free of makeup, streaked with tears, made her seem terribly frail and very young, even childish, but she did not act childish. She began tearing Jack's clothes off him because he was moving too slowly for her; then she pulled him to the bed. She didn't want touching or fondling or messing around, she wanted him in her, and when he entered, he felt both their bodies tighten with the shock of connection. True, he was the axis on which her life turned, but she was the globe around him, the world around him, and without her he was lost in a void, with his life blowing emptily by.

Christie invited Jack to stay with Carey Ann at the farm overnight and Jack gratefully accepted. He wasn't quite ready to confront Carey Ann's parents. He wasn't sure just what he wanted to confront them with. But the next morning, the Hamiltons drove back into Kansas City, and while Carey Ann was at her parents' with Lexi, Jack paid a call on Clayton French, his good friend and head of the English department at the university.

"Well, Jack, ol' buddy," Clayton said after hearing his friend out, "nothing would please me more than to offer you a position here. But it doesn't work like that, you know. Next year for sure we have no openings on the faculty. The year after that, maybe. We've got an arrogant young dude from California who just might move back out there if the rest of the faculty don't kill him first. It's perfectly possible his position will be available, but not for a year, and then there would be all the formalities, advertising the position, you know how it goes."

"Mmm," Jack said. "I understand. I knew this was a long shot. I was just thinking of making some changes and hoping some things might . . . oh, sort of just fall into place for me."

"Kind of change you're talking about doesn't usually happen that fortuitously," Clayton said. "Specially not in the academic world. Hey, you know I could always give you some freshman-English sections. Not glamorous, and hard work, and you'd have to be part-time, no benefits, no tenure, but you'd have some money coming in."

"Part-time freshman English," Jack said ruefully, smiling.

Clayton held out his hands, palms up, in response. "What can I say? But you could probably line that sort of thing up at the other colleges around here. It would probably do to put bread on the table."

"I don't know," Jack said. "I mean, I'm grateful for anything you can do, Clayton. I'm just thinking aloud right now. I'm sort of feeling my way along. What it is, is that I can't stomach the thought of being dependent on Carey Ann's parents for anything."

"I know, I understand that. But don't you think it's kind of a selfish attitude on your part, Jack? I mean, they've got all that money, and what they really want to do with it is make their daughter's life nice. That doesn't mean you'd be a freeloader in their eyes."

"I know," Jack said. "I guess. Oh, I don't know."

"Let's go have lunch and a beer," Clayton said, clapping his friend on the shoulder.

That afternoon, back at the Skragses' house, Jack sat on the carpeted family-room floor with Lexi, putting together a large wooden puzzle of the Old Woman Who Lived in a Shoe. His daughter had been delirious to see him again, but that first rapture had passed and now she more or less ignored him, assuming he'd be there forever, helping her get the puzzle right. She smelled of baby powder and shampoo. Carey Ann came into the room and knelt down next to them.

"Mmmm," she said, wrapping her arms around Jack. "This is heaven, having you with us."

Lexi eyed her parents suspiciously, perhaps considering whether to be jealous of their attention to each other, but turned back to the puzzle.

"*There!*" she said triumphantly, fitting a wooden head on top of a wooden body.

"Good girl, Lexi!" Carey Ann said. "Now, where does this piece go?"

"I've been thinking," Jack said. "I've been

465

thinking that maybe we all should move back to Kansas City."

Carey Ann looked at him suspiciously. "What do you mean?"

"Just what I said. We should move back here. That way you could be close to your parents and friends and Jelly Roll . . . "

"But what about you?"

"Well, I talked to Clayton today. He said he could give me some sections of freshman English, and I could probably pick up some others around at the local colleges — "

"Jack, you'd go crazy," Carey Ann said. "I can't ask that kind of sacrifice from you."

"Well, it wouldn't be that bad," Jack began, but Carey Ann interrupted him.

She rose from her sitting position onto her knees and, putting her hands on his shoulders while he sat cross-legged in front of her, said, "Jack. Don't. Don't even begin, okay? I mean, I know you want to make me happy. I know your heart's in the right place. But we've gone over all of this before, a hundred times. It's just not fair of you to get my hopes up again."

"Carey Ann — " Jack began, but then Mr. Skrags walked in.

"Hello, there, everyone!" he said heartily, and Carey Ann jumped away from her husband as rapidly as if she were a teenager caught making out with her boyfriend.

"Hi, Daddy!"

Mr. Skrags was a large man who wore cowboy boots and string ties. This gave him the appearance of being just a down-home old boy, friendly and easygoing, but Jack knew what kind of near-genius dynamo thundered along inside the man.

"Good to see you again. Glad you could find the time to come out," Mr. Skrags said, shaking Jack's hand. He bent over and kissed his daughter on the cheek, then picked up his grandchild and threw her up in the air a few times. He seemed to have endless strength and energy. He had thick silver hair and sparkling blue eyes — Carey Ann had gotten her blond good looks from him. He looked like what he was, a handsome and powerful man. He didn't even have a potbelly. Jack wished he could look like him. He wished he didn't see his father-in-law as his enemy.

"Um . . . sir? I wonder if I could speak to you a moment. Um, alone," Jack said. Jack's parents had told Carey Ann to call them by their first names, but Carey Ann's had offered no such intimacy.

"Of course, of course," Mr. Skrags agreed readily, without a trace of surprise at the request. "Girls, will you excuse us?"

The "girls" left the room. Jack got up off the rug.

"How about a drink, Jack? Scotch? Bourbon?"

"Bourbon's fine," Jack said, only because he knew that was Mr. Skrags's drink. Jack hated bourbon, thought it was too sweet, but he wanted to score any points he could.

"Sit down, sit down," Mr. Skrags said, handing Jack a heavy glass and sinking into a wing chair. With his free hand he indicated, with a generous, majestic gesture, the opposite chair. The king in his castle.

Jack took a sip of his bourbon. He cleared his throat. He took a deep breath. "I've been thinking, sir, about moving back to Kansas City after this semester's up." There, Jack thought, I've completed an entire sentence. Mr. Skrags's expression did not change — nor did it give anything away. Jack had hoped his announcement might at least bring a smile to the older man's face. Jack plunged forward. "I know how much Carey Ann means to you, and, well, now that I have a daughter I guess I can understand more clearly just how much you miss Carey Ann and how much she misses you, and also how nice it would be if you and Mrs. Skrags could watch Alexandra grow up, and I know how much it would mean to Carey Ann to be near her family and friends." Still no response from the old goat, even though Jack paused, waiting, sipping his bourbon. "So. Well. I've been talking to Clayton French, the head of the English department here at UMKC, and he said that although he couldn't promise me a position on the faculty he could probably dredge up some freshman-English sections, and I could probably get some from some other colleges, and so I'd make enough to keep the wolf from the door. . . . I haven't exactly thought this all out, but I'm sure we could sell the house in Vermont and use that money to make a down payment here, and . . . well, we'd get along. We'd manage." Jack felt himself winding down like a top, spinning more and more slowly, ready to topple over on his side from lack of energy. "So. So . . . I just thought you might like to know."

Jack waited. He took another drink of bourbon, which was beginning to taste pretty good. Mr. Skrags had such relentless eyes.

"Why, Carey Ann told me she was getting pretty happy up there," Mr. Skrags said. "Told me things were working out. Said she'd made some good friends and was enjoying her courses."

"Well, yes, that's true enough," Jack replied. "But I know she'd be happier here. She's said any number of times she feels more at home here, and she's always talking about how much she misses Christie and Jelly Roll — and you and Mrs. Skrags."

"And what about you, son? How do you like it there, at that school? That was the important thing — the *crucial* thing, as I recall — that you had a fire in you to teach at that school."

Jesus, the old man was hard, Jack thought. He wasn't going to give Jack an inch. "I like it a lot," he answered, frantically reassuring himself that Mr. Skrags, all-powerful as he was, couldn't possibly know what had happened between Jack and Daphne. Was Mr. Skrags trying to turn Jack's generous change of mind into a sign of failure? "Things are going very well for me there. I've had a large enrollment in all my classes."

Mr. Skrags shook his head. "I think it's a big mistake to make a career change of such magnitude just because of an unhappy wife." He looked dour.

Well, fuck it, then. We'll just stay back east and you can never see your precious daughter again! Jack remained silent, helpless.

"I thought you were hankering to write a novel," Mr. Skrags went on. "I thought Carey Ann told me the two things you wanted were to teach at Westhampton College and write a novel."

"That's right," Jack said. "That's correct. But — "

"But you've got a family to support. I know. Well, son, I've told you, I'd be more than willing to support you and your family for two or three years while you wrote your novel. You know I've got more than enough money for all of us."

Why did he have to make such a generous offer with such an ugly, mean look? Frustrated, Jack said nothing.

"Seems to me," Mr. Skrags went on, "if you were living in Kansas City, working on a novel, you'd be happy, and Carey Ann'd be happy, and everyone would have what he wanted."

"Well, I don't know," Jack said. "I mean, there's the matter of respect. I'd hate for Carey Ann or you to not respect me because I was living off your money."

"Maybe it's more a matter of confidence," Mr. Skrags said.

"What?"

"Maybe you're not so sure you could write a really good novel. If I thought I could write a decent novel, why, then, I'd know I was deserving of respect, never mind whose money I took to write it."

"I know I could write a good novel," Jack said indignantly.

"Then you should reconsider my offer to help you and Carey Ann out a little bit for the next few years while you work on it. That's the only way all this moving-around stuff makes any sense to me."

Jack's head was full, as if his thoughts were swaying back and forth, bumping into each other. The bourbon, of course, but also Mr. Skrags, who was pinning Jack down like a worm on a hook with his piercing, steely blue-eyed stare so that everything in Jack was trying to wiggle free.

"I'll think about it," he said. "It's very kind of you to make the offer, sir, and I'll think about it."

"Good. You do that," Mr. Skrags said. "Now, let's go find the girls."

That night was New Year's Eve and at nine Jack and Carey Ann and her parents left a sleeping Lexi with Beulah and went to the country club for dinner and the party. Two live bands set up, one at each wing of the club; one played jazz and nothing newer than Sinatra; the other played the latest rock. Jack hadn't danced for a long time, and he loved moving to the music, feeling the music move in him until something stirred, then boiled, then burst free. The women wore glittering jewelry with evening gowns and exposed more skin in one night than Jack would see in a year back east. Carey Ann was wearing a strapless pink satin thing that flew out around her legs as she danced, and her hair, which she had had done in a formalized coiffure for the evening, had come undone and down, and streaked and flashed out around her head like a wild woman's. What would the college faculty think of Carey Ann now as she hammed it up, flicking her body to "Sledgehammer"? What would they think of him as he slid backward, trying to do the moonwalk? Waiters passed through the crowd distributing flutes of champagne. It was almost midnight. Now both bands played "Auld Lang Syne," and then the bells and noisemakers razzed through the air, and Carey Ann grabbed Jack and kissed him hotly, while a marvelous thing happened. From above, someone released a net of what Jack at first thought was confetti, and some of it was colored paper, but there were flower petals in the mixture, and soon, while everyone stood yelling and clapping and kissing and toasting, their shoulders and hair and the floor they stood on were sprinkled with the fragrant, vivid leaves of poinsettias and roses and carnations. "Ooooh!" the crowd called out. "Aaaah!" The lights dimmed then, and the band played a slow song, and Jack took his wife in his arms. Now, he thought, now it should come to me with a lightning bolt of clarity, the decision about my life, whether to take the old fart's offer and write, or to stay in Westhampton and teach, or move here and teach and *not* write — *now* the answer should strike me. But the answer did not strike him, and he entered the new year undecided.

The Hamiltons didn't return to Westhampton until the middle of January, the day before Jack had to start teaching. Jack planned to call Daphne from his office at the college to see if she was all right, but as soon as he arrived at home, before he'd had time to unpack his suitcase, Shelby Currier phoned them with the news: Hudson Jennings had left his wife and was now living with Daphne in her cottage, and rumor had it that they were looking at houses together and planning to get married as soon as Hudson's divorce came through.

"Jesus," Jack said, whistling through his teeth.

"It's a real shocker, isn't it?" Carey Ann said. "Who'd ever think those two old dried-up sticks could be capable of passion? I guess it shows that you just never know."

"Jesus," Jack said again. He couldn't seem to assimilate the information. It was stuck —

he could feel it — a prickly mass at the top of his brain. When Carey Ann hung up, he went to the front window and stared out, as if he could see all the way down the road and into Daphne's house and mind.

SPRING

SPRING

13

At the end of February, Daphne and Hudson moved into their new home. They weren't married yet, and wouldn't be for a few more months, when Hudson's divorce was final, but Daphne's cottage was too cramped for them both, and Hudson needed to be down in Westhampton, close to the college. The odd old Victorian they bought was empty, so they moved into it, and Hudson went about his administrative and teaching duties, and Daphne set up the house for their new life together. She unpacked her grandmother's crystal into Hudson's grandmother's china cupboard. She filled the refrigerator with fresh fruit and vegetables so she could keep Hudson alive forever. Everywhere she went, Dickens went with her, keeping so close he often tripped her. He was confused by so many moves in such a short time . . . but not too confused, for when Hudson came home from the university, Dickens shadowed him too, and at night, when Daphne and Hudson sat talking, Dickens curled up on Hudson's feet, as if to keep him where he belonged. So Dickens, in his doggy way, understood.

Daphne had decided that in the fall, once she and Hudson were settled into their routine, she would start work once again toward her Ph.D. One of the new pleasures in her life was talking over with Hudson just which period of English literature she should specialize in.

But there were many new pleasures in her life. Having Hudson, warm and solid, sleeping next to her, was heaven. She had insisted on a queen-size bed. Daphne wanted to share all the intimacies of sleep with Hudson. He had told Daphne that he and Claire had always had twin beds because of Claire's bad back, and Daphne feared that Hudson, used to years of that, would out of habit cling to his side of the bed and his privacy. He did go to sleep that way, settling on his half of the bed, flat as a saint, on his back, hands crossed over his chest, always in pajamas, never nude, but every morning Daphne awoke to find him curled around her somehow, a leg over hers, or an arm around her waist, or his entire body molding hers in one long embrace. So the bed worked its charm.

Daphne had been afraid that any man after twenty-five years in Claire's chaste and repressive presence would have become impotent, but Hudson hadn't. He was not wildly imaginative and innovative, but that wasn't what Daphne wanted. Well, she hadn't even thought what she wanted with Hudson — just as she had never dreamed of how she might grow a garden on the moon: it had always been beyond the possible. But *if* she had thought, then this would have been what she wished for: the way he slowly explored her body, running his hands over her arms and legs and hips and breasts as if he'd never seen such things before, then surrendering himself to Daphne's touch and kisses, giving himself over to her love, giving himself up to feelings he had forgotten he had. They couldn't be in bed with each other enough. At night, by candlelight or in the dark, they talked and touched and took their time, making up for lost years.

The days were different. Hudson had lived for all his adult life in the center of a sphere of serenity that moved with him as he moved; it was as if he were a planet ringed by stillness. He was not spontaneously affectionate, and although he loved Daphne and the access he now had to her body, he was more often than not jarred rather than pleased by her impetuous embraces. When he sat down for his breakfast and coffee and morning papers, he was unprepared for Daphne swooping down upon him in a flowing negligee, hugging him so hard his coffee slopped into the saucer.

"Ouch," he would respond. "You mashed my earlobe."

"Hudson, you wimp," Daphne would reply. She was determined not to be put off by his stiffness. She was a toucher, and with Cynthia gone, she needed someone to touch, so now, with Hudson in her life, and happiness all around her, she felt like touching and kissing and hugging him all the time. And it was not that Hudson didn't like the affection. He was just always so startled by it. Daphne finally agreed to stop kissing him on the ear or rubbing his thigh when he was driving; Hudson was afraid he'd have an accident. In turn, Hudson promised to try to relax and stop wincing when Daphne crushed him in one of her hugs.

It was perplexing for Hudson, all this change; Daphne could see that. It was as if his love for her were a geyser that had finally burst free but still had to force itself through layers of restraining rock. Old habits were not easily broken. Hudson was not used to excess, and what he felt for Daphne was excessive, and what he often showed her, at night, was, at least for Hudson, extravagant — and then he had to go back to the college in the

482

daytime, back to his former, tame self.

It was important that he remain as he had been, reasonable, available, tactful, clever, attentive. He still had a department to run, and students, and colleagues. And now all this was complicated for the first time by unpopularity. More than a few of the older professors and their wives looked upon Hudson's desertion of Claire as scandalous, cruel, dastardly, and they made this clear to Hudson in various ways. Some took it upon themselves to speak to Hudson. Others were less obvious and merely snubbed Daphne and Hudson, not inviting them to parties, only nodding to them at social functions. This did not particularly hurt Daphne, for these people had never included or recognized her in the first place, but she was hurt for Hudson. At least the Whites remained loyal friends and even champions of Daphne-and-Hudson.

Claire behaved as only Claire would, with stoic dignity. As soon as she could, she planned to move to England to live with relatives.

Hudson told Daphne that before he had come to Daphne that winter's night to tell her he loved her, he first told Claire what he was planning to do. He told Claire that he loved Daphne, and wanted to divorce Claire in order to marry her.

Claire had said, "Hudson, I know that in many ways I haven't been a good wife to you. One can't help certain deficiencies of body or instinct or disposition, and if you have suffered from lack, I also have suffered from guilt."

"She really said that?" Daphne asked. "In just those words?"

"In just those words," Hudson replied.

"What a marvel she is," Daphne said.

And Claire *was* a marvel, behaving in a much more civilized way toward Hudson than Daphne had toward Joe. Claire met Hudson for lunch to discuss the division of their property and the legal procedures for their divorce. She did not call him names or curse him. She did not seem to hate him. If Daphne answered the phone when she called, she always said politely, "Hello, Daphne. May I speak to Hudson?"

Still, Daphne felt awkward because of the commotion she and Hudson had caused. She had never wanted to be the center of a scandal. She had always wanted to be liked. She kept away from college functions as much as possible, but at the end of February the president held a formal cocktail party in Peabody Hall in honor of a visiting humanities lecturer. At the last moment, Hudson called Daphne to tell her to go without him; he was tied up in a budget meeting and couldn't get away.

"Well, I just won't go either. I don't need to go, darling," Daphne said sweetly, feeling cowardly.

"Please go, Daphne. You have to represent me. You must give my regards to Mr. Scalas," Hudson replied, and Daphne acquiesced.

So she entered Peabody Hall that cold winter evening, feeling nervous and insecure. A slightly hysterical phrase was running through her head: Hello, Mr. Scalas, I am Daphne Miller, an almost-Ph.D. student in English, an ex-wife of an English professor, an ex-secretary of the history department here, and an almost-wife of an English professor. An almost-and-ex, an ex-and-almost, she thought, slipping into the ladies' room to scrutinize her hair. How had she ever before managed to enter social occasions on her own? She looked fine, appropriate, in a plain gray dress with white cuffs and pearls. An almost-and-ex, and ex-and-almost; she'd find the Whites and she'd be all right. Her mind was going.

The faculty lounge was crowded. Grabbing up a glass of white wine, Daphne took a moment to look around. She didn't see the Whites. But there was Madeline Spencer, thank heaven, and the Van Lieus were across the room in a corner. She would head their way.

"Daphne," an arctic voice said.

Daphne turned toward the voice. "Aah," she said, stifling a scream. She was as startled as if a creature had risen dripping from the dead before her, and hadn't she in a way already consigned Claire to those departed from us? She hadn't thought she would see Claire here — or, rather, she hadn't thought of Claire at all.

"You seem surprised to see me."

Claire was wearing a mustard-colored wool suit that had to be thirty years old; it had that kind of iron-strong stern cut to it. She had lost weight, and her color was not good, not that any human being alive could have good color in that suit.

"Hello, Claire," Daphne said, trying to be civil, thinking: Oh, God. "How are you?"

"Since you ask, Daphne, I am not well. I am heartbroken. I am lonely, and frightened, and humiliated."

Daphne stared at Claire. She could not believe Claire was saying this. She would never have thought Claire capable of such a thing. "But, Claire," she began, "Hudson said — "

"That I took the news well? That I faced the firing squad with dignity? Of course I did.

Did you expect I would grovel, or plead, or debase myself, and beg him to stay?"

Daphne stared at Claire in horror. Claire did look awful, the whites of her brilliant eyes yellowish now, her skin puffy and wrinkled, her shoulders slumping.

"I'm so sorry," Daphne said, almost whispering.

"Are you really?" Claire sneered. "I don't think so. I think you are in fact quite happy. After all these years of chasing him, you finally got him."

"That's not fair!" Daphne snapped. "I never chased him!"

"Of course you did, in your own way. I'm not a fool. Neither are you. You weren't brazen about it, but you chased him all the same. I know it, everyone knows it. Now you've caught him. Don't pretend you're sorry."

"Well, I'm not sorry about that," Daphne said. "I mean, about Hudson. I mean, I didn't chase him, but I do love him. But I am sorry you are so unhappy, Claire, and I never meant — "

"Did you think that because I am old now it would be easy for me? Or that because I am proud and particular I have no feelings? Do you really believe that my relatives and dogs will console me for the loss of a husband of twenty-five years? Yes, I shall survive, but I'll never be happy again in my life."

"Oh, you will," Daphne said. "Oh, I'm sure you will."

"You have no right to contradict me!" Claire said. "Don't demean my feelings, you do not have the right. I am telling you that losing Hudson is horrible for me, and I shall never recover from it, and I shall never be happy again. I want you to know that, Daphne Miller. I want you to remember that you have bought your happiness with my grief."

"I'm so sorry," Daphne said again, pleading.

"Your apology is not accepted," Claire replied. "I shall never, ever forgive you."

Then Claire walked away. She moved slowly, as if in pain, and Daphne realized then that several people had been watching her and Claire. Now one of the older professors came forward and took Claire by the arm and assisted her across to a chair. Claire took the drink the professor handed her. She looked terribly aged, aeons older than Hudson.

Daphne was certain of only one thing at this moment: she could not stay at the party. She was shaking, and the least she owed Claire was the rest of the night in this room without her. She hurried out of the main room, found her coat, and went into the night.

When Hudson came home after his long meeting, Daphne told him about the encounter. Hudson was baffled.

"I'm sure she'll be all right, Daphne," he said. "I can't imagine her saying such things to you. She's never been given to dramatics before."

"Hasn't she ever cried about all this?" Daphne asked. "Or called you names or cursed you? Hudson, I don't want details, I just want to know whether she's shown any anger."

"Not really," Hudson said. "Perhaps Claire's more angry with you than with me."

"But that's not fair!" Daphne cried.

"Perhaps she sees you as a seductress," Hudson said. He smiled. "While I am only a poor simple man, helpless in my masculine lusts."

Daphne was glad when, in March, Claire went away to England. But very soon after the move, Claire began to write to Hudson; at least once a week Daphne would find one of Claire's pale blue airmail envelopes in their mail. It drove Daphne crazy each time Hudson glanced at the envelope, then casually stuck it in his briefcase to read in his study with his university papers. When she questioned him, he said only, "More legal affairs,

Daphne, nothing important." One day, seeing her expression, Hudson said, "Would you like to read the letter, Daphne?"

"Oh, no, no, of course not!" Daphne replied, horrified that he would realize how nosy and insecure she was. After that she tried to pretend she didn't notice the letters.

But one day she could stand it no longer and sneaked into Hudson's study while she knew he was teaching. There in his beautiful old wooden filing cabinet, in a manila folder, was a file labeled "Claire," and in the folder were the letters. And Hudson had not been lying. The letters were about legal matters for the most part, but Claire also wrote about her new life, chattily and wittily. Daphne's heart was pounding so heavily that she feared she'd have a heart attack and be found dead on Hudson's floor, Claire's letters in her hand, so she put them back and left his study. But whenever a new letter came, she found herself as obsessed as a maniac, until she had once more sneaked in and read it. There was no passion in the letters, no sign of love or sexuality, nor of grief or pain or temptation. Nor was there any sign that Claire was receiving letters from Hudson. What was Daphne to do? Confront Hudson? Ask him if he were writing to Claire? Ask him not to write to Claire? If what Hudson had said was true, that Claire was angry with Daphne and not with Hudson, then how clever Claire was being, how sneakily vengeful, writing these plain newsy letters to Hudson, sending them to Hudson and Daphne's home, where she knew Daphne would note their presence, rather than to the college, where Daphne would never know. The letters were only an irritation in Daphne's life, but how clever of Claire to be so irritating. In a way, Daphne was grateful — Claire's letters kept Daphne's life from being perfect. Daphne knew that nothing perfect could last on earth, and her life was becoming dangerously close to that.

In March, Cynthia said during one of her casual phone calls that she would like to come back to live with Daphne and Hudson instead of remaining with Joe and Laura. She missed her friends, her school, even the East Coast.

"But, darling," Daphne said, "what about living in England? What about RADA?"

"Mom, I really don't think I'd make it into RADA. That was just a dream. Even I can tell I'm too inexperienced."

"Still, you never know until you try — "

"Mom, I didn't even get cast as the lead in the high-school play."

"Heavens, Cyn, you can't give up because of — "

"I'm not giving up, Mom! I'm just becoming, oh, more sensible, I guess. More realistic about my abilities."

Thank heaven for that much, Daphne thought. Cynthia was actually learning some humility.

"Besides," Cynthia went on, "I wouldn't want to act in Hollywood anyway. It's so tacky. I want to be a real actress, I want to act onstage, on Broadway. Well, I'll have to start off-Broadway, of course. And you and Hudson live so close to New York."

"So much for humility."

"What?"

"Nothing, darling. We'll be glad to have you with us."

That was true. She and Hudson had chosen their house with the thought in mind that Cynthia might come back, and before school was out Cynthia was with them, installed in her bedroom on the third floor of their gingerbread Victorian, where she could have girlfriends spend the night and play her stereo full volume without disturbing Hudson and Daphne. Cynthia had become fairly independent of Daphne, and although she was around Daphne less — always out with friends or in her room — when she was with Daphne she seemed more loving and relaxed.

Cynthia loved Hudson. She thought he

was sophisticated.

"I think it's awesome, Hudson marrying you," Cyn said one day to her mother when they were folding laundry.

"Why?" Daphne asked, amused.

"Well, Hudson's so brilliant and important and . . . debonair."

"Well, I'm no frog!" Daphne snapped.

But her anger was short-lived. She knew it was only natural that Cynthia should take for granted any charms Daphne had, balanced out as they were by all the times Cynthia had seen Daphne in a rage or a fit of red-eyed self-pity. She was fortunate that her new husband and her daughter liked each other.

In fact, she was fortunate in every way, which was the difficult part: whenever one of Claire's blue airmail envelopes arrived for Hudson, Daphne would be reminded of Claire facing her old age alone, and she would feel overcome with guilt. Daphne could not help but compare Hudson's desertion of Claire with Joe's desertion of her, so long ago, and she hoped that someday she would become more forgiving of Joe and Laura, at least in her own heart. Bitterness was such a waste of spirit.

She did not dwell on the bitterness much anymore. Now she pondered guilt. It had always been a point of pride in her life that when faced with a choice, she chose the action that would hurt the fewest people, even if that meant she was the one who was hurt most. For that reason she had not slept with Jack. For that reason she had refused to marry David, because she knew the pleasure of his company would be ruined by the times of drunkenness, which would frighten Cynthia.

One rainy morning in April, when Cynthia was at school and Hudson was at the college, Daphne sat finishing her second cup of coffee and looking out the window at the rain. With a sort of melancholy pleasure she was worrying at the thorn of guilt that had lodged very physically in her heart. She made herself think about the last time she had been with David.

He had been dying, for months, of cirrhosis of the liver. It was not an easy death. During his forty-seventh year of life, David had lost weight because he was unable to eat. For a while he only grew more brilliant-eyed and handsome, but finally he had begun to look skeletal, his face a death's-head, his complexion jaundiced and mapped with broken veins.

During the last few days, Daphne had sent Cynthia to stay with a friend so that she could be with David constantly. She was with him when he entered the hospital. By then, the doctors had told him there was nothing they could do for him except to make him more comfortable. Really, they could not do even that. He was nauseated, and vomited from time to time, with blood in his vomit. His liver had simply shut down, and his spleen was enlarged, he had edema, so that his limbs and stomach were swollen grotesquely. He had to work to breathe.

Daphne had sat next to him, holding his hand. She had wanted to be brave for him. She had pretended that they both understood that soon, suddenly, miraculously, he would be well. In his turn, he had tried to act light-hearted and carefree.

But once, when he smiled, and she saw how rusty his teeth looked, because of his bleeding gums, her anger broke forth. Her anger and her grief.

"Oh, David, damn you!" she said. "I'm so angry with you. You should have stopped drinking. You could have stopped drinking! Now I'll miss you so much. I'll be so sad and lonely. You're not doing this just to yourself, you know, you're doing it to me. Why didn't you stop drinking! Don't you feel guilty?"

David had thought about her question. Holding her hand, gasping as he fought to breathe, he had thought, staring in a blurry, melancholy way, as if truly looking over his entire life. Finally he had said, "Guilty? No. I don't feel guilty. But I do feel . . . regret."

Shortly after that he had slipped into a coma and died.

Now, in her kitchen, her new kitchen in her new Hudson-and-Daphne life, Daphne mused on David and his words. After his death she had felt guilty. Perhaps, if she had married him, he would have stopped drinking. Perhaps, if she had married him, he would not have died.

Perhaps. Perhaps not. She had certainly wrestled with this question many times before. David had already had two loving wives who had left him because of his drinking. He had always known that Daphne would marry him the moment he stopped drinking. What it all came down to was that Daphne had had to bet her life and Cynthia's — and David's — that if they married he would continue to drink, and ultimately inflict his ugly scenes on Cynthia. Daphne had had to make a choice.

When she had agreed to marry Hudson, she had once again made a choice, and this time she had chosen her own happiness over someone else's. She and Hudson were guilty of causing Claire sorrow.

Did that mean she loved Hudson more than she had loved David? Or was it simply that she realized at last — and it was about time, for she was getting old — that almost everyone on this earth, in order to be happy, must choose at times to do something that hurts someone else. Everyone on this earth must live with some degree of guilt.

Very well, then, she had chosen to take her happiness at the expense of Claire's. She was guilty.

But about this choice, she did not feel regret.

Carey Ann was having her period and having cramps and feeling awful, so Jack was in Grand Union buying Doritos and chocolate ice cream for her, and bananas and frozen chicken patties for Alexandra, and he didn't know what for himself. This was what had become of him. He couldn't even decide what he wanted to eat for dinner. Slouching over his metal cart, inching drearily up and down the aisles, he castigated himself: he wasn't a man, he was a slug. An adult, with money in his pocket, he could have anything he wanted for dinner. He could buy a frozen gourmet dinner of clams in tomato sauce. He could stop by Burger King and buy five thick cheeseburgers and all the crisp french fries he'd ever wanted in his life, and now he wouldn't break out in pimples. He could choose the freshest vegetables and expensive boned skinned chicken breasts and make himself a healthy stir-fry. He could get really wild and drink a six-pack of beer along with cream cheese, bagels, hot salted pretzels, and bacon sandwiches. But he didn't have the energy to make the decision, let alone fix his own meal.

He stood by the meat bin for a while, hoping inspiration would strike. A whole dead chicken was truly a repulsive thing, all puckered and goose-bumped. It was the end of May. It was warm enough out to cook something on the grill, but they were moving in a week, and the grill was stuck behind packed cardboard boxes in the garage. He had done that much; he had decided to go back to Kansas City to teach. But he hadn't managed to feel relaxed about the decision.

"Hello, Jack."

Daphne's cart rolled up against his, metal clinking companionably.

"Daphne." First he just looked at her. He hadn't even seen her for over a month. Life with Hudson obviously agreed with her. She sort of glowed. But then, hadn't she always? She was wearing a blue dress that set off the dancing blue of her eyes.

"Hudson tells me you're not staying on at Westhampton. That you're going back to Kansas City."

"Um, yes, that's right." They sounded so formal, Jack thought, so terribly proper, as if he'd never had his hand up her skirt. But he had come to attention at the sight of her, come out of his slouch and into an almost military stiffness, his body of its own accord going into this attitude of respect. "It will make Carey Ann happy to be around her family and friends. And I'll be able to teach freshman English, and even, eventually, I hope, teach literature there. In any event, I knew I wouldn't have a chance in hell of getting tenure here."

"What about your writing?" Daphne asked.

"Oh," Jack said. It surprised him that she remembered that he wanted to write, that she spoke of it as if it existed: "your writing." "Well. That will happen sometime, I suppose. I have a family to support and all that."

"I thought Carey Ann's father offered to support you all for a while so you could write."

"Yes, he did, that's true, but — I mean, you know, man of the house and all that. Pride and responsibility, you know."

"What about happiness?" Daphne said.

Jack looked down at his cart, shifted it slightly, as if it had been in someone's way. "Of course it would make me happy to write, but I've got others to think about."

"Don't you know Carey Ann and Alexandra will be happy if you're happy? And as for her father — well, Jack, don't you know *now* that the ultimate happiness in life comes from making our children happy? I'm sure Mr. Skrags would be just thrilled to give you a chance you'd never have otherwise in life."

Jack stared at Daphne. Suddenly a shiver passed over him, streaking down his spine, and he went cold all over. Here it was, the message from fate, Daphne in her toga passing along the wisdom of the ages, and he was chilled with comprehension. Or perhaps it was just the refrigerated air from the meat cooler wafting up his left arm. But he had never thought of it that way, that helping him out would make Mr. Skrags happy. Why hadn't he thought of that? People generally liked to help others if they could.

Still, would it be the *right* thing to do?

"Still," Jack said, "would it be the *right* thing to do? To let myself be supported by my father-in-law?"

Daphne laughed. "Jack. Life is far too short to limit yourself to doing only what is 'right.' Good Lord, do you think I'd be living with Hudson now if I'd paid attention to what was 'right'?"

"Hello, Daphne! I've been calling you all day! Where have you been? I wanted to chat

500

with you about the spring dance."

Jack turned savagely toward the fat old biddy waddling up toward them with *her* cart, wanting to yell at her: "Not now! *Not now!*" But Marcia Johannsen came inexorably on, unaware of the fact that she was interrupting one of the most crucial conversations of Jack's life.

"Marcia, Jack, I think you know each other," Daphne said graciously.

Jack realized he was glaring at the woman who was extending her hand with a smile.

"Yes, yes, hello," he said, taking the woman's hand and shaking it. "Nice to see you again."

"Nice to see you. Daphne, the committee meeting for the dance is going to be on Thursday night instead of Wednesday. Will you still be able to make it?"

"Let me check," Daphne said. She reached into her handbag and pulled out a small leather appointment book. Taking her time, she flipped through till she found the right date. "Umm," she said. "I have something that evening, but I can rearrange it. What time?"

Were these two women going to stand here talking about a fucking dance *forever?*

" . . . at Linda Hutton's," Marcia Johannsen was saying. "Since she's going to be in charge next year, it seems only — "

"Excuse me, ladies," Jack said politely, wanting to murder them both. They all shifted their grocery carts so that he could roll away from the meat section and down the aisle to frozen foods. Despairingly he reached in and grabbed a brightly colored cardboard box destined for a hungry man and tossed it in his cart. Dutifully he picked out the items for Carey Ann and Alexandra and wheeled off zombielike to the checkout counter.

Well, he was a fool, wasn't he? After all, Daphne Miller, soon to be Daphne Jennings, was only a mere woman, a former college secretary, as lost in the whims of the world as every other human being. Why had he endowed her with special powers? Because he had needed to, he guessed. And that was foolish. Really, when was he going to grow up? Right now. He'd grow up right now, and start making his own decisions! And his first decision was that he'd stop by the liquor store for a six-pack and some of the huge salted pretzels they sold from a glass jar. He'd buy something for Carey Ann too, to help with her cramps. Korbel wasn't too expensive and Carey Ann really loved champagne. It would be a nice gesture, and she'd be pleased that he had been so thoughtful. Then he'd tell her that he'd decided to take her father up on his offer for a year or two, and see how she reacted. She'd already said seven hundred times before, that if that was what he wanted to do, it was fine with her. He'd just check to see her reaction to be sure it really was okay.

He loaded his groceries into the car, then walked down the little mall to the liquor store. He bought the beer, the champagne, the pretzels, and carried them to his Honda and stashed them carefully on the floor of the passenger side. As he was going around the front of his car to the driver's side, someone honked at him. He looked up. There was Daphne, driving up the parking lot in the brown Volvo. She waved. Jack waved back.

Daphne was now almost in front of Jack's car, her head bent at an angle as she rolled down her window. She didn't stop her car, but she did slow down.

"Hey, Jack!" she yelled, as if they had never been interrupted, as if they were still in the midst of a conversation. "Do it! Take it! Go on! Be brave! It's all right. You can take what you're offered!"

Jack watched, speechless. The brown Volvo passed on up the line of parked cars. Daphne stuck her head out the window and looked back at him.

"Go on!" she yelled. *"I dare you!"* Her smile was brilliant.

Then she drove away.

THORNDIKE-MAGNA hopes you have enjoyed this Large Print book. All our Large Print titles are designed for easy reading, and all our books are made to last. Other Thorndike Press or Magna Print books are available at your library, through selected bookstores, or directly from the publishers. For more information about current and upcoming titles, please call or mail your name and address to:

THORNDIKE PRESS
P.O. Box 159
Thorndike, Maine 04986
(800) 223-6121
(207) 948-2962 (in Maine and Canada call collect)

or in the United Kingdom:

MAGNA PRINT BOOKS
Long Preston, Near Skipton
North Yorkshire,
England BD23 4ND
(07294) 225

There is no obligation, of course.